FROM HERE
TO
SUSTAINABILITY

Real World Members

bassac
Black Environment Network
Campaign Against Arms Trade
Charter88
Christian Aid
Church Action on Poverty
Community Action Network
Electoral Reform Society
Forum for the Future
Friends of the Earth
International Institute for
  Environment and Development
The Iona Community
Medact
National Peace Council
Oxfam
Pesticide Action Network UK
Population Concern
Quaker Peace and Social Witness
Save the Children
Town and Country Planning
  Association
Transport 2000
UK Public Health Association
United Nations Association
The Wildlife Trusts
World Development Movement
WWF-UK

FROM HERE
TO
SUSTAINABILITY

Politics in the Real World

By

The Real World Coalition

Written and edited by
Ian Christie and Diane Warburton

EARTHSCAN
London and Sterling VA

First published in the UK and USA in 2001
by Earthscan Publications Ltd

Moved to digital printing 2004

A catalogue record for this book is available
from the British Library

ISBN: 1 85383 735 0

Edited, designed and typeset by
BDP Book Development & Production
Penzance TR20 8XA

Printed and bound in the UK by
Antony Rowe Ltd, Eastbourne

Cover design by Richard Reid
Cover photo by Tony Stone Images

For a full list of publications please contact:
Earthscan
8-12 Camden High Street, London, NW1 0JH, UK
Tel: +44 (0)20 7387 8558
Fax: +44 (0)20 7387 8998
Email: earthinfo@earthscan.co.uk
http://www.earthscan.co.uk

22883 Quicksilver Drive, Sterling, VA 20166-2012, USA

Earthscan is an imprint of James and James (Science Publishers)
and publishes in association with the International Institute for
Environment and Development.

This book is printed on elemental chlorine-free paper

Contents

Preface

The Real World Coalition comprises over 25 leading UK campaigning organizations. Its mission is to lay the foundations for change by raising and maintaining understanding in UK public and political debate of the causal links between, and therefore the solutions to achieving:

- environmental sustainability;
- social justice;
- eradication of poverty;
- peace and security;
- democratic renewal.

These are the key policy constituencies of sustainable development. The coalition set out its arguments in its first book, *The Politics of the Real World*, which was written for us by Michael Jacobs. Published by Earthscan in 1996, it has sold over 15,000 copies. The book has played a significant role in shaping public debate about the need for genuinely 'joined up' policy if the issues on which Real World member organizations campaign are to be resolved once and for all.

All member organizations have contributed to this book through witness boxes and comments on various drafts. Particular thanks go to the editorial panel: Kevan Bundell, Christian Aid; Oliver Buston, Oxfam; Duncan McLaren, Friends of the Earth; Sally Nicholson, WWF-UK; Sara Parkin, Forum for the Future; and to the two authors who wrote and edited the text.

Ian Christie is Associate Director of The Local Futures Group, and is a researcher and writer on environmental issues, sustainability and social policy. His publications include *Managing Sustainable Development*, 2nd edition (with Michael Carley, Earthscan, 2000) and *Sustaining Europe* (Green Alliance/Demos, 1999).

Diane Warburton is a researcher and writer on sustainable development, specializing in community participation. She is also currently Principal Research Fellow on the ESRC Democracy and Participation Programme. Her publications include *Community and Sustainable Development* (Earthscan, 1998).

Real World is supported mainly by subscriptions from member organizations. However, the writing of this book would not have been possible without the additional generosity of the following people and organizations:

- The Polden-Puckham Charitable Foundation;
- the Elmgrant Trust;
- Forum for the Future;
- the late Margaret Mawson;
- the Methodist Church;
- WWF-UK.

Most Real World members are charities. It is inevitable that the remit of this book will go beyond the stated aims and objectives of most member organizations. In endorsing this book, therefore, each organization is indicating its formal agreement only in those areas where it has specific competence. At the same time, each endorses the overall argument of the book as a whole. Each also acknowledges the expertise and authority of the other member organizations of Real World in those areas where they themselves do not have specific competence.

Sara Parkin
Chair, The Real World Coalition
January 2001

Foreword

> '*There has indeed been enormous progress on all fronts over the last decade, but rarely proportionate to the accelerating destruction of the natural and social capital on which all our lives depend. If anything, the gap between need (what has to be done to take our aberrant species forward into a genuinely sustainable way of life) and response is growing.*'
> Jonathon Porritt[1]

> '*Globalization of the economy implies globalization of responsibility.*'
> Kofi Annan[2]

The agenda of The Real World Coalition is for radical reform in national and international politics and economic policy. Its members work for environmental protection and security, the elimination of poverty, and the renewal of democratic institutions and processes. They promote the global and national agenda of sustainable development – economic and social development which respects, and works within the limits of, the environmental systems that support all life; which promotes peace, justice and civil liberties; and which contributes to a richer quality of life for all.

Politics in the UK and beyond has consistently failed to invest energy, imagination and resources in meeting the challenges of reversing economic and social trends now recognized as unsustainable. In the coalition's first report, *The Politics of the Real World* (1996),[3] we highlighted critical issues that are still largely pushed to the margins of public debate and political manifestos:

- the risks of catastrophic environmental degradation, both locally and affecting the whole Earth;
- gross inequalities between the developed and developing countries;
- endemic poverty and conflicts in the developing world;
- growing economic inequality in the UK, and the persistence of major gaps in economic and social opportunity between different groups, according to race, gender, age and disability;
- widespread disaffection towards the political system at local and national levels, towards political parties and, for many at the bottom of the economic ladder, towards society as a whole;

- a pervasive sense that community life and families are being damaged by changes in the economy and the operation of organizations;
- the gap between standard measures of economic success and the realities of quality of life.

These issues are intertwined. We cannot reverse the trends of environmental degradation without tackling the deep economic and social inequalities between the rich and poor worlds. We cannot ignore the contribution of ecological crises to economic turmoil and risks of international conflict. If we want stronger communities and family life, we need to overcome the alienation of so many people from politics and local decision- making, and to bridge the gap between work and family life, and between businesses and communities. And if we want a political debate that faces up to the challenges that the new century poses to our ways of life and consumer values, then we need a revitalized culture of democracy and a new generation of informed and empowered citizens.

This poses fundamental challenges to mainstream politics and to the divisions and assumptions which characterize our decision-making systems. As Ken Worpole has argued:

> '*Throughout the world where forms of representative democracy operate, the historic counter-oppositions – left and right, state and market, public and private, conservationist or developmental – are proving inadequate to cope with the complexity of problems facing communities (including nation states) and the choices which press upon them.*'4

Since Real World's first report was published in 1996, the UK political landscape has been radically changed by the advent of the New Labour Government. Our hope that the issues raised by Real World in 1996 would reach the mainstream political agenda has been fulfilled in part. Much of the Government's vision of 'modernization' embraces the need for environmental protection, social cohesion and justice, and democratic renewal. At the international level there is growing acknowledgement of the need for radical reform of global governance; to help poor countries escape from extreme poverty and conflict; to make economic globalization fairer and environmentally sustainable; and to prevent conflicts rooted in poverty and injustice.

But no one could claim that sustainable development; as a guiding philosophy for governance and economic strategy, has arrived at centre stage in politics, business and the life of citizens. The gap between world leaders' aspirations and reality is huge: they have the resources to act on their diagnosis of the need for change, but many lack the will and political courage. The challenges are growing more urgent as we learn about the risks of global environmental degradation – especially of climate disruption – and as extreme poverty and suffering persist, despite the rising wealth of the globalized economy and the huge advances in modern technology.

The 'new economy' of information technology, 'knowledge enterprises' and globalizing markets cannot be developed in isolation from social and environmental policies. It has much to offer – potentially it can support environmental protection and a cleaner, more efficient productive economy, and it could help shape a more 'inclusive', better educated and informed society. But it could, without political courage and strong strategic guidance from governments, business leaders and civil society as a whole, widen the gaps still further between the economy and the real world, between a global 'superclass' and the poor, and between gross domestic product (GDP) and quality of life. Indeed, there are already many signs that this is happening.

'Modernization' cannot simply be about embracing globalization, open trade, new technology and competitive challenges, and working ever more 'flexibly' to cope with them. It must, if it is to be environmentally, socially and politically sustainable, also be about rethinking our political and business cultures. We need to recognize our responsibilities to future generations and to the poor of the world, and our need to respect and sustain the environment on which we all depend. Globalization and modernization which fail to deal with deepening inequalities between the rich and poor worlds, and with ecological degradation, are self-defeating. Global development as we know it will face severe crises, if not environmental catastrophes, within decades, which will undermine economies and social stability across the world.

Real World's members have come together again to underline their conviction that the issues which we tackle are related, domestically and internationally, and that we cannot deal with our particular concerns unless we are part of a wider framework for action – the concept of sustainable development – which addresses all of these challenges. Only by working with this strategic vision will we be able to close the gap between aspiration and action among decision-makers in government, business and other sectors. We are not arguing for a rejection of modernity, for an anti-business stance, or for a Utopian 'fundamentalist' vision of environmentalism. We see much to support in the modernization agenda promoted by New Labour. But we believe too that this programme for combining a dynamic economy with a fairer society can only succeed both here and overseas if it has sustainable development at its core, in both theory and practice.

Our conviction, then, is that taking sustainability seriously is not only right, it is in everyone's long-term interests. A programme based on the goals of democratic sustainable development could help improve people's lives in Britain and across the globe, and could begin the vital task of repairing and stabilizing the ecosystems and social fabric on which we all depend.

Real World believes now, as it did in 1996, that there is a hunger in the public at large for a politics that takes seriously the great challenges of environmental sustainability, democratic regeneration, inequality and the revitalization of community life. Once more, Real World aims to provide a non-party political forum in which these issues can gain a fresh hearing and reach new audiences. We do so in the context of a positive vision for the UK, at home and on the world stage.

This book updates the core thinking that lies behind the Real World initiative. It offers an analysis of the Coalition's key themes; assesses recent progress in making a reality of the ideas of sustainable development; and proposes ideas for further reform and modernization of policies. We offer an account of current politics that assesses the work of Government and business and the voluntary sector against the aspirations of the members of Real World. Success is acknowledged honestly, and we offer positive suggestions and constructive criticism to try to help close the gap between where we are now, and where our aims for sustainable development suggest we should be. But we do not hide our mounting concern that greater urgency is needed in tackling the deepening, connected crises of environmental degradation and human deprivation, at home and around the world.

For The Real World Coalition

Ben Hughes
Chief Executive
bassac

Niall Cooper
National Coordinator
Church Action on Poverty

Judy Ling Wong FRSA
Director
Black Environment Network

Andrew Mawson OBE
Co-Director
Community Action Network

Ann Feltham
Joint Co-ordinator
Campaign Against Arms
Trade

Ken Ritchie
Chief Executive
Electoral Reform Society

Pam Giddy
Director
Charter88

Sara Parkin
Programme Director
Forum for the Future

Daleep S Mukarji
Director
Christian Aid

Charles Secrett
Executive Director
Friends of the Earth

Nigel Cross
Executive Director
International Institute for
Environment and
Development

Peter Beaumont
Development Director
Pesticide Action Network UK

Revd Norman Shanks
Leader
The Iona Community

Wendy Thomas
Chief Executive
Population Concern

Dr Robin Stott FRCP
Chairman
Medact

Linda Fielding
General Secretary
Quaker Peace and Social
Witness

Mike Aaronson
Director General
Save the Children

Rosemary Bechler
Co-Chair
National Peace Council

David Bryer
Director
Oxfam

Gideon Amos
Director
Town and Country Planning
Association

Stephen Joseph
Director
Transport 2000

Simon Lyster
Director General
The Wildlife Trusts

John Nicholson
Chief Executive
UK Public Health Association

Barry Coates
Director
World Development
Movement

Malcolm Harper
Director
United Nations Association

Robert Napier
Chief Executive
WWF-UK

List of Acronyms and Abbreviations

Aids	acquired immune deficiency syndrome
bassac	British Association of Settlements and Social Action Centres
CAAT	Campaign Against Arms Trade
CAN	Community Action Network
CAP	Church Action on Poverty
CEDAW	Convention on the Elimination of Discrimination Against Women
CSO	civil society organization
DDA	Dangerous Drugs Act
DDA	Defence Diversification Agency
DESO	Defence Export Services Organization
DFID	Department for International Development
DSS	Department of Social Security
DTI	Department of Trade and Industry
EC	European Commission
ECE	Economic Commission for Europe (United Nations)
EDC	endocrine disrupting chemical
EQS	environmental quality standard
ERS	Electoral Reform Society
ETI	Ethical Trading Initiative
EU	European Union
FDI	foreign direct investment
FOE	Friends of the Earth
FTSE	Financial Times Stock Exchange
GDP	gross domestic product
GM	genetically modified
GMO	genetically modified organism
GNP	gross national product
GPI	Genuine Progress Index
HIV	human immunodeficiency virus
ICPD	International Conference on Population and Development
ILO	International Labour Organization
IMF	International Monetary Fund
IPPNW	International Physicians Against Nuclear War

ISEW	Index of Sustainable Economic Welfare
LETS	Local Exchange Trading Systems
MAFF	Ministry of Agriculture, Fisheries and Food
MAI	Multilateral Agreement on Investment
NATO	North Atlantic Treaty Organization
NGO	non-governmental organization
NHS	National Health Service
NPC	National Peace Council
NWC	nuclear weapons convention
OAU	Organization of African Unity
OECD	Organisation for Economic Co-operation and Development
OSCE	Organization for Security and Co-operation in Europe
Oxfam	Oxford Committee for Famine Relief
PAN	Pesticide Action Network UK
PHA	Public Health Association
QPS	Quaker Peace and Service
QPSW	Quaker Peace and Social Witness
QSRE	Quaker Social Responsibility and Education
RDA	Regional Development Agency
RSPB	Royal Society for the Preservation of Birds
SD	sustainable development
SSSI	Site of Special Scientific Interest
TCPA	Town and Country Planning Association
TNC	trans-national corporation
TRIPS	Trade-Related Aspects of Intellectual Property Rights
UDHR	Universal Declaration of Human Rights
UN	United Nations
UNA	United Nations Association
UNDP	United Nations Development Programme
UNED	United Nations Environment and Development
UNEP	United Nations Environment Programme
UNHCR	United Nations High Commission for Refugees
VSO	Voluntary Service Overseas
WDM	World Development Movement
WHO	World Health Organization
WRI	World Resources Institute
WTO	World Trade Organization
WWF	World Wide Fund For Nature

Introduction:
Millennial Hopes and Fears

'As a result of all the "progress" of the last 50 years,
many have done well, but many not so well, even in
the rich societies. In the world at large, the rich still get
richer and the poor get poorer, in spite of our best
intentions.'
Charles Handy[1]

'By the end of the new century, if we are both lucky
and wise, we will exit in better shape than we entered...
People everywhere will have acquired a decent quality
of life, with the expectation of more improvement to
come... Whether it happens... depends fundamentally
on the shift to a new ethic, which sees humanity as part
of the biosphere and its faithful steward, not just the
resident master and economic maximizer.'
E O Wilson[2]

What State are We in? The Paradox of Our Times

The Millennium celebrations at the end of 1999 were intended
to display a new sense of national purpose and energy in
Britain. In the event, we ended the old Millennium with a bang
and entered the new one with a whimper – or rather, with a
whinge. Spectacular firework displays were followed by rows
over the transport delays and queues which marred the party at
the Millennium Dome, and by questions about what exactly we
were meant to be celebrating. And as soon as the celebrations
ended the Labour Government entered a period of political trou-
bles which left its strategists agreeing with its critics that it was
failing to make its purposes clear.

The Dome at Greenwich became a target for deeper criticisms of the state of Millennial Britain. It came to symbolize a
country eager to put energy and investment into 'modernization'
in order to meet the future, but unclear about what kind of future
it is heading for. The Dome was soon widely regarded as a col-
lection of exhibits without a theme, a celebration of an economy

and a society which lack a story about where we have come from and what kind of world we want to make. To its critics, it did not point the way to a *better* world, nor open up debate about the society we wish to create for our children and grand-children. Rather, with its inevitable McDonalds outlet, its desperation to meet its targets for admissions and revenue, and the difficulty of travelling to its Docklands home, to its many critics the Dome summed up *fin-de-siècle* Britain all too well. Whatever our big ideas about the future, they are undermined by the present reality of homogenized consumerism, the relentless competitive pressures in workplaces, and the sheer effort involved in using our shambolic public transport.

But the unease and confusion amid the celebrations are connected to a greater paradox, which defines our times. Our world has seen, especially for the majority of citizens in the rich industrial countries, a spectacular increase in living standards, longevity and opportunities to fulfil potential.

Yet this world has failed, despite having the knowledge, wealth and capacity to do so, to lift the absolute poor out of poverty, reduce the divisions within and between societies, and reverse the trends which threaten the global environment. We have the resources to create genuine progress for all; governments everywhere lack the will to implement the changes made urgent by mounting evidence of environmental degradation and widening gaps between rich and poor. We have grounds simultaneously for unprecedented optimism and pessimism about the human prospect.

The paradox of our times affects the deeper currents of public attitudes and values, in ways which our politics has yet to reflect. In February 2000 the international development charity Voluntary Service Overseas (VSO) published a report on the state of the British psyche at the turn of the Millennium.[3] VSO had been startled by a 61 per cent increase in applications for voluntary work in developing countries from business and management professionals in the second half of 1999. It commissioned research to find out what was behind this upsurge in interest. The research indicated deep dissatisfaction with the 'stress and spend' culture of Millennial Britain: people feel driven to acquire money and status in an intensely competitive society but are often unable to enjoy their affluence. The pressures to spend, and the pressures of work, allow many people little time to assess their priorities, and leave them questioning the value of their careers and material achievements. Yet few can imagine positive practical alternatives to 'stress and spend' as a way of life.

This study reinforces findings from many others carried out in the 1990s. Repeatedly, researchers have identified a tension between the demands of work and the claims of family life, a growing divide between official yardsticks of progress and citizens' anxieties and priorities and a search for more meaning in life than 'consumer choice' can provide.[4] At the same time, there is no doubt that living standards are higher than ever, and that we live in historically exceptional times of good fortune and plenty.[5]

In part, this set of results merely points to an ancient truth – that money and status cannot buy happiness, and that 'getting and spending' will not make a meaningful life. It also reflects the realization – across the political spectrum – in the UK that the drive for liberalized markets and lower tax rates since 1979 have been accompanied by a failure to invest in the public realm: we have, to quote J K Galbraith, 'private affluence alongside public squalor'.[6] It also reflects a growing sense of strain within modern societies – the idea that for all our genuine and unprecedented gains in living standards, we have many ways of producing, consuming and working which are unsustainable. They are undermining the environmental, moral and social common resources on which we all depend.

Moreover, our politics and media largely fail to give voice to these ideas. Both are fixated on consumption as the key to success – how we can generate more spending power for consumers and what they can do with it.[7] Politicians who pride themselves on managerial competence and 'spin', and their ability to appeal to as wide a range of constituencies as possible, are unlikely to be good at asking fundamental questions about the purposes of growth and consumption and their moral dimension, let alone at offering answers. Media obsessed with ratings and celebrity are part of the problem rather than a force for overcoming it. There is a vacuum in our politics where we should find passionate debate and leadership on the goals and costs of economic development, the collective consequences – material, moral and spiritual – of private consumption, and outrage at the degradation of the environment and the devastation of species worldwide, which will diminish the wealth of the world we are leaving to our children.

What the Millennial confusion underlined was that the boom in Britain's economy in the late 1990s was not being translated directly into a sense of optimism and purpose. The principal indicators – GDP growth, inflation and unemployment – all looked good, and the credit was claimed by the Government for its 'prudent' management of the economy. For millions, of course, affluence is still bringing real gains to their quality of life. But by the 1990s there was an unmistakable break with the past: politicians and economists could no longer rely on the formal measurements of the economy being related closely to the public's sense of well-being and meaning in their lives.[8] And indeed, in reality the link between these things had been weakening for many years.

The cause is the 'decoupling' of the economy from our quality of life: growth does not always translate into affluence, nor affluence into satisfaction and meaningful living. The economy can grow without creating secure or satisfying jobs, or investing in public services which enhance quality of life. Rising average incomes hide widening gaps between rich and poor. Low inflation is applauded by policy-makers, but the official measure is disconnected from important aspects of quality of life – for example, housing. Low inflation has not been experienced by anyone trying to buy or rent a home in the 'growth' regions of Millennial Britain, placing great pressures on those starting out in work or family life.

In the real world, the economic indicators that count are not only those that make sense to Government and the City. Our accumulation of economic capital is now all too capable of being disconnected from the crucial environmental goods or 'capital' on which our health and wealth depend, and can undermine the 'social capital' or relations of trust, goodwill and altruism essential for a decent society and fulfilled lives.

This lesson is all the more stark across the developing world. There, many economic policies approved by financial markets and international agencies have little or nothing to do with real gains for the poor. The sustainable economic growth with social equity that is vital for future quality of life, and especially for the poorest people, remains out of reach for many developing countries.

Mind the Gaps: The Fault Lines in the Politics of the Real World

The first Real World book, published in 1996,[9] opened with an account of the UK's drift towards the Millennium. The diagnosis of the state we were in was bleak: we argued that 'the body politic frequently seems rudderless, swinging to and fro on passing waves, mesmerised by the smallest movements'. When *The Politics of the Real World* appeared, its analysis of the gaps between politics and people, present policy and future needs, was compelling. Opinion polls and low election turnouts suggest that the gaps loom as large in many people's lives now as they did then.

Real World's claim is that these gaps in our economic and political outlooks and policies are profoundly dangerous for the future quality of life of British citizens, and of the world's peoples as a whole. The gaps we identified point to a basic disconnection between the priorities and policies of decision-makers, and the world as experienced and endured by the mass of citizens across the planet:

- *The Quality of Life Gap:* while standard measures of the economy tell us about change in GDP, inflation and employment, they fail to tell us about the long-term sustainability of our economic development, and how it translates – or fails to translate – into quality of life. Fixated on traditional quantitative measures of growth as a yardstick of progress, our economic worldview has become decoupled from the realities of well-being for the mass of people, and from the realities of what levels of exploitation our environment can sustain, and how much inequality our society and economy should tolerate.[10]
- *The Environmental Gap:* human activity is almost certainly leading to disruption of the global climate – yet the action planned and taken by governments and corporations falls hopelessly short of what is needed and feasible to prevent severe damage to economies and environments, and to make beneficial changes in energy use; and intensive production and consumption are increasingly damaging the environmental 'services' on which we all depend, breaching environmental limits, eliminating the diversity of wildlife, habitats and crops, and introducing risks to human health (such as toxic chemicals) into the food chain and wider environment.[11]

- *The Poverty Gap:* for the last two decades, economic change in the industrialized world has, in many cases, widened the gaps between the richest and the poorest groups, compounding the disadvantages suffered by people on low incomes and leading to the growth of a 'super-class'[12] of hyper-affluent people. Not only have inequalities increased, but the rise of individualism and the loss of identification with the public realm and public services on the part of so many electors mean that increasingly politics is a matter of responding to private wants, focus groups' perceptions and sectional interests, rather than negotiating the public good.[13]
- *The Development Gap:* immense inequalities exist within nations, but these are overshadowed by the gap between the rich industrialized world and much of the 'South' – the developing world of Africa, Asia and Latin America. The gap in living standards, access to technology, finance, trade, energy, healthcare, education, civil liberties, social stability and environmental security remains huge, and dangerous (see Table 1.1).[15] The post-Cold War era has not inaugurated a shift towards a sustainable and fair 'new world order'.
- *The Democracy Gap:* the UK and the developed world in general have seen a striking decline in public confidence in political institutions and politicians over the last 20 years – reflecting the trends in the economy that have heightened inequalities, insecurities and environmental risks. Just as democracy is increasingly embraced and sought in the developing world, so it seems to be viewed with cynicism and apathy by many citizens in the Organisation for Economic Co-operation and Development (OECD) countries.[14]
- *The Security Gap:* long-term well-being and better development for the poor are threatened by civil conflicts, made worse by the arms trade and low investment in United Nations (UN) peace-keeping, and in conflict prevention measures. Ending and preventing conflicts is a precondition for sustainable development and spreading good democratic governance.

Table 1.1 *The Development Gap: Inequalities in Financial and Industrial Resources Worldwide, at the Beginning of the 21st Century*

	Consumer group: OECD countries	Middle income group of countries	Low income group of countries
Current population	1.1 bn persons	3.4 bn persons	1.2 bn persons
Percentage of world population	19%	60%	21%
Percentage of world GNP	82.7%	15.9%	1.4%
Percentage of world trade	81.2%	17.8%	1.0%
Percentage of commercial lending	94.6%	5.2%	0.2%
Consumption of foodstuffs/ fertilizer	50% of global grain production and 60% of artificial fertilizers	Around 30–40% of world fooodstuffs	500–800 mn chronically undernourished; limited access to fresh water
Transport and household technologies	92% of private cars	2 bn persons with no household electricity or telephone	
Consumption of energy and industrial production per year	75% of energy use; 80% of iron and steel; 81% of paper; 85% of chemical production; 86% of copper and aluminium	Around 10–15% of world energy and industrial production	Mainly meeting energy needs by cutting fuel wood at higher than replacement levels; 100 mn without adequate fuel

Sources: UNDP, WRI, Worldwatch Institute, cited in M Carley and P Spapens, *Sharing the World: Sustainable Living and Global Equity in the 21st Century* (London: Earthscan, 1998)

The analysis in *The Politics of the Real World* was clear-cut: these gaps point to a serious disconnection between the world of politicians, economists, big business leaders and the rich, and the real world in which the mass of people seek to make a living, raise families, find meaning and live a decent life. If we want sustainable development for the new century – that is, economic development that brings a higher quality of life for all, without doing it at the expense of future generations, the poor and the environment – we have to close these gaps. That is the challenge of the politics of the real world, and it defines the priorities for decision-makers in the 'sustainability transition' we need to make in the next half century.[16]

What state are we now in? The arrival in power of the New Labour Government in May 1997 took place to the strains of the pop song 'Things can only get better'. Have they? Unquestionably, in New Labour the UK has a government with more sympathy with the ideas of Real World than many expected. Britain's political culture and business environment are being changed, in many ways for the better. New Labour has recognized many of the profound challenges arising from developments across the globe. But the radical modernization it has promised is, as yet, an incomplete set of projects.

It is not simply that the Government's programme will take years to secure the hoped-for improvements in the environment and public services, because of chronic under-investment for decades. A deeper issue is that the projects of 'modernization' do not hang together consistently, so Government's aspirations to sustainable development do not always translate into action. Indeed, the action taken sometimes undermines the stated aims. Devolution is accompanied by a tightening of control over local government, schools and health care; the aspiration to be a leader in policy to mitigate climate disruption is subverted by fear of measures which could upset 'the motorist'; and the Government's vision of an environmentally friendly economy is undermined both by its lack of energy and ambition in promoting the growth markets and technologies of the new century – such as renewable energy, waste minimization and organic and low-impact farming, and its dogged support for old or unsustainable technologies such as nuclear power. The Real World argument is that we need to see modernization through the prism of sustainable development if we are to have a coherent strategy for reform that meets the challenges and opportunities facing us.[17]

We contend that the failure to embrace sustainable development fully as a truly 'joined up' framework for policy accounts for many of the problems faced at home and in international governance. Domestic and international policy-makers still pursue economic development in isolation from environmental and social problems, guaranteeing difficulties in hitting economic, environmental and social targets together. Without the perspective of sustainable development, we will continue to give perverse incentives for environmental and social damage and under-reward economic development which protects and enhances environmental and social capital.

The New Context for the Politics of the Real World: New Labour's Progress

9

The Real World story in 1996 was dominated by frustration over the great gap between politics and the citizen, and between the official measures of the economy and the real state of our quality of life. Real World members are glad to report that in many ways the picture in 2000 is more positive. As indicated by our 'witness boxes' in the following chapters, Real World members acknowledge some genuine progress in their areas of concern. How has the context changed?

First, the idea that much of the current economic growth and 'business as usual' in production and consumption are environmentally and socially unsustainable, has gained important ground. New Labour came to power promising to put the environment 'at the heart of government', and has radically revised and improved the UK's sustainable development strategy.[18] Government has begun to develop a wide-ranging set of indicators of quality of life, intended to supplement the standard measures of economic performance and to map our progress towards more sustainable development.[19] And on the most urgent and threatening issue – climate change – the Government has accepted the need for radical long-term action. In 1997 the Kyoto Summit committed the industrialized world to significant cuts in emissions of 'greenhouse gases' implicated in the threat of climate disruption – albeit far short of the reductions needed in coming decades. In this, the UK has played a leading role within the European Union (EU).

In transport policy, New Labour initially attacked the idea that road-building could solve our chronic problems of road congestion, and signalled a long-term shift towards an 'integrated transport strategy', in which public transport would receive much more investment and measures would be taken to cut the growth in road traffic and reduce dependence on cars.[20]

Progress is slow, however, and there has been a retreat from the radicalism of the Government's 1998 White Paper on transport. The Government has also announced its intention to reverse the long-term trends which have damaged the countryside – subsidized pesticide-dependent intensive agriculture, the spread of suburbs and out-of-town shopping centres, and planning policies which have failed to regenerate our cities and make them attractive places to work, live and raise families.

Second, the inequalities that have grown at home and overseas have been recognized as dangerous and unjust. In the UK, the Government has made the assault on 'social exclusion' – the accumulation of damage done to people and neighbourhoods by poverty, unemployment, crime and ill-health – the challenge by which it wishes to be judged. A wide range of initiatives has been launched to analyse social exclusion, and to produce 'joined up' policies intended to avoid the fragmentation of previous approaches to poverty. Government has introduced a 'New Deal' programme of measures to help unemployed people into work and learning, and to regenerate the worst-off public housing estates.[21] Ambitious targets have been set for the halving, and then the elimination, of child poverty. Measures have been introduced to improve the incentives to move from welfare into paid work, and to boost the incomes of low-paid workers. The Government has also launched initiatives to modernize the education and health services, accompanied at last by realistic levels of investment.

In overseas development policy, some progress has been made on debt relief for the poorest countries. Britain has been a prime mover in shifting the policy of the industrialized world towards large-scale forgiveness of debt for the heavily indebted countries of the South. The UK responded positively to the powerful international campaign for debt forgiveness, Jubilee 2000, in which Real World members played a leading role. In the year 2000, the leading industrial democracies are committed to write-off US$100 billion of the debt burden on the poorest developing countries – although progress has been painfully slow (see Chapter 5).[22] The Government has endorsed the UN target of halving the proportion of the world's population living in 'absolute poverty' by 2015. And it has pledged itself to increasing the value and quality of overseas development aid, pursuing the goals of sustainable development.[23]

New Labour entered power aware of the need to regain and foster public trust in the process of government, and to renew the UK's moth-eaten constitution. The Government has launched a policy of modernizing local democracy, through the introduction of elected mayors (starting in London), and through improved local services. We now have elected assemblies in Scotland and Wales; the potential for more autonomy in Northern Ireland; the prospect of regional assemblies in England; and a partially-reformed House of Lords. The result is an inconsistent, quasi-federal system that needs many more reforms. Despite this, constitutional reform has arrived at last.

11

Finally, what has happened in the field of security and peace? On the positive side, the Government has made determined efforts to end the conflict in Northern Ireland and create a new framework for cooperation with the Republic of Ireland. It has established a fund to support international conflict prevention and peace-keeping. Famously, the Government announced from the start that it would bring an 'ethical dimension' to foreign policy, determined to uphold human rights and social justice around the world. This became part of the justification for Britain's role in the North Atlantic Treaty Organization (NATO) intervention in the Balkans, waging war on Serbia and helping to drive the Yugoslav army from Kosovo; but it has also been one of the areas in which the gap between ambition and reality has been most glaringly visible, as we discuss later in this chapter and in Chapter 7.

In each of the policy areas sketched above, some real and welcome progress is being made. But optimism must be tempered. In many ways, the gap between what we know must be done to reverse the unsustainable trends in the economy and society and what we still do regardless of this knowledge, has remained as wide as ever – or even grown.

The Gap between Ambition and Reality

Despite genuine progress in some areas of policy, huge gaps remain between ambition and reality. First, the idea of 'sustainable development' remains marginal in political life, even while it gradually gains influence among policy-makers, major businesses and international development agencies (see Chapter 2 and Panel 3). Labour does not yet treat sustainable development as a central organizing concept that shapes its programme: rather, it is acknowledged as one goal among many for bodies such as the Regional Development Agencies (RDAs).[24] And 'the environment' remains a policy issue confined for the most part to the sidelines, regarded by Government, citizens and media as something to worry about only after attending to the core issues of the economy, jobs and public services. The realization that the quality of the environment, and its connections to economic and social development, is profoundly relevant to all these areas has, even now, yet to dawn in parts of the policy-making and opinion-forming worlds.

Chapters 3–5 examine the connected challenges of environmental sustainability, poverty reduction and sustainable economic development: there is real progress to report. Awareness is growing, but not yet at a pace to match the rate of environmental degradation, especially of climate disruption, and to make a real difference to the problems of deep poverty and inequality. In 1999 the United Nations Environment Programme (UNEP) published its review of the state of the global environment.[25] The conclusions were blunt:

> 'the global system of environmental policy and management is moving in the right direction, but much too slowly... on balance, gains by better management and technology are still being outpaced by the environmental impacts of population and economic growth. As a result, policy actions that result in substantial environmental improvements are rare. The present course is unsustainable and postponing action is no longer an option' *[emphasis added]*.

Most alarming, the evidence mounts that the world is heading for major climate disruption as a result of the flow of greenhouse gases, such as carbon dioxide, into the atmosphere from fossil fuel use (by power stations, households, businesses, motorists and so on). Although the UK has taken a lead among OECD countries on this major issue, the sense of urgency and the scale of action here and worldwide are nothing like enough to control the risks of climate disruption and immense environmental, economic and social damage. Klaus Töpfer, executive director of UNEP, made this plain in launching the UNEP analysis of the global environment:

> 'A series of looming crises and ultimate catastrophe can only be averted by a massive increase in political will. We have the technology but are not applying it.'[26]

The gap between our traditional measures of economic development and the realities of what makes for quality of life, remains large. The Government's new set of sustainable development indicators is a welcome and substantial achievement – but so far they have not been fleshed out with new data, or been used to challenge the dominance of GDP in assessing our progress and prosperity. Daily life confirms the gap between the headline indicators and the reality of quality of life, or lack of it. Britain is experiencing the long-term effects of decades of under-investment in maintaining the public realm: the roads are clogged; the railways decrepit; the hospitals in crisis; many public spaces are felt to be unsafe; and state schools are under strain. What this amounts to is a crisis of public health in the broadest sense: the polluting effects of many of our consumption habits often make us sick; the rundown in public services and spaces makes for an unhealthy and unattractive public realm in our poorer areas, and in many affluent ones too; and the worst-off neighbourhoods and social groups are those with the worst health and the most dangerous and sickly environments.

These problems are far worse in many of the ex-Communist and developing countries, where ill-maintained infrastructure, polluted environments and the damage done by poverty and conflict to public health combine to hold back sustainable development and keep billions impoverished. At the same time, economic growth based on unsustainable exploitation of resources, which rewards a minority with wealth and power, proceeds apace in the same countries. On narrow measures of growth and development, parts of China, Russia and South-East Asia are booming; but viewed through the prism of sustainable development, countries such as Indonesia have been undermining their future through rapacious exploitation of their natural resources, and Russia is in the grip of a huge long-term crisis of public health, as a result of pollution, poverty and under-invested infrastructure – a threat acknowledged by President Putin on taking office.

In the West, subtler issues are becoming important too. The gap between the official story of prosperity and the reality of everyday living is not simply about the gulf between rich and poor, or between private consumption and under-investment in public services. It is also about the gap between the promise of affluence and its failure to deliver real satisfactions and a sense of worthwhile endeavour. The legacy of two decades of 'Thatcherism' in the UK includes more dynamic enterprise, but it also involves more insecurity and more 'hurry-sickness' in a hyper-competitive world of work and consumption. The pressures are intensified by computer technologies and by globalization of competition. As Matthew Engel has noted, barely exaggerating, we live under a new economic law: 'An organisation that employs people who are not, all the time, racing around like blue-arsed flies must, *ipso facto*, be inefficient'.[27]

The inequalities in British society exacerbate these pressures in daily life. The gap between the richest and poorest segments of society is greater than it has been for many decades. Large majorities across income groups believe that the gap is too large and should be narrowed by Government action.[28] But while the Government has taken many steps to improve the position of the poorest, as discussed in Chapter 4, it rejects the idea that there might be limits to how relatively rich the affluent can become. It expresses concern over excessive boardroom pay rises, but says that, in a free and dynamic market economy, no action can be taken against them. Our national debate about taxation and income remains evasive and unrealistic, as we argue in Chapter 2.

The gulf between the rich and the poor shows no sign of being narrowed by voluntary restraint by the hyper-affluent classes of the modern UK. In March 2000, Barclays Bank announced thousands of job cuts along with the closure of hundreds of bank branches, leaving many communities without access to banking services. This sounds like the behaviour of a firm in deep trouble. But, far from being in crisis, it was at the same time posting record profits, and announced also that its Chairman's salary had quadrupled to £1.75 million in the previous year. The gap between what counts as economic success to the 'superclass' and what is experienced by workers and communities was starkly illustrated.

The problem of disconnection between the superclass and the rest of society is hardly new. It was highlighted in the recession and corporate 'downsizing' of the early 1990s, and was a key issue in the first Real World report. But it is an issue that Labour has refused to tackle with the same vigour it has shown in offering new rights to, and demanding new responsibilities from, the poorest in our society. Corporation taxes on business have been lowered, and business has been courted, rightly, by the Government as a valued partner in strategic policy-making. But there has been little debate and less action on the social responsibilities of the private sector which might be expected in return.

In particular, despite the Government's review of company law, we have yet to see a serious debate on the reform of corporate governance to reflect the concerns and rights of stakeholders in the wider community as well as shareholders; or proposals to regulate and increase the accountability of transnational corporations, which have more scope than ever to avoid national taxes and to dilute attempts to regulate their behaviour. We rely on the voluntary initiatives of business to improve their accountability and push for more sustainable development, and this leaves too much scope for foot-dragging by many companies, while a group of enlightened corporations take a lead in social and environmental policy. This is not in the long-term interest of big business: its public image is damaged by the rapacity of many multinationals in exploiting key resources (such as forests and fisheries), and by the greed of the high-profile minority of executives whose astonishing pay packets bear no visible relationship to their performance.

15

Its unbalanced approach to business has created problems for Government in relation to 'consumer power'. It was badly wrong-footed over genetically modified (GM) foods, seeming to back uncritically the corporate wisdom of Monsanto until late in the day, and belatedly recognizing the force of citizens' concerns over the introduction of GMOs (GM organisms) into the food chain (see below). It has yet to offer adequate support for the development of organic farming, despite the explosion of consumer demand (70 per cent of our organic produce is imported), and the very modest funds available for supporting farmers to convert are greatly over-subscribed.

On security and conflict prevention, the Government faces tough criticisms about the lack of substance behind its claims to have an 'ethical dimension' in its foreign policy. While the attempt to introduce ethics into foreign policy is welcome in principle, the Government faces controversy over continuing arms sales and over the use of export credits to support this trade, criticisms of levels of development aid, and accusations of inconsistency in standing up for embattled ethnic groups in Kosovo, but not in (say) Kurdistan. These controversies have undermined confidence in the chance of narrowing the gap between ethical aims and pragmatic 'realism' in foreign policy. Achieving results in conflict prevention means taking a much more radical approach to curbing arms production and sales, as argued in Chapter 7.

Finally, one result of the continuing gaps between rhetoric and reality, between promises and actual policy, is that Government is making little progress in revitalizing democracy. Electoral reform has been minimal, and devolution partial. Most hereditary peers have been removed from the House of Lords, but radical options for an elected second chamber have been rejected – as have ideas to make citizens' juries and other forms of participatory democracy more central to the second chamber.[29] The Government faced accusations of centralist 'control freakery' after its ill-fated attempts to manipulate the politics of devolved systems in Scotland, Wales and London. The modernization of local government has so far been all about organizational efficiency within councils, not the regeneration of the democratic link between citizen and local government, or the decentralization of genuine power and resources to the local level. The public continues to display deep disillusion and apathy towards politics, and this is especially marked among the young. Political engagement is, if anything, declining, with a growing gap between the more affluent and educated groups and the rest of the population.[30] Reversing this will take a radical effort to revitalize the world of politics, beyond anything New Labour has so far achieved or even proposed.

An illustration of this has been the continuing potency of protests and citizens' campaigns developed outside the framework of party politics and representative democracy. Since 1996, citizens' use of their consumer power against unsustainable trends and inequitable development has been mobilized in dramatic ways. At the time of the first Real World report, grassroots protests against road-building were helping reshape transport policy by challenging the orthodoxy that growth in car use must always be accommodated. Since then consumer activism has won further ground. There has been a rapid growth in demand for organic foods as more people have recognized the unsustainability of our intensive agricultural sector and the damage it does to the environment, health and local diversity of produce. There has been a significant growth in the take-up by supermarkets and shoppers of fair-trade goods, which guarantee a decent price to producers in the developing world; and 'ethical trade' initiatives, improving labour standards in global supply chains, are developing. The potential for new alliances between consumers, producers and retailers is beginning to be realized, but mainstream politics is slow to respond and engage in this.[31]

Most spectacularly, consumers have revolted against the introduction of GM foods to the UK market – and their resistance has led to a worldwide crisis for the proponents of GM crops. 1999 saw a powerful campaign by NGOs against the introduction, without systematic and careful testing, of GM foods into consumer markets. Consumers and the media, and then the supermarkets, turned against the powerful interests – Government and corporations – backing the new technologies. By early 2000 the UK Government had acknowledged the strength of public misgivings, and accepted the need for more careful trials of GM crops. Moreover, Monsanto, the corporation spearheading the development of GM technologies, lost public and market confidence to such an extent that it was taken over by Pharmacia/Upjohn at the end of 1999, and continues to exist as their agro-chemical division.[32] The development of GMOs continues, as does the debate over the need for and safety of them, and there are no guarantees that wise precautionary policies will prevail in business and government policy around the world.

The GM fiasco demonstrated the reality of the trust gap between consumers and policy-makers. As in the Brent Spar clash between Shell and Greenpeace, decision-makers in business and Government discovered that, however sound their expert arguments might seem to them, they cannot impose decisions on citizens. Public fears over GM technologies may prove to be exaggerated, but that is not the nub of the matter. The point is that in the 'X-ray' environment of modern media and intense scrutiny of policies and organizations, trust in risk assessment and management has become a vital asset.[33] Policy-makers, scientists and business leaders increasingly acknowledge the need to earn trust from the public, and that means more open dialogue and a willingness to understand why citizens see risks where the experts see benefits.[34] Gradually, such dialogues are becoming established as part of the process of innovation, and of some corporations' relationships with their stakeholder communities. Fundamentally, the GM case opens up a key question about the revitalization of democracy, to which we return in Chapters 2 and 6: how do we create better processes for making complex choices about issues which connect individual consumption to long-term collective impacts?

The upsurge in direct action and consumer protest also points to another 'democracy gap' – the lack of grip by national governments and democratic processes on globalization and the power exerted by transnational corporations. The globalizing economy is beyond the regulatory reach of nation states: we urgently need an accountable and coherent system of global governance to apply rules to the new global market which safeguard the environment and are fair to developing countries and the poor. The lack of governance for globalization is fuelling alienation from traditional politics and scepticism about the capacity of democracies to make a difference to the big issues shaping our future. The apathy aroused in the UK by elections, and in the USA by the domination of the American political process by corporate funding and identikit parties, are warning signals that the formal political system cannot ignore.

Richer Choices, Richer Futures: Connecting Sustainable Development and Modernization

Unsurprisingly, the balance sheet is mixed, and we write at an early stage in what most people expect to be at least a two-term period of government. New Labour has set out an agenda for change which in many ways deserves applause and co-operation. Government cannot transform a modern nation on its own, and the agenda needs constructive criticism and practical support from business, NGOs and individual citizens.

However, the development of the programme so far has also generated much frustration, confusion and disillusionment as Government and public face up to the problems of 'delivery' of radical change, and the fact that promised improvements in public services will take years to be realized. What concerns Real World most is that the Government, and many of its partners in the OECD countries, have barely begun to take on some of the most serious problems and challenges we face, globally and at home.

A recent Government-funded exercise in futurology projected a vision of British life towards 2010 based on current trends:[35] this suggested a future of even more 'fluid' individualism and ever looser family and community bonds, with self-interest and insecurities increasing as change in technology and work speeds up. This Britain would be creative and innovative, but could be marked by yet deeper social polarization and more rootlessness. The report was notable for its failure to consider the wider context which will help shape our future – the development of the rest of the planet, and our impacts on the environment – and to explore the changes in values and behaviour which could make for a more humane, environmentally friendly and outward-looking society. The implicit, fatalistic message is this: the future will bring us more of the social fragmentation, market-led individualism and loss of trust and engagement in civic life that we have experienced for the last generation.

This is not a future that the present Government would wish to see; nor would the citizens which gave it power on their behalf. Yet debate about the future all too often fails to open up a rich range of alternative choices. We have, as Tom Burke among others has said,[36] an 'impoverished theory of choice' in our economics and systems for assessing technologies and planning applications. But the options before us do not boil down to a simplistic battle between a check-list approach to modernization, and what Tony Blair has termed 'the forces of conservatism' blocking progress. There are different paths available to the outcome we want – namely sustainable development that shapes a modernized, cleaner and fairer economy, and a more democratic governance of globalization. We need better ways to explore 'alternative modernizations' that will open up more imaginative and innovative solutions to present problems.[37]

Real World argues that sustainable development can provide a vision of the future we all want: a fair and decent society; a rich and diverse environment; and a prosperous economy. It can also provide a robust framework for debate and policy design, helping to identify outcomes and targets to which a wide range of innovations and initiatives can contribute. It allows policy-makers to avoid false choices – such as between environmental protection and economic competitiveness – and it requires them to face up to real challenges which they are tempted to duck – such as the need to plan for reductions in traffic and in the volume of household waste. Sustainable development can provide new development models for poorer countries which will enable them to raise their quality of life without risking growing inequality and environmental degradation. And finally, it focuses policy-makers on alternative ways to achieve desired goals and on innovations in production and consumption which are otherwise marginalized.

Real World aims to set out a vision of qualitatively richer futures for Britain and its relationship with the rest of the world,[38] and to highlight the problems and opportunities for change in Government policy. However, we emphasize that the issues are not simply the responsibility of Government. We are moving into a world in which business and consumers not only share much of the responsibility for making positive change but can also have increased power to bring it about. Increasingly, it is recognized that this capacity for shaping change needs to be enhanced by greater democratization: making companies more publicly accountable; empowering the poor to make decisions about local planning and the renewal of neighbourhoods; and equipping people to make choices not only as consumers but also as responsible citizens. This second Real World report is intended to help shape the agenda for change to which all sectors and all parts of society can and must contribute.

Five areas for action stand out, to which we return in the following chapters:

1 *Making a Low Carbon, High Value Economy:* promoting business innovation in technology to achieve a tenfold increase in the productivity of our energy and material use, dramatically reducing waste, pollution and greenhouse gas emissions, in order to respect the environmental limits we are already, or are in danger of, breaching.
2 *Reducing poverty and key inequalities at home and abroad:* attacking the causes and consequences for individuals, families and communities (including whole regions and countries) of persistent poverty and social exclusion – lack of access to the resources, services and rights which make full citizenship and social contribution possible.
3 *Promoting sustainable development in the international economic system:* reforming global economic governance – above all the trade system – to ensure that developing countries can grow equitably and in an environmentally sound way; leadership from the rich world in reducing resource consumption, and in redesigning debt and aid strategies to promote sustainable and fair globalization that ensures that market forces serve the public good in the rich and developing worlds alike.
4 *Promoting security, peace and conflict prevention:* seeing sustainable development strategies as a vital force for long-term international security and prevention of conflicts; and helping promote security through debt relief, strengthening of the UN, curbs on arms production and the arms trade, better development and humanitarian aid, and peacekeeping.

5 *Renewing democracy for richer choices:* innovating in democratic processes at local, national and international/global levels, in order to improve public engagement in decision-making and to foster national and international debate on innovations, risks and long-term impacts of our choices as consumers and citizens.

If our political system and markets can be reformed to engage creatively and energetically with these agendas, we will stand a far better chance of aligning the programme of modernization with the vision of sustainable development, of moving from here to sustainability in the course of the new century.

21

The Rest of this Report

The next chapter provides an overview of the politics of sustainable development today. We go on to look at global and local environmental issues (Chapter 3); poverty and social exclusion in Britain and overseas (Chapter 4); strategies for fair and sustainable global economic development (Chapter 5); the renewal of democracy in the UK and beyond (Chapter 6); and international peace and security (Chapter 7). Finally, in Chapter 8 we identify key issues for Government, business and civil society to pursue in the run-up to the UN Earth Summit 2002.

Britain has the opportunity to be a leader and an exemplar to the world at Earth Summit 2002 – ten years after the Rio Earth Summit which focused global attention on the ecological and social costs of global industrialization. Our aim is to encourage Britain's decision-makers, in all sectors, to seize that opportunity, and to make the UK a pioneer in building an innovative, sustainable economy and vibrant democratic society fit for its purpose in the new century. This is a Millennial ambition that does justice to the challenges facing the people and the environment, here and around the world.

2 Richer Futures:
The Politics of Sustainable Development

'Today, the central issues for thoughtful and successful industries – the two being increasingly identical – relate not to how best to produce the goods and services needed for a satisfying life – that's now pretty well worked out – but rather to what is worth producing, what will make us better human beings, how we can stop trying to meet non-material needs by material means, and how much is enough.'
Paul Hawken, Amory B Lovins, L Hunter Lovins[1]

'Capitalism was transformed and reshaped by the socialist challenge; if the green challenge has a similar effect, it will in time produce a world economic and trading system vastly different from today's... Progress is infuriatingly slow and conventional politics remains clogged with old thinking. There will be many reverses to come. But the trend is one way.'
Andrew Marr[2]

Western Dominance: The End of History?

Looking back on the 20th century, it seems to be divided between a dark age and what has been, by historical standards, a golden one – for the West, at least. Between 1900 and 1950 humanity endured two world wars, the Depression, and totalitarian regimes. But the last half-century has seen a period of unprecedented peace and plenty in the West, crowned in 1989–91 by the end of the Cold War and the disappearance of Communism as a rival to capitalist democracy. Francis Fukuyama's book on 'the end of history' and the triumph of markets and liberalism summed up the mindset of many Western policy-makers in the 1990s.[3]

The dominance of the Western model of progress is unquestionable. Globalization – the spread of industrial production and consumption, of new technologies, and of the influence of Western cultural and political models – seems to create a single, enormous process of development. It has led many to conclude that anyone concerned with the human costs of capitalism has to abandon old ideas about regulation and redistribution, seeking the so-called Third Way between free-market ideology and 'outmoded' social democracy and socialism.[4]

We argue, as before, that for all its power the dominant model is unsustainable. Liberal capitalism has seen off its greatest enemies, but has yet to overcome the risks to its future from its very success in bringing unheard-of levels of innovation, production and consumption. The efforts by the New Labour Government to create a programme of 'modernization' that will revitalize society, the economy and the democratic process itself, are not yet radical enough in analysis and implementation. First, they fail to face up consistently to the tough issues facing us because of the unsustainable features of the present model of development. As argued in Chapter 1, this is because modernization needs the framework of sustainability to give it coherence. Second, they leave little room for alternative visions of modernization that permit richer choices about the paths to a sustainable future. In this chapter we enlarge on these points.

'Business as Usual': The Ideas Behind the Dominant Model of Progress

Michael Jacobs sums up the prevailing model of progress, deeply internalized by politicians, policy-makers and many citizens worldwide:

> 'The principal purpose of economic activity is to raise incomes. Income growth makes people better off: it enables them to consume greater quantities of ... goods, and through taxation enables governments to provide essential public services such as education, health care and social security ... free trade and growth lead to "modernization" – the increasing productivity of agriculture, the movement of people into towns and cities and the transformation from traditional to modern cultures. In the North, and in the South to come, scientific advance drives technological change, and thence both

> *economic growth and social development. Social and*
> *environmental problems … are gradually tackled'[5]*

This model is now 'going global'. It has helped create the conditions for unprecedented prosperity for hundreds of millions of people across the world. It has been a force for greater economic well-being, social liberalization and technological advance. In its most progressive, democratic and socially equitable forms it is practically and morally superior to the remaining regimes which resist it, whose alternative models invariably involve repression, poverty and no vision of progress for the poor. But this superiority does not mean that the present Western model of development is sustainable, for us or for developing countries, or that globalization of the narrow 'free market' version of capitalism is inevitable or desirable. Quite the contrary.

Globalization is hardly new. Arguably, we are living through another phase in a long process of interpenetration of economies and societies that began in earnest with the Western exploration and colonization of the Americas five centuries ago. But there are new elements to globalization that make the present trend of integration of economies profoundly significant:

- the global spread of industrial production, trade, consumption and competition, and the integration of more markets into one system of rules governing trade, investment and finance;
- the diffusion of modern technologies to developing countries;
- the increasing reach of telecommunications – telephones, television and the internet;
- the growing recognition of the importance of well developed civil society and good governance (democracy, legal systems and a rich range of community organizations) to securing sustained and sustainable economic progress;
- the globalization of environmental problems, from locally 'visible' hotspots of pollution and loss of habitat and species, to 'invisible' problems affecting ecosystems on an international scale – climate disruption, spread of toxic chemicals, loss of biodiversity, ozone-layer depletion and over-exploitation of fisheries and freshwater supplies.

Globalization has often been discussed by policy-makers, business leaders and free market economists as if it were a force of nature, an inevitable trend that national governments and citizens must accept – or else be marginalized in the new economy.

But the present process of global economic development is neither inevitable nor unalterable. Indeed, sustainable development requires that we learn to govern the globalization of markets, rather than letting it dominate societies the world over.

Questioning 'Business as Usual'

Despite its acceleration and seemingly unstoppable character, globalization on the present 'neo-liberal' model of market deregulation, privatization and 'free' trade has come under fire from two directions. First, its tendency to increase inequalities in society and marginalize large numbers of people economically and culturally, has led to a backlash, manifest in the election in the late 1990s of more liberal and social democratic governments in Europe, and in confessions of failure from the World Bank and other international agencies. The naïve application of neo-liberal economic policies developed in the USA and the UK to the complex and fundamentally different context of post-Communist Russia or impoverished societies in Africa has not led to widespread improvements in well-being and economic capacity. In many ways it has entrenched and worsened inequalities, corruption and organized crime.[6] The lesson has been that markets need a social foundation – good government, respected laws and a framework of corporate regulation and business ethics – to humanize capitalism. It is a lesson spelled out by Adam Smith which many 'economic advisors' from Western consultancies and global agencies have failed to heed.

Second, the model has faced mounting criticism of a more profound kind. Increasingly, people are arguing that the progress delivered by Western 'business as usual' is subject to diminishing returns. Higher growth and consumption are treated as ends in themselves by governments and business, but many citizens now feel that more of the same kind of affluence is no longer a way to a better quality of life. Growth is not the same thing as progress; and what counts as progress to economic decision-makers may not feel like it to citizens. New approaches to valuing economic activity indicate that growth in GDP has diverged sharply from gains in quality of life – see Panel 1 on the Index of Sustainable Economic Welfare (ISEW).[7]

Alternative approaches to valuing economic activity stress the need for policies to tackle the downside of growth and the collective impacts of individual consumption choices. More pri-

25

Panel 1

Growth Does Not Always Mean Progress: The Index of Sustainable Economic Welfare (ISEW)

The ISEW, inspired by work by the US environmental economists Herman Daly and John Cobb, has been developed over the last few years by researchers at Surrey University's Centre for Environmental Strategy and the New Economics Foundation. The ISEW aims to provide a new measure of economic development, overcoming the well-known limitations of GDP as an indicator of progress. Similar indices have been developed in other countries, notably the Genuine Progress Index (GPI) devised by John and Clifford Cobb in the USA.

The ISEW seeks to place a value on aspects of well-being and to take account of the environmental and social costs and benefits of production. For example, it values unpaid labour (such as childcare) and treats it as a positive contribution to the economy, whereas GDP ignores childcare, except as a paid service. The ISEW also makes deductions from GDP to reflect the costs to society and the environment of activities which GDP simply adds in to the total of contributions to economic activity. Thus, for example, ISEW subtracts from GDP the cost of 'defensive spending' (such as the cost of crime or the healthcare costs of road accidents) and of damage to the environment (such as the cost of cleaning up oil spills).

ISEW is open to a range of criticisms. Like other attempts to revise GDP, the ISEW suffers from a degree of arbitrariness in the valuations it places on intangible good and the weighting it gives to social and environmental factors. But ISEW is a powerful catalyst for debate, providing a graphic way of illustrating the fact that economic growth cannot be used, as it so often has been by policy-makers, as a proxy for a larger understanding of progress.

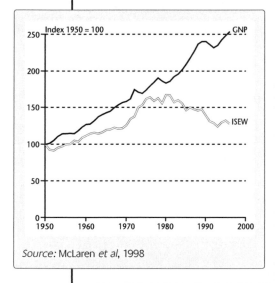

Source: McLaren *et al*, 1998

Sources: T Jackson *et al*, *An Index of Sustainable Economic Welfare for the UK 1950–96* (Guildford: Centre for Environmental Strategy, University of Surrey, 1998); D McLaren *et al*, *Tomorrow's World: Britain's Share in a Sustainable Future* (London: FoE/Earthscan, 1998) H Daly and J Cobb, *For the Common Good*, (London: GreenPrint, 1989)

vate choice is of little use if the 'commons' on which all depend are degraded by the very process of growth: if the air is polluted; the roads are chronically congested; the water and soil are damaged by pesticides, and the climate is dangerously disrupted as a result of fossil fuel consumption. There is mounting concern that the 'social commons' too have been degraded: that the vast increase in private choice and individualism has been purchased at a high price, damaging the 'social capital' of trust, neighbourliness, community spirit and respect for others on which decent social relations depend.

27

This critique also points to the global scale of these environmental and social 'externalities' – costs generated by 'business as usual' which fall on everyone, and especially on the most vulnerable. The dominant economic model has succeeded in many ways in tackling local problems of pollution and in reducing many inequalities and injustices. But its global reach exposes the limits to its capacity for problem-solving and overcoming challenges to its legitimacy. Real World argues that the model has a structural incapacity to respond to clear signals of unsustainable development: it is not a 'self-correcting' system in which market forces always automatically develop optimal outcomes. Consider for example global environmental degradation and the plight of the world's poorest.

It is becoming clear that global ecological problems have emerged which do not respond to incremental, technological fixes – global warming, the loss of biodiversity on a huge scale, the crisis in global fisheries, and the inexorable rise of road traffic and pressures of congestion, pollution and loss of countryside. The design of present markets fails to give incentives to conserve key resources and to promote forms of governance that prevent damaging over-exploitation.

In relation to poverty, the last two decades have seen not only phenomenal growth in wealth in the West and in many developing countries, but also persistent and often worsening divisions between rich and poor, within and between countries. The UN Development Programme's 1999 report on human development showed that in the second half of the 1990s the world's 200 richest people had more than doubled their wealth to over US$1 trillion; meanwhile, the number of 'absolute poor' people living on less than US$1 dollar per day was unchanged at some 1.2 billion.[8] These and other indicators of gross inequality pointed to a world of 'grotesque' divisions in living standards and prospects for well-being and environmental gains, as the report flatly said. The gap between the richest fifth of the world's population and the poorest fifth has widened over the last three decades. Far from 'trickling down' from the entrepreneurial classes around the world, wealth has coagulated around them, and the poor have been left to languish.

What has been missing is a realization that there is no such thing as 'the market' – an autonomous mechanism which allocates resources optimally without intervention from Government and civil society. Markets depend on a social and political foundation of rules, incentives and values. It has been this which has been lacking or under-developed in many countries, and above all at the global level.

Critiques of the neo-liberal model, acknowledging this point, now come from the very international agencies most eager to apply its economic medicine to developing countries and the ex-Communist world in the 1990s. The OECD and World Bank now accept that the gross inequalities exacerbated by neo-liberal economic policies have undermined the prospects for stable economic development. Progress cannot be secured without reversing environmental degradation, reducing inequalities, devising policies that improve the lives and prospects of the poor, ensuring good government through sound institutions and a strong civil society.[9] The persistent arguments of NGOs, citizens and consumers against the effects of neo-liberal globalization have begun to be heard by international policy-makers.

To an encouraging degree, these arguments have made an impact on the modernization programme of the New Labour Government: as we note in the next section, this means there are important affinities between the programme and the goals of Real World. But a fundamental point has yet to be acknowledged in the self-criticisms by global economic agencies and in the aspirations of governments, including New Labour. This is that it is not only the neo-liberal model of globalization and economic development that is unsustainable but also, more generally, the conventional model of progress through economic growth alone. As Michael Jacobs has argued, the problems of environmental degradation and deep inequality:

> '*are not... symptoms of the model's failure, but of its success. The conventional wisdom needs to be exactly reversed: the better the model performs, the worse these problems will get... Moreover, since each is relat-*

*ed to the others, they cannot simply be dealt with sep-
arately and incrementally. They require more fundamental changes in the patterns of economic and social
development.'[10]*

It is this recognition that is at the heart of the tensions that exist
between New Labour's agenda for change and the Real World
vision of sustainable development (see Panel 2). The affinities

---

Panel 2

Sustainable Development

The idea of sustainable development has been defined in many ways,
but the most familiar definition remains that given in the Brundtland
Commission report, *Our Common Future* (1987): 'development which
meets the needs of the present without compromising the ability of
future generations to meet their own needs'. For the UK Government, in
its 1999 sustainable development strategy report, it is about 'ensuring a
better quality of life for everyone, now and for generations to come'; this
means meeting four objectives at the same time, at home and around
the world:

1 social progress that recognizes the needs of everyone;
2 effective protection of the environment;
3 prudent use of natural resources;
4 maintenance of high and stable levels of economic growth and
   employment.

Another definition, from the Real World member Forum for the Future,
sees sustainable development in this way:

*'Sustainable development is a dynamic process which enables all people
to realize their potential and improve their quality of life in ways that
simultaneously protect and enhance the Earth's life-support systems.'*

The starting point for definitions of sustainable development is the diagnosis of unsustainable trends in the economy, and in our exploitation of
natural resources. The core concepts behind the term now have wide
acceptance. They are that:

• the environment, globally and locally, must be protected so that the
  critical life support services it provides are maintained for present
  and future generations;
• environmental policy and economic policy must be integrated if
  this is to happen;
• the main goal of economic development should be to create conditions for people to enjoy a better quality of life, not simply the pursuit of quantitative growth in the economy;

- the pursuit of sustainable development must include policies to eliminate poverty, in the industrialized and developing worlds alike;
- all parts of society must be involved in decision-making about the measures that will bring about the transition to sustainable economic and social systems over the coming decades.

The aim of sustainable development was endorsed by 149 countries, including the UK, at the UN Earth Summit on environment and development at Rio in 1992. This conference agreed a global action plan for sustainable development – Agenda 21. Nation states and municipalities have since produced many national and local Agenda 21 strategies. In the UK, all local authorities were to have drawn up a Local Agenda 21 plan by the end of 2000. Since Rio, many international organizations, businesses and other bodies around the world have also endorsed the goals of sustainable development.

Sustainable development is a political process. It requires judgement and trade-offs about what counts as essential environmental 'capital' and what does not, and how much of the Earth we are prepared to share with other species. Thus it is full of contested ideas and ethical dilemmas, as well as being concerned with techniques for assessing our environmental impact and evaluating risks and choices in as objective a way as possible.

Sources: WCED, *Our Common Future*, (Oxford: OUP, 1987); Forum for the Future, *Understanding Sustainability*, (London: Forum for the Future, 2000); DETR, *A Better Quality of Life for All*, (London: DETR, 1999); UNEP/WWF/IUCN, *Caring for the Earth*, (London: Earthscan, 1991)

and differences between them, and the implications for the direction of policy, are highlighted in the next two sections.

The Modernization Project and Sustainable Development: Affinities and Shared Agendas

The New Labour Government in the UK bases its programme on a far-reaching analysis of the reasons for previous Labour electoral defeats and the changes wrought by New Right governments in the 1980s. This analysis pointed to the need for a radical reappraisal of centre-Left politics and the abandonment of many aspects of social democratic programmes which, it was argued, had been rendered obsolete by social, economic and technological change.[11]

Some of this reassessment makes important concessions to the neo-liberal view of the world. Labour and its counterparts elsewhere have largely accepted the arguments that the State should not attempt to run enterprises; that income inequalities are not a key problem providing that the poor are able to gain opportunities for work and higher incomes; and that taxes on income should be contained and reduced. New Labour's thinkers point to the transformation of the economy by deregulation and privatization: there is no way back to the social democratic past.

This leads to plentiful criticism that the Third Way amounts to little more than dressing up neo-liberal 'business as usual' in flimsy social democratic clothing.[12] Much of this is well founded: in particular, New Labour has been far friendlier to business than to the beleaguered public sector, and has displayed many of the crude, and sometimes populist, reflexes of its predecessor in relation to immigration and criminal justice. But there is more to the Third Way vision of modernization than its concessions to the New Right. Its defenders argue that it is about the pursuit of traditional, social democratic goals – freedom, community, fairness and equal rights – in a transformed economic and social world which requires that social democrats use new means to achieve these ends.[13]

The project of modernization is complex. It is partly an attempt to rethink social democracy, partly an acceptance of the primacy of markets in economic policy and partly an overhaul of institutions to make them deliver better outcomes. New Labour's programme is a confusing spectacle not only for 'old style' socialists and many radicals of the centre and Left, but also for conservatives – and no doubt for some of the Third Way's proponents themselves. For every progressive policy, there is a concession to vested interests or to populist prejudices (as in the case of policy on refugees and asylum-seekers). The elements of the package seem ill-assorted, and hard to connect to a coherent set of values. Much of this stems from New Labour's overriding desire to remain in power long enough to usher in an era of dominance for progressive parties. The long-term vision is thus constantly accompanied by short-term positioning intended to keep the Government popular with tabloid newspaper editors and as many electoral constituencies as possible – an approach that means that everyone is offended at least as often as they are pleased.

But despite the Government's tendency to follow public opinion rather than lead it, and all the consequent inconsistencies between vision and short-term action, much of New Labour's programme is a genuine attempt to get to grips with

31

big changes. As Jacobs notes, the Third Way has not been simply about accommodation of business-led globalization, individualism and new technology regardless of their social and environmental impact: the Government does want to direct these forces in positive directions.[14] It argues that we need radical change in the process of policy-making and far-reaching constitutional reform, in order to re-energize democracy and bring politics into renewed contact with citizens' key concerns. It accepts that traditional compartmentalized policy-making has failed to deal with the most complex 'joined up' problems – of the environment, of social exclusion and poverty and of welfare.[15] It embraces the idea that policy-making needs to focus on good outcomes and learning about what works, rather than simply on inputs and outputs. It is easy to point to a gap between the emphasis on 'holistic' policy-making, learning lessons and 'joined up government' on the one hand, and practical action on the other hand. Examples of fragmented policy are still thick on the ground. But at least an attempt is underway to bring about a radical change in the culture of policy-making and delivery, especially in combating social exclusion.

So where do we see a need for a more radical, courageous and imaginative approach? In the chapters that follow we highlight specific issues, but it is important to explore the more general problems that the Third Way approach has yet to overcome.

The Sustainability Gap: Why the Third Way Falls Short of Sustainable Development

In Chapter 1 we listed several 'gaps' that mark the faultlines of Millennial politics. These have been acknowledged, but not yet bridged by New Labour. As Tony Blair writes in the foreword to the Government's Sustainable Development Strategy:

> 'The last hundred years have seen a massive increase in the wealth of this country and the well being of its people. But focusing solely on economic growth risks ignoring the impact – both good and bad – on people and on the environment... Success has been measured by economic growth – GDP – alone. We have failed to see how our economy, our environment and our society are all one. And that delivering the best possible quality of life for us all means more than concentrating solely on economic growth.'[16]

32

Witness Box 1: Forum for the Future

The UN Conference on Environment and Development (Earth Summit) in Rio in 1992 shifted the whole debate about sustainability for everyone. It was no longer a matter of arguing whether evidence of a rapidly degrading environment, and persistent human poverty and inequality of opportunity should be on the policy agenda or not. It was. The challenge became one of designing and implementing policies that converged the social and economic goals of well-being and wealth for all, with the fundamental need to sustain a life-supporting environment.

Forum for the Future was set up to help people make sense of that challenge, for their business or organization, and for themselves. The starting point had to be where they were now; the process had to be both realistic and cognisant of the degree of urgency that the evidence – in particular from the climate scientists – seemed to dictate. For this reason the Forum works through partnerships and at strategic level.

Our work with our partners who are mainly, but not exclusively, in business, government and higher education, confirms that sustainable development is not something that they plan to embrace in the future. In very different ways, they have started. All are already operating in a rapidly changing and increasingly complex world and sustainable development, with its emphasis on integrating social, environmental and economic goals in an ethical framework, does offer an overarching logic that can help shape strategies for the future. Some have been able to embrace it quickly and frankly. Others are taking a more measured and cautious approach.

Shifting institutional thinking is hard. Few work-forces have encountered even the most basic scientific principles that underpin environmental sustainability at any stage of their education or training, and many organizations are structured so as to prevent the integrated, cross-disciplinary approach that is at the heart of identifying and implementing sustainability solutions. Everywhere though, pressures to change are growing. The environmental evidence is mounting; the demand for corporate responsibility is growing, as is the demand for better value in the provision of public services. Consumers are increasingly interested in the environmental and ethical provenance of the food they eat and the goods they buy. In the usual muddled and chaotic way that society engages with change, sustainable development is forcing its way from the conceptual margins into the mainstream of the practical reality for more and more people.

And, to be fair, as this book points out very well, Government is beginning to respond. But for our partners, as for others in the vanguard of change, there remains too much of a dislocation between what Government is exhorting people and organizations to do, and the positive frameworks and incentives that need to be put in place to actively support and reward those who do change to a more sustainable way of doing things.

> *From Here to Sustainability* sums up this 'gap' very well. Forum for the Future would argue that sustaining the effort of the first movers in the UK, and bringing others on board at a speed that both social and environmental indicators, and the economic markets of the future, indicate we should, will require Government to exercise much more vision in its leadership than it has to date. If sustainable development is to become a reality in the timescale that evidence suggests, then it must be at the heart of Government in an integrated and very practical sense, not just a rhetorical one.
>
> Key policy targets for closing the sustainability gap are:
>
> • *Resource productivity should be a key economic performance measure.* Factor-10-type improvements in the efficiency with which we use resources are required. We see this as a tremendous opportunity for new business and industries as well as for transformation of existing ones.
> • *Making that ethical foreign policy a reality.* Without pretending things can be sorted out overnight, policies for aid, trade, security and all foreign relations based on sustainable development principles will be vital if change is to work at a global as well as a local level.
> • *Restoration of public trust in systems of justice and governance.* Public confidence in politics, business, professional bodies and public institutions has probably never been lower. This trust can only be regained through a much more frank and open approach to all decision-making, standard-setting and accountability procedures. The public needs to be re-engaged in democratic processes through the sort of discourse that is honest and embraces the complexities and difficulties of decisions. All the evidence from deliberative and participatory processes suggests that, even over issues that require highly specialist understanding, 'common sense' usually prevails.

This represents a huge advance in thinking, reflected in the Government's indicators of sustainable development. But the radical change in perspective needs to be reinforced in all the key areas of policy-making. In the Government's programme, and across business and society, there is a 'sustainability gap' between current policies and attitudes and the changes we need if we are to bring an end to unsustainable trends.

A major problem, noted in Chapter 1, is that sustainable development is not yet treated as the unifying framework that gives coherence to the pursuit of interrelated economic, social and environmental goals. Without this, the modernization project misses connections between these areas that must be made if the right kind of reform is to be made and maintained. It means that policy-makers are prone to react to emerging evidence and to twists and turns in public moods, rather than focusing on the connections between issues and developing policy against a 'big picture' analysis, as provided by the framework of sustainable development. The result is that however impressive individual policy initiatives and White Paper analyses may be, they do not add up to a cohesive and strategically designed vision of change and implementation.

In addition, there are inhibitions and inconsistencies in New Labour's approach that work against sustainable development goals. We identify six blindspots that inhibit progress:

1 the perception of environmentalism as a problem rather than a force for progress;
2 an uneven approach to balancing rights with responsibilities;
3 a narrow view of the 'new economy' and globalization, and of the nature of market forces;
4 over-centralization and the crisis of local governance;
5 the tension between 'individual choice' and collective well-being; and
6 risk, innovation and alternatives: an impoverished idea of choice.

The Fear of Environmentalism

First, Labour perceives environmentalism as a problem rather than as a force for progress. Michael Jacobs has analysed possible reasons for this:[17] a dislike of what is seen as a 'deep Green' rejection of capitalism; a fear that environmental policies impose burdens on business; a perception of radical environmentalists as 'anti-growth' and hostile to 'modernity'; and a view that tougher environmental policies will hurt the poor (for example, through raising fuel prices). Environmentalism is still not seen as a source of innovation and opportunities to pursue the outcomes shared by the Third Way and proponents of environmental sustainability (see Chapter 3).

As Jacobs notes, this kind of response to environmental campaigners is in many ways unfair to much of the green movement, which has greatly refined its thinking on environmental sustainability, and which has become a valuable partner to

Government and business in designing policy.[18] Environmentalism is not, except at the margins, fuelled by deep-seated dislike of progress, market forces or modernity *per se*. Nor does it imply blanket hostility to growth and markets. Rather, it is about alternative forms of progress and modernization, based on the argument that conventional approaches to these ideas fail to face up to environmental constraints and to measure accurately the social and ecological costs of economic development. It draws attention to the fact that there is no such thing as 'the' market, which is independent of society. Rather, markets do what we ask them to do, and reflect the conditions and regulations we place on them. Environmentalists want markets designed to reflect better the social and environmental costs of economic development, and to support society's non-economic goals. They also make the point that while the sort of economic growth that delivers better quality of life for developing countries and low-income groups is desirable, we need to be highly selective about the forms of growth that can be sustained by the rich countries.

Nor is it fair to characterize environmentalism as backward-looking and 'anti-progress'. If one is driving fast towards a cliff edge, it is not a concession to the forces of conservatism or nostalgia to brake and swerve. The diagnosis of many trends in economic development as unsustainable does not entail policies that involve regressing to a pre-affluent world (although it does point to some policies that mean going 'back to the future', such as the revival of organic farming, support for cycling and walking, and the revival of town- and city-centres as residential places). Rather, it is the basis for innovation and redesign of the products, services and markets that have brought real progress for millions, so that they can continue to offer gains in quality of life instead of threatening it for future generations.

But many politicians and policy-makers still see environmental policies as constraints and burdens, not as catalysts for radical changes that will enhance our quality of life and open up new economic opportunities. This places serious limitations on the ways in which economic policy is being modernized, and to which the environment is, as promised by New Labour in 1997, placed 'at the heart' of government.

Whose Rights, Whose Responsibilities?

Second, the modernization project is uneven in its thinking about rights and responsibilities. In principle, the need for a balance between rights and responsibilities has great resonance in sustainable development thinking and in environmentalism: individuals owe duties of care to their communities and environments as well as having fundamental human rights. The Government's approach also owes much to a recognition that we cannot always afford to leave judgements about the way to live solely to individuals. Personal choices have collective consequences, and insistence on being 'non-judgemental' about lifestyles risks ignoring this. We know a good deal by now about what makes for a wasted life and one potentially rich in fulfilment, and policy for social 'inclusion' should be aimed at helping people avoid the former, with all its impacts on self and others, and at gaining the skills and relationships that provide the possibility at least of the 'good life'.[19]

But there are serious flaws in the approach to rights and responsibilities taken so far. For many people who are 'excluded', it is necessary for there to be an extension of rights in order for them to be in a position to make a social contribution. Consider the position of many disabled people: their benefit rules have been tightened and pressure to take employment opportunities increased. However, unless their rights are better recognized, in the form of action to end discrimination and to make transport and buildings accessible, then talk of fulfilling responsibilities is hollow and coercive. The Third Way has been tougher on reminding people of their 'responsibility' than on the implementation of their accompanying rights.

Government has also been more interested so far in restricting traditional rights – such as trial by jury – and in emphasizing its toughness in dealing with refugees and asylum-seekers, than in extending the agenda of civil liberties. It has retreated from its pre-1997 position on freedom of information, placing heavy restrictions on its proposals for reform of access to public-sector information. And it has yet to grasp the potential of the idea of extending rights as a means of raising people's awareness of the relationship between their private freedoms and their responsibility to others. For example, consider the possibility of a bill of environmental rights, as proposed by Friends of the Earth in Witness Box 6 (Chapter 3, page 71). This would

37

enshrine rights to environmental health – and to information on pollution and redress for breaches of environmental quality. It would emphasize people's responsibilities to each other and to the environment, as well as personal rights, connecting the collective and the individual realms, which have been forced apart by the relentless promotion of individualism and consumerism.

Moreover, the Third Way notion of 'rights with responsibilities' has so far been applied almost wholly to the socially excluded poor: welfare recipients have been left in no doubt of their social responsibilities, but what about the rich? Big businesses have seen a massive extension of their freedom of operation in recent years, but we have yet to see a 'New Deal' that requires of them commitments to social and environmental responsibility as a quid pro quo for tax breaks, cuts in corporation tax and relaxation of regulations. While more coercive policies are applied to the poor, there is little pressure from Government on big business and the most affluent classes to show more responsibility towards the environment, the communities affected by their decisions, and their workforces.

The message from the recent Committee of Inquiry on a new vision for business was that the gap between business success and corporate responsibility could be closed. Many steps can be taken to promote more sustainable and ethical business which will benefit companies as well as the communities and the environment.[20] But while some corporations are developing impressive policies for social and environmental responsibility, many are not, and we lack a coherent set of standards to judge progress by business towards tackling unsustainable development and fulfilling social responsibilities. Despite evidence of public support (see Panel 3), Government's review of corporate governance has backed away from serious measures to enshrine the importance of corporate responsibility towards the environment, and to communities beyond company shareholders.

What Kind of Modernization, What Kind of Growth?

The growth in the rewards and privileges for market 'winners', and the failure to focus on their social responsibilities, are connected to the third issue – the risk of taking a fatalistic view of the economic and technological developments lumped under the headings of 'globalization' and the 'knowledge economy' of new technologies and services. At times, the Government and its

---

Panel 3

Good Business? Corporate Social and Environmental Responsibility

Over the last 20 years there has been a steady growth in debate, initiatives and reporting about the environmental and social responsibilities of business. This has been fuelled by the increase in the political and social influence of business following the market liberalization of the 1980s in the UK and the USA.

But reporting by companies on social and environmental performance is still in its infancy, lacking statutory backing and agreed standards. Some multinationals now produce detailed social and environmental reports, while others produce general statements, and many have taken no action. Over one-third (37 per cent) of the FTSE 100 companies in the UK still do not publish an environmental report. Pressure for more transparency, standard processes for social and environmental accountability, and investment in social and environmental initiatives by big business is certain to go on growing. As the table here indicates, public opinion rates corporate responsibility as a major issue. In this context, it is in companies' own interests to try to improve their performance rather than wait to be targeted by NGOs, media and consumer boycotts.

The Importance of Corporate Responsibility: Results from a MORI survey, summer 1999

When forming a decision about a product or service from a particular company or organization, how important is it to you that it shows a high degree of social responsibility?

	Very important	Fairly important	Total
1998	28%	49%	77%
1999	41%	40%	81%

Base: 1,011 British adults, July–August 1999

Source: MORI, London

---

advisors appear to view these developments as a massive external force to which we have to adapt, like it or not. Charles Leadbeater reviews the transformation of labour markets, organizations, careers and institutions demanded by the IT-intensive knowledge economy and concludes that there is no way around it – we have to 'go through it'.[21] It is odd that Government makes no bones about the tough choices and the costs of transition to prosperity in the 'new economy' of digital services, but finds it hard to communicate a similar vision of the benefits of shifting to a sustainable economy which would harness IT for environmental and social benefit as well as economic dynamism.

The radical nature of the changes wrought by IT and other technologies is not in doubt. And Government has not taken a wholly fatalistic view of them: for example, it is committed to ensuring universal access to the Internet in order to prevent 'information exclusion' among the poor. But the prevailing model of modernization adapts people to the demands of global corporations and of the new technologies. It stresses flexible labour markets, more private provision in welfare, rapid adoption of new technologies and the need for workers to adapt to further acceleration of change. It places much less emphasis on reciprocal steps by employers and regulators to help workers and local economies thrive, and to reconcile the demands and satisfactions of work with those of home and wider citizenship.

What this points to is a greater tension between our role as consumers and our futures as workers, citizens and family members – all roles in which, for many people, control and choice seem to be diminished by prevailing forms of modernization. More choices in the shopping malls for those who can afford the price, but more pressure to work long hours, and more tension between the demands of being a worker and being a parent. What sense of 'being in control' we might gain as consumers – and much 'consumer choice' is experienced by citizens as confusing and frustrating – we tend to lose in our other social roles.[22] And we lack the tools to act on our preferences for collective goods, having been encouraged for years to value private consumption choices above all. More is said about this later.

Adapting to the forces of global change and new technology, like economic growth, can be seen as an end in itself. Unless there is a clearer political vision behind the process of modernization, we will end up with results that contradict the outcomes Government says it wants. IT-driven economic change will not on its own make a better environment or richer work for the unemployed and underpaid. We need to know what goals we want to accomplish by going through upheavals in working life and economic organization. When Government says that economic growth is essential to sustainable development, we need to ask: what kind of growth? When innovations are presented as part and parcel of an unstoppable process of modernization – as with GM foods – we need to ask: who is going to benefit, and what alternative forms of modernization and market design are open to us, and to the developing world?

A case in point is the controversy in spring 2000 over the sell-off of Rover and the closure of the Ford car plant at Dagenham. The debate was framed as a choice between accepting the decisions of BMW and Ford about the lack of a profitable future for their plants, and between finding ways to carry on producing exactly the same kinds of product. Yet we know, from Government's forecasts of traffic growth, from daily experience of road congestion and pollution, and from over-supply in the world's car markets, that this is unsustainable environmentally and economically. An approach both sustainable and modernizing would have been a far-sighted initiative from Government to explore investment with business partners, workers, local government, local communities and NGOs in a new enterprise in low-pollution, non-fossil fuel vehicle design and production. This could secure many jobs and help create a UK-based centre of excellence in what we know must be the new direction for car manufacturing in the 21st century. Third Way thinking in this important case was incoherent because the problem was not viewed through the lens of sustainable development. As a result, the politicians' immediate response was at odds with their own long-term aspirations for a sustainable economy.

41

What needs to be questioned, then, is the idea that 'alternative modernizations' for sustainable development are not available.[23] So far, welfare and labour market reform have focused on getting people off benefits and into paid work, but this is not possible for every welfare recipient: we can imagine reforms that allow more creative combinations of benefit and work, or that provide benefits in return for community volunteering, caring and other social contributions currently under-recognized.[24] Can we not imagine a more rapid adoption of new technologies for environmental sustainability, and a slower take-up of those innovations that could pose serious risks to future generations – instead of the reverse case, which is the current model? Or a modernization which provides more support for people to contribute to the economy as carers, parents and volunteers, rather than simply as knowledge-workers in a fast-moving digital economy? Or an extension of cooperative local enterprise organized for mutual benefit, and not simply policies to support private business start-ups? Government has yet to fully recognize and effectively support the mass of local innovations in the new 'community economy' which already embrace sustainable development ideals and practices.[25]

The point here is that a narrow approach to the dynamics of modern economic change can lead to a simplistic acceptance that the global will always override the local; that the development of a modernized economy is always best done by the private sector; that proliferating market choices always expand real choice for citizens; and that there is no holding back the 'ever-increasing pace of change', as policy-makers and business gurus never tire of telling us. In reality, accepting these positions condemns us to missing out on many alternative paths of development and progress which could promote better technologies, higher quality of life and a fruitful connection between local production and global development.

The Crisis of the Local

Our fourth 'sustainability gap' is about centralization of policy-making and the crisis in local governance. One effect of globalization is disorientation and a sense of loss of control for many individuals. This fuels demand for more local autonomy, politically and economically, in many areas.

Under New Labour there has been a radical departure in some ways from the centralism of traditional British government. New Labour has partially reformed the House of Lords, and established elected assemblies and devolved governments of varying autonomy in Scotland, Wales and Northern Ireland. It has set up RDAs in England that could be the seedbed for a new tier of regional assemblies and authorities. London now has an elected Mayor and assembly, and other cities could follow suit. And the Government has launched reforms in local government to improve the consistency of services and promote more engagement by citizens in local authorities' work. It wants to see a renewal of local democracy and has taken interest in new forms of participatory democracy (see Chapter 6).

Nationally, the new order is messy – a quasi-federal system in which the status of England and its regions is problematic. But while there is potential for further positive developments in the national constitution, there is a familiar crisis in local governance. Local autonomy is at odds with Government's desire to influence the quality of outcomes in education, health, housing and other areas, and with the deep distrust of local government inherited from the Thatcher and Major periods. It is easy to see why distrust persists: the quality of basic public services varies greatly from place to place, and inefficiency is widespread. Local authorities are subject to stringent controls over funding and have seen many powers removed to other agencies. The demands of over-complex systems of evaluation of local projects and services are in danger of preventing them from working well. Room for local innovation and experiment, 'bottom-up' solutions, and engagement of local people are essential in complex areas such as regeneration, planning and social housing, as is universally acknowledged.26

43

The result is a crisis in local governance. Government has devolved many responsibilities and problems to local level – such as the task of achieving reductions in congestion and increases in recycling – but has not followed up with sufficient powers and resources. This means that much of local government grows ever more demoralized, and seems less and less relevant to citizens, as shown in the miserably low turnouts in most local elections.

This matters for sustainable development. We know from theory and practice in environmental policy, urban regeneration, education and transport that 'top-down' solutions from the national level rarely achieve all the desired results. National blueprints can do no more than set out broad frameworks for action and specify standards and targets, especially in complex areas such as sustainable development planning, where we know that we need to do as much experimentation and learning as possible on how to change production and consumption patterns. Local conditions differ, and securing good outcomes depends on the cooperation and commitment of organizations that have detailed local knowledge.

Sustainable development needs strong local governance. Britain has a sustainability gap in this area because of the failure to devise a comprehensive and coherent settlement between local and central government, and between local representative democracy and the emerging movement for participatory governance. We say more on ways to bridge this gap in Chapter 6.

Consumer Choice and Collective Well-Being: The Politics of Individual Demands and Public Services

Perhaps the most complex and politically difficult issue facing the Third Way project is the tension between individual consumption and collective well-being. Governments are fixated on increasing individuals' capacity to consume, and policies that would restrain some kinds of consumption by large sections of the population are viewed with alarm. Faced with constraints on consumption – such as lack of road space or landfill sites – we have expanded supply. But now we face the reality that supply cannot be expanded indefinitely, because of problems of pollution, health risks and loss of amenity and land that we are increasingly unwilling to accept.

44

The problem for Government, and also for voters, is that citizens seem to want things both ways. People resist fuel taxes and road pricing, but rage against congestion and pollution from cars; there is much dislike of the erosion of countryside by executive housing developments, but continued movement out of cities in search of 'better' places to bring up families.[27] If sustainable development involves less car use and more urban living, then governments face immense problems of demand management – changing long-established patterns of consumption and aspiration.

Transport and housing issues highlight key problems facing modern affluent society – how to balance short-term individual and sectional interests against long-term collective ones, and how to reconcile economic development with environmental sustainability? The scale of car ownership makes governments wary of policies that might alienate 'Mondeo Man'. The growth of car-dependency gives car ownership and driving the force of a social necessity, the badge of adult status and a civil liberty. The problems of demand management were highlighted in Fred Hirsch's famous analysis of the 'social limits to growth': free use of the road, and homes in unspoiled countryside, are 'positional goods' that decline in quality the more that others have access to them. The politics of demand management forces politicians and public to face up to these limits to the power of consumer choice, which has been viewed as indefinitely expandable. As Hirsch puts it, 'The life depicted in the glossy magazines clearly is attractive to many of us. The snag is that much of it is unavailable to very many of us at once, and its diffusion may then change its own content and characteristics'.[28]

Part of the solution to the dilemmas of demand management is to emphasize the benefits to both the community and the environment as a whole, and also to individual consumers of new approaches to meeting particular needs. Curbing demand for unsustainable goods and services is not all about 'sacrifice': it frees time, money and imagination for meeting needs and wants in new and better ways. It is not about suppressing consumption, but about redirecting it. Thus it is possible for new approaches to mobility – making available more alternatives to car use, and funding them from more realistic pricing of road use – to provide better results for all. And if we can provide safe, reassuring, pleasant urban environments for families, we can reduce and redirect much unsustainable demand for rural housing.

Clearly, part of the answer will involve a comprehensive and positive approach from Government, educating public opinion and funding visible and attractive alternatives to present demand – making public transport far better, making walking and cycling easier and safer and investing in an 'urban renaissance' that will make city living affordable and reassuring to families[29] – in advance of 'stick' policies that price people out of cars and make greenfield housing developments costlier. Otherwise, in the absence of carrots, we face yet more policy gridlock, with citizens unable to change to more sustainable consumption and policy-makers fearful of the electoral consequences of wielding sticks to promote change. The dangers of failures to lead public opinion, and to make a clear link between fuel duties, environmental protection and new investment in more sustainable forms of transport, were brought home to the Government by the fuel tax protests of autumn 2000.

Part of the resolution of dilemmas could come from more and better public spending on public services. Britain needs long-term investment in public services, as announced in New Labour's Comprehensive Spending Review in July 2000. If the Government's plans are realized then great progress could be made, especially in our worst-off areas.

But another vital part of any approach to managing the tensions between individual wants and collective quality of life is a richer debate on the nature of the choices available to people and communities, and the outcomes of our private and public spending. 'Choice' is a term now associated mainly with the endless multiplication of options in the private sector – ever more identikit wine bars, bewildering mobile phone tariffs, still more options in private pensions. It looks like a cornucopia, but such multiplication is not always empowering for consumers, nor is it the same thing as an expansion of choices to allow new ways of living to flourish that can reconcile individual wants better with the needs of the public as a whole.

Witness Box 2: Transport 2000

Transport trends are unsustainable – in social and economic as well as in purely environmental terms. Traffic growth, if continued at past rates, will produce high levels of congestion with big economic consequences and environmental damage, especially with growing carbon dioxide emissions. Traffic divides communities, and increasing car dependence, exemplified by out-of-town shopping centres, widens social exclusion for those without access to a car. Meanwhile, alternatives to cars and lorries – walking, cycling, buses, trains – suffer from under-funding and neglect.

The Government is taking some action to tackle all this. Local and regional transport plans, increased rural bus funding, a new strategic rail authority with new rail franchises, quality bus partnerships and contracts, and powers for councils to charge for road use and workplace parking. But this is not enough. Sustainable transport requires Government action in three key areas:

1 *Civilizing traffic:* This means high quality street design, including greater priority to pedestrians, disabled people, cyclists, buses and trams. Home zones and quiet lanes – low speed areas with priority for pedestrians over other traffic – should become widespread. We need bus priority networks with proper enforcement; effective enforcement of speed limits; a crackdown on anti-social driving; and management of lorry traffic, with controls on larger and heavier vehicles. Further tax reforms are needed to reduce incentives for people to drive (like mileage allowances for business use of private cars) and to charge lorries sensibly. Wider charging for road use, perhaps instead of vehicle duties, should be considered.

2 *Improving choice:* Government needs to be far more active in promoting and funding a high quality public transport network. This is not just about extra and better trains and buses, but about quality – improved information, integrated ticketing, good interchange, improved personal security, better accessibility and simple fare structures. This has been treated by politicians and the public as an unattainable dream, yet applying the best practice from the UK and Europe would make a huge difference. Greater choice for freight could be offered, with good rail freight terminals, 'piggyback' services and fast coastal shipping routes.

But public transport is not the only – nor in many cases the main – alternative to car use. Many car journeys are very short; for these, improved conditions, priority for pedestrians and good cycle networks are likely to provide the main alternatives. Safe routes to schools, stations, hospitals and other such important destinations need to be developed and properly funded.

In addition, a number of other more radical ideas should be tried, such as flexible public transport services (taxi-buses, etc) that come to your door, local car clubs or 'street fleets' that give you low cost local car hire, and personalized travel information.

3 *Improving accessibility:* People travel to access goods, services and other people, not for the sake of it. We need to help people and goods travel less and more efficiently, and to promote access for everyone. This means better land use planning, with less car-based development. The Government should also do more – through tax relief, regulation and direct funding – to promote partnerships to reduce car dependence with those that generate travel. Travel plans by employers, schools, hospitals and leisure facilities, home deliveries from shops and new communications technologies can make travel easier for everyone. Social exclusion needs to be tackled through lower fares on public transport, safer streets and better services for outer city and rural communities. Trains and buses, and the stations and stops they serve, must be made more accessible for those with disabilities, children, shopping or luggage.

More fundamentally, we need to question the trend to big centralized services and the withdrawal of local services – schools, health centres, police stations, banks, post offices and shops. Too often the imagined savings from these changes result in making employees and users travel more. Similarly, the 'just in time' manufacturing and distribution orthodoxy, which results in useless freight transport and downgrades local production and sourcing, needs to be challenged and tackled through taxation and regulation.

Finally, we need – in transport as in energy and many other areas – to get away from thinking big. Traditional transport policies have relied on big infrastructure projects, built to meet forecast demand or the need for political monuments, and on questionable computer models that include only what can be counted. In practice, small-scale measures that manage demand and provide practical choice for the large number of local journeys would be far better value for money and far more sustainable.

47

The same is true for the effects of much public spending. In the public sector, we are promised a massive injection of money into investment-starved services such as health, education and transport. This is welcome in many ways, but much of the effort will simply go to making good the damage done by years of neglect. And much will also be spent on dealing with the consequences of damaging forms of consumption – poor diets, work patterns dependent on long commuter journeys, addiction, dependence on cars and exposure to pollution.

A fundamental question must be asked: how well will the spending plans be tested against the aims of the Government's Sustainable Development Strategy, to ensure that the investment helps deliver the outcomes we want? For example, spending on new and wider roads, and on better railways (beyond essential safety improvements), offers short-term relief to commuters, but will simply provide more road space to be used up rapidly by growth in car use. The costs of buying such relief are high. The director of the Pedestrians Association, Ben Plowden, notes the costs of the Government's transport plan:

> 'The plan's aim is a 50% increase in rail passenger journeys over the next decade. Rail travel accounts for less than 1% of the trips we make annually. So the Government will invest £60 billion to increase rail travel from 1% to 1.5% of trips. Hardly a bargain (although perhaps better value if reducing impacts of air travel). What about urban tram networks, costing up to £350m each? For the price of seven of 25 such schemes, safe walking and cycling routes could be provided for all 25,000 schools in the country.'[30]

Will the investments in transport produce patterns of mobility that reduce pollution, congestion and greenhouse gas emissions, and improve public health by promoting walking and cycling? If not, what are we achieving? Similarly, spending on the National Health Service (NHS) will benefit those on waiting lists, but will we find ways to improve public health so that pressure on hospitals reduces?

Will we, having spent hundreds of billions of pounds during the Government's ten-year plan, have an economy and infrastructure fit for a world which, we know, needs radical cuts in fossil fuel use, waste generation and pollution, and which offers major opportunities in renewable energy, cleaner production and much less damaging forms of transport? If the spending strategy is not designed and run within a coherent framework for sustainable development, it will produce many outcomes we do not want, and we will continue to incur the costs of environmental and social damage from economic policies that are not tested for sustainability.

Towards a Healthier Debate on Taxation and Public Goods

What all this points to is the need for two major developments in our political conversations and civic education. First, that governments need the courage to promote a richer understanding of quality of life. This means emphasizing that collective services and the taxes to pay for them make us all better off, and that personal quality of life is liable to suffer in the end if the collective services are not supported. Ultimately, individual consumption that damages the 'commons', and a culture in which income tax increases have become politically unthinkable, are unsustainable: they undermine public goods on which decent social relations, environmental quality, strong enterprises and individual thriving all depend. Public goods benefit us to varying degrees, not only directly as individual consumers, but also in our social role as citizens, employers, workers and family members.[31] We are always more than simply consumers, and we therefore need more than simply the goods we can buy as individuals. We need the public goods – healthcare, policing, shared institutions – that only collective investment supplies. The under-valuing of these services, and of the public sector workers who provide them, has to stop.

49

This message needs to be brought back unapologetically into our political debates. The Government's failure to make sense to the public of its policies on indirect taxation, and the public's resentment of levies such as petrol duty, as shown in the fuel crisis of September 2000, show the urgency of a more sophisticated, mature debate on public spending, tax and public goods. But still deeper changes are needed. Civic and moral education, and public debates, need to be more open to discussion of the values, hopes and fears influencing our choices about spending, work, family life and the environment, and about the changes in lifestyles and priorities needed for a sustainable society and a just global economy. Politicians and other opinion leaders need to speak openly on the ethical and spiritual dimensions of consumption and public goods. New participatory mechanisms are needed that allow citizens, politicians, experts and others to discuss these issues and identify new ways forward – and begin to develop the 'moral fluency'[32] that is lacking in many current debates.

Second, we need still greater willingness among politicians in all parties for open and mature debate on the role of taxation in achieving a good quality of life. New Labour has revived the language of public goods and has broached the previously unthinkable topic of limits to growth in car use – arguing, rightly, that it is ultimately 'anti-motorist' as well as anti-social and environmentally damaging to go on as we are. But it fears that the public is not ready for the message that high quality public goods, funded by taxes and well maintained, are the key to a decent, sustainable society, even though the evidence that neglecting them is disastrous is all around us in congested streets, rundown schools and dilapidated hospitals. The fear of the new politics of demand management has been evident in the Government's first-term approach to transport, acknowledging the unsustainability of traffic growth but failing to innovate in road charging and invest significantly in public transport.[33]

The national debate on tax is evasive and irresponsible, with politicians on all sides reluctant to mention income tax or hypothecated eco-taxation, and eager to suggest that with enough 'efficiency savings' and 'growth' we can afford more consumption while reducing taxes – which are always referred to as a 'burden' rather than the means of collective investment in well-being. Governments are reluctant to accept the survey evidence that consistently shows that a majority of the public backs higher taxes, even on income, in return for better services. This approach rests on cynicism about the link between statements to pollsters and the real views of those polled, and perhaps on a fear that the civic bond of trust between Government, public agencies and citizens has been eroded so much that few people have faith in the ability of the State to spend tax revenues well. Tax and trust are intertwined – regaining confidence in the former as something other than a burden is linked to measures to restore the latter, through a revitalization of citizenship.[34]

Real World believes that the public is ready for debate and a confident lead from Government on the place of tax and changes in lifestyle in renewing public services and bridging the sustainability gaps. We have reached a point where some of the limits to 'going private' are being reached: no-one can insulate themselves utterly against degradation of the environment and the social fabric, no matter how much they try to 'opt out' of public services. What is lacking is political courage and willpower to open up public debate on how we make the changes.

Short-Term Choices, Far-Reaching Risks: Processes to Open Up Long-Term Thinking and Richer Choices

Finally, there is a major gap between the processes of decision-making and the outcomes associated with sustainable development. Collective decision-making is focused on the short term, through two processes: consumer choices in the marketplace and the periodic votes in local and general elections. Consumer choices are informed by longer-term considerations in limited ways, through labelling of goods as to their environmental impact or provenance, by NGO and Government information campaigns and through consumer panics driven by the media and by governmental and business incompetence. Our election results are usually a judgement on the recent past and a protest about the present, rather than a response to open and wide-ranging debates about the long-term futures we want.

51

What this gives us is a political culture that fails to face up to the long-term implications of collective choices. Forecasting is the province of think tanks and planners in government and business. Yet the implications of new knowledge and consequent innovations can affect whole societies and future generations (as in the case of human genetics knowledge and gene engineering); learning how to assess new knowledge and technology can no longer be left to policy-makers alone. The long-term implications of GM foods were aired via a public panic, resulting in an informal 'regulation' of the market against GM technology through a *de facto* alliance between NGOs, retailers and alarmed consumers against the decisions made behind the scenes by Government and the producers. Government and business have begun to be forced into the kind of precautionary, open testing and debate they should have chosen in the first place. The outcome made sense – more or less – but the route by which we reached it did not. It points to the need for a better, less volatile process for assessing risks and, as noted in Chapter 1, an escape from our impoverished idea of public choice.

Too often, the public is forced to accept a choice simply between status quo and top-down modernization, with little attention to long-term implications. The debate on GM foods is framed in many ways as a clash between Luddite rejection of progress and GM technology as the inevitable route to future food supplies. In the land use planning system we encourage zero-sum games between developers' proposals and councils' powers to turn them down, rather than creatively exploring a range of alternatives for the use of local spaces.

The outcome of 'either/or' planning and short-termism has been, over decades, a tendency towards monocultures – places and economies that have lost their diversity and are thus vulnerable to economic decline and damage to environmental quality. In farming, intensive production of subsidized crops has squeezed out wildlife, wild flora and local varieties. In housing, we have consigned poor people to monotonous estates where social exclusion and low quality environments go hand in hand, and where contact with diverse networks of work and social life is difficult. In town planning, the outcome has been a standardized and tedious urban realm, dominated by cars and national chain stores, giving people some of what they want as consumers, but leaving many dissatisfied with the design of public spaces and the loss of local distinctiveness. We now live with the consequences of short-sighted decisions and poor debate about choices. What we fail to explore is a range of alternatives to achieve outcomes that people want – wholesome foods, convenient mobility and access to services, decent work, a liveable environment.

52

Bridging the sustainability gap between short-term choices and long-term assessments, and between the simplistic alternatives offered, is a vital task. It means finding ways to give citizens choices about public goods as well as about consumer items, and to inform and educate about the trade-offs and possibilities they involve. It means radically rethinking land use planning, housing and urban design. It means stretching the timescale for planning, explicitly asking what an innovation or development proposal means for our children, grandchildren and later generations.[35] Much local experimentation is going on to make planning and policy-making more responsive to these ideas, and to develop new indicators of progress and participatory approaches to engage citizens in decisions once confined to expert secrecy.[36] But so far they are piecemeal and marginal to mainstream constitutional reform. Moreover, the greatest challenge of all – climate disruption – poses serious problems for the decision-making processes and capacity for long-range debate in modern societies, requiring tough decisions now about risks that threaten the well-being of future generations and the diversity of wildlife and habitats worldwide. There are few signs yet that our politics is capable of facing up to this issue. Only in the face of the worst floods for decades, accompanied by extreme transport problems, did politicians feel compelled to start talking about the probable links between our energy consumption, fuel costs and climate disruption.

Redefining Progress: Towards a Politics of Quality of Life

Bridging our sustainability gaps demands a rich variety of policy innovations, not only from Government but also from business and the voluntary sector; and it means that policy-makers and citizens need to face up to the unsustainable consequences of much current consumption. The rest of the book explores the ways in which the gaps can be overcome – ways that will bring costs and trade-offs as well as 'win–win' developments, and which require much experiment, learning and willingness to fail, but which also promise a greater overall quality of life.

Government and many businesses acknowledge that we need new concepts of growth and progress, no longer neglecting the public commons and the long-term interests of society and the environment. This is a major advance. But Millennial politics is failing to inspire the public, because it remains largely disconnected from visions of greater quality of life, environmental care and decent social relationships.

The NGO movement for sustainable development has a responsibility to help raise public awareness and understanding. Governments can only move so fast; the problems of implementing radical policies for change, for example in environmental strategy, are rooted in politicians' fears of alienating electors who are unconvinced of the need for a shift from many current habits of consumption. NGOs such as the Real World member organizations need to play a more effective role in increasing public awareness and willingness to embrace change.

We aim to build on the progress made in recent years, to encourage further action and positive rethinking which will help create a new politics of quality of life that can produce innovations and modernization for genuine progress. At present the agenda of modernization is strong on analysis of key problems, but weak on consistent and coherent implementation of solutions that reverse unsustainable trends and point us towards sustainable development. The Government has signed up to sustainable development in theory, but in reality New Labour's inhibitions hold it back from embracing the vision of sustainability, and from using it as a guiding framework for policy and new partnerships across British society and across the world. The following chapters set out ideas for closing the gaps between aspirations and action, and for harnessing the potential of sustainable development as a movement for fair and long-lasting progress worldwide.

53

3 Sustaining the Environment: From Crisis to Opportunity

'To knowingly cause large-scale disruptions to climate
would be unjust and reckless. We stand on the threshold
of doing just that. If the United Kingdom cannot
demonstrate that it is serious about doing its part to
address this threat, it cannot expect other nations – least
of all those which are much less wealthy – to do theirs.'
Royal Commission on Environmental Pollution[1]

'On ... welfare and education, the Government has
sought to lead public opinion... It is leadership of this
kind which the environment now demands. New Labour
needs to explain to the public the importance of taking
action, the adjustments that will be required and the
huge gains that can be made. It must make the environment part of its overall political project. In the end such
leadership can only come from the highest level.'
Michael Jacobs[2]

Introduction

The rise of environmental policies has been propelled by disasters and the fear of calamity. Environmentalists have played an
indispensable role in reminding us of our dependence on the
Earth's services and the great risks of undermining them. But this
approach brings problems. It makes campaigners dependent on
disasters and warnings to win a hearing – with all the risks of
crying wolf and generating cynicism and indifference in the
mass media and among politicians. Our politics and media show
no signs of urgency in their treatment of environmental issues.

Yet the evidence is mounting that 'business as usual' is
unsustainable, threatening to degrade environments and destabilize the climate in dangerous ways on a global scale.[3] The Rio
Earth Summit of 1992 established an international consensus
on the importance of the issues and led to global accords on climate change and biodiversity protection. There is a scientific
and governmental consensus on the reality of climate disruption

resulting from human activities such as fossil-fuel burning. Melting polar ice and glaciers, and more violent storms around the world send warnings that climate changes are already with us. The huge costs and disruption caused by storms and floods in the UK in autumn 2000, drew attention to the potential for disastrous consequences from climate change. We know that many species are at risk worldwide, especially in the tropics, from loss of habitat, over-exploitation of resources and climate disruption. Humanity is helping produce a mass extinction of wildlife on a scale unseen for millennia. We know that industrialization in the South is producing the same appalling problems of pollution, waste disposal, loss of habitats and threats to public health that arose in the developed world in previous decades. We know that there must be a limit to the harvesting of resources such as fisheries and to the growth in road traffic in the congested cities. We know that the 'holes' in the Earth's ozone layer have grown.

The message from these developments is clear. The environment is under severe and growing stress from human activities. The warning signs – such as floods, droughts and fires – are damaging human communities and health now on a huge scale.

The Real World argument is that urgent, strategic action is needed at all levels from the local to the global. We need to act on what is now a shared analysis, with ever more visible evidence, of environmental degradation that threatens economies and health worldwide. While much remains uncertain about the risks of global environmental damage, especially about climate disruption, prudence dictates that coordinated action should begin now to tackle the major global problems.

There can be no excuses for inaction. To ignore the warning signs and cling to gas-guzzling 'business as usual', as powerful US industrial lobbies have done, is both selfish and self-destructive. The costs of measures to mitigate climate disruption will be dwarfed by the costs of coping with the worst scenarios for environmental and economic damage worldwide. A 'no-regrets' policy of measures to insure against this is right – morally and from the perspective of long-term economic self-interest. And there are, as will be discussed later, real economic benefits to be gained from taking serious action to reduce fossil-fuel use and greenhouse emissions.

As explained in the next section, there are serious political challenges to be overcome before governments, businesses and citizens do consistently what they need to do. Although most policy-makers now acknowledge the need for action, and although the longer-term benefits of embracing environmental sustainability vastly outweigh the short-term costs, there is a serious gap between aspirations and practical measures.

Increasingly, politicians make encouraging speeches about the need for environmental sustainability, and the benefits from pursuing it – such as Tony Blair's welcome speech on the environment in October 2000. But despite these positive messages, the economic signals received by businesses and consumers say something entirely different. We know we need to reduce carbon emissions, but the price of fuel – however high it seemed to the demonstrators in the 'fuel crisis' of September 2000 – tells consumers and businesses that energy saving is not worth the effort. We know we should favour public transport over car use, but the price of rail tickets, and the state of the rail network, tells us to stick to our cars. We know we need to minimize waste and recycle materials, but the economic signals in the waste industry contradict the policy message (Figure 3.1).[4] The key challenge is to reform our market frameworks to favour resource

Waste industry hierarchies

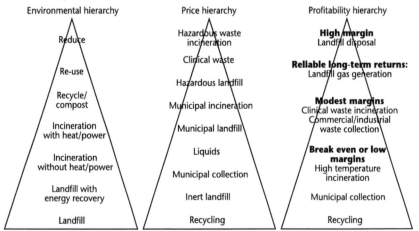

Figure 3.1 *Hierarchies in the Waste Industry*
Source: Merril Lynch, 'Pollution Control', September 1998, cited in R Murray, *Creating Wealth from Waste* (London: Demos, 1999)

conservation and efficiency, and to harness the power of environmental policy to improve quality of life and create jobs. Doing this is tough politically but the gains for the economy and for quality of life will be great. The next wave of environmental policy must be about its full integration with economic and social development.

Environmental Policy: From the 'Easy' Issues to the 'Hard' Politics of the Environment

Environmental problems used to be seen largely in terms of the rundown of finite resources such as oil, or of population growth. While it is true that finite 'non-renewable' mineral resources can and may in many cases 'run out', it is now acknowledged that we have the technical capacity to find substitutes and adapt the economy. And while local population pressures are severe in many places, it seems that the global population is beginning to stabilize, with a downturn in the growth rate. These issues are important, but not decisive. The loss and degradation of renewable resources, and the destabilization of whole ecological systems – the 'services' of Nature on which we rely – are far more serious, and impose more pressing limitations on our economic activities.

The greatest of these threats is signalled by the growing evidence of climate disruption stimulated by fossil-fuel burning and other human activities that send greenhouse gases such as carbon dioxide into the atmosphere (see Figures 3.2 and 3.3, pages 58 and 59). Extreme weather events have increased dramatically in frequency worldwide over the last two decades, and this seems to be linked to the rise in greenhouse gas emissions. Global warming is likely to affect the climate at every level from the local to the global, disrupting economies, societies and ecosystems. It threatens political and economic stability, and also poses immense problems for wildlife, unable to migrate from rapidly changing environments as readily as people.[5] Moreover, the cumulative effect of emissions is what matters, so reductions in the annual rate of damage are not enough; and even radical action now will not prevent future effects occuring based on the existing accumulation of emissions in the atmosphere. We need to make rapid reductions in our use of fossil fuels well before they run out, and to shift to using renewable sources of energy. The world faces the imperative of reducing

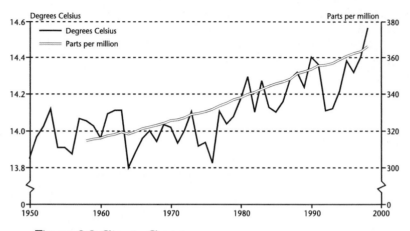

Figure 3.2 *Climate Change*

Source: Goddard Institute for Space Studies (temperature) and Scripps
(carbon dioxide), cited in L R Brown et al, *Vital Signs 1999–2000* (London:
Earthscan, 1999)

carbon dioxide emissions by at least 60 per cent from current levels by 2050 in order to stand a chance of stabilizing the climate, and much deeper cuts are needed in the main industrial countries if the task is to be shared fairly among nations (Figure 3.3).

Like carbon dioxide emissions that can't be 'seen' until the impact is actually felt either physically or economically, other 'invisible' problems are rising up the agenda. A huge issue of concern for long-term health worldwide is the high level of pollution from toxic chemicals, especially pesticides and hazardous wastes. Some 400 million tonnes of hazardous waste are generated annually worldwide, and pesticides are implicated in loss of biodiversity in intensively farmed land in the North and also in human health risks. Increased use of pesticides stimulates insects, bacteria and weed plants to evolve resistance, and pesticide-resistant species are on the rise, mainly as a result of overuse of chemicals in agriculture. Toxic chemicals now circulate globally and accumulate in the food chain. The damaging effects on health from chemical pollution include proven and suspected impacts on human and animal reproductive systems from the spread of endocrine-disrupting chemicals, many found in household products.

The effect of hormone-replicating chemicals, pesticides, dioxins and so on, now cause as much concern as the old problems of visibly polluting 'hotspots' of production (such as smokestack factories). An individual car might be 'cleaner', but the growth in traffic means that air pollution is diffused ever more widely, and efficiency gains are swamped by growth in car mileage. Our health may not be at risk from gross pollution incidents as much as it was, at least in the West, but we now rightly fear the effect on health of the accumulation of chemicals in soils, water, waste dumps and the food chain.[6]

The threats to wildlife across the globe are also changing. The menace of extinction in the wild of 'charismatic' species such as the tiger and chimpanzee is bad enough, but it is accompanied by the loss of whole habitats and food chains – from insects to major predators. This is what is putting environmental security at risk. The over-exploitation of so many fishing grounds seriously threatens not just the targeted species, but also all those that feed on it, and the capacity of stocks to recover at all.[7] The signs are mounting that many fisheries exploited to the limit may struggle to recover even if fishing is banned.

Biodiversity is threatened above all by the destruction of key habitats, such as rain forests in the tropics and temperate zones, woodlands and grasslands, mangroves and other wetlands, and coral reefs. Habitats are destroyed to make room for farming or urban development, or are degraded inadvertently

59

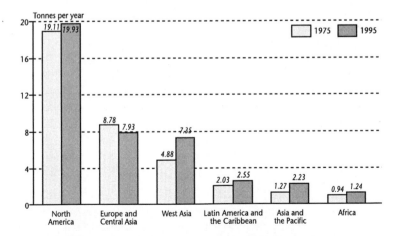

Figure 3.3 *Carbon Dioxide Emissions per Capita*
Source: UNEP, *Global Environment Outlook 2000* (London: Earthscan, 1999)

by human activity (for example through pollution, the introduction of non-native species or over-exploitation of land or water). Some 65 million hectares of forest were lost in the period 1990–95, due to logging, ranching and new settlements. Although an increase of forest area in the North slightly offset this loss, these new plantation forests offer little scope for richer animal and plant life. More generally, the quality of forest biodiversity is threatened by pollution, crude logging practices, fires and water abstraction.

Animal and plant biodiversity is at great risk in many areas of the world, and many scientists contend that humanity is the catalyst for a mass extinction of species without parallel since the end of the age of the dinosaurs. The extinction rate at the start of the Millennium is some 50 times the natural rate, according to the International Conservation Union; In 2000 some 25 per cent of the world's mammal species and one in eight of bird species were estimated to be at risk of total extinction.[8] The great apes – our closest relatives – could vanish in the wild within a decade, according to the world's leading primate research and protection bodies.[9]

The areas of richest diversity – such as rainforests in South America, South-East Asia and central Africa – are often those at most risk from expanding human activities (agriculture, war, pollution) and from climate disruption. A new concern is the advent of transgenic (genetically engineered) crops and livestock. These could affect other species in unexpected ways, and also promote further loss of agricultural genetic diversity, at risk as habitats are lost and seed variety is diminished as crops are rationalized by the spread of transnational 'agribusiness' in the developing world as they have been in the North.

Dealing with these challenges makes the work of the previous phases of eco-politics appear simple by comparison: as Tom Burke has argued, we now face the 'hard politics' of the environment.[10] These challenges are much tougher to deal with, both politically and economically. They focus attention on the damaging impacts not of particular industrial processes, but of entire productive systems – on the need for restructuring whole sectors of energy- and materials-intensive industry to reduce radically their consumption of resources. It is the old energy- and materials-intensive sectors that are proving slow to appreciate the opportunities – for quality of life and business development – from embracing change.

Witness Box 3: Pesticide Action Network (PAN) UK

Pesticides are different from many other chemicals. They are toxic, intended to harm living systems; they are the only chemicals released deliberately into the environment for their toxicity. They are widespread – residues are found at the Poles, in air, sea, food, soil and water. They have impacts in small quantities: residues in food are measured in parts per million; residues in water in parts per billion; and parts per trillion of some pesticides have adverse impacts on marine fauna. Pesticides have brought benefits in the relatively short term to the production of food and fibre. What is at issue is the costs to the wider society in producing these benefits, and whether they are sustainable. The misuse, overuse and abuse of pesticides can lead to adverse effects on human health and the environment. According to the Ministry of Agriculture, Food and Fisheries (MAFF), one tablespoon of herbicide used carelessly near water can pollute drinking water for 200,000 people; and over 30 per cent of the UK arable acreage is sprayed by operators who have no training. However, the ordinary everyday legal and continuing use of pesticides according to current label directions is a more challenging threat.

Government policy is to 'minimize' the impacts of pesticides, but this is clearly not working. Although pesticides have been in widespread use in the UK for 50 years, increasing regulation has barely kept pace with increasing use and increasing pollution. The number of pesticides exceeding environmental quality standards (EQSs) in waters in England and Wales almost doubled in 1996, to 14 per cent of the total monitored by the Environment Agency. According to Ofwat, the total cost of removing pesticides from drinking water is £1,000 million, and the annual cost £50 million. The Royal Society for the Protection of Birds (RSPB) and others noted an 89 per cent decline in sparrow numbers from 1969 to 1994; 82 per cent for grey partridge; and 58 per cent for skylarks – the decline is based on herbicide and insecticide use destroying the birds' food chains. Many factors have contributed to agricultural change; pesticides are not the sole cause but are clearly implicated.

Internationally, the largest proportion of the health and environmental costs of pesticides use is borne by developing countries. Environmental pollution knows no boundaries: the use of hazardous pesticides in developing countries causes environmental pollution, ozone depletion, endocrine disruption and residue exceedences worldwide.

The three targets for Government action that we propose are:

1 Promote the reform of the Common Agricultural Policy so that it rewards farmers for the way they farm, not just the volume they produce. This would enable environmentally friendly production to be as profitable as 'conventional' production.
2 Ensure the direct and indirect costs of pesticides are reflected in the price of the chemicals. A tax on pesticides, provided it is returned to the agricultural sector and provided it is designed to fit with

61

> other economic instruments affecting farm incomes, could stimulate employment opportunities and alternative technologies.
>
> 3 Target aid in agriculture to support sustainable rural livelihoods, based on generation, innovation and promotion of ecological alternatives to pesticide use, especially organic agriculture, and support governments to regulate pesticides effectively.

Responsibility for change is massively diffused in this new context. As Burke puts it, 'the buck stops everywhere'. There are potential losers, at least in the short- and medium-term of a transition to sustainable development. This helps explain the widespread sense of denial and paralysis in the national and international response to the diagnosis of problems such as climate disruption.[11] We can (nearly) all agree on the issues, but their vastness, complexity and uncertainty, and the political risks of radical action as perceived by mainstream parties, block comprehensive measures to bring environmental sustainability into the heart of policy-making and business strategy.

So we have a national and global problem of implementation: almost everyone acknowledges that a major long-term programme to reorient the economy is needed, and we know we have many of the technological and policy answers; but no-one can summon up the will to begin the work seriously. Meanwhile, the problems of diffuse pollution and loss of environmental quality continue to pile up, in the UK as well as globally.

Facing Environmental Limits: The Nature of Environmental Sustainability

The challenge of environmental sustainability is threefold. First, to improve radically the efficiency with which we use fossil energy, water and materials: most materials do not get converted into products, but become waste by-products. Second, to make absolute reductions in use of fossil energy and in waste output. Third, to do these things while maintaining or enhancing living standards, employment and competitiveness – all traditionally seen by business and governments as threatened by radical environmental policies. In short, we need to improve enormously the efficiency with which we use the environment to get the benefits and services that support the economy and our quality of life.

Witness Box 4: The Wildlife Trusts

The Wildlife Trusts have two aims. The first is to achieve a UK richer in wildlife – to protect and enhance species and habitats, both common and rare. The second is to achieve greater public understanding and appreciation of wildlife. Engaging people in all sectors of society, in urban and rural areas, is fundamental to the ethos of The Wildlife Trusts. Environmental, social and economic considerations are invariably interlinked, and The Wildlife Trusts recognize the need to work with local communities, the private sector, government agencies and other organizations to achieve their aims.

Key priorities of The Wildlife Trusts are:

- *Agriculture:* A top priority for wildlife in the UK is to change agricultural policy. Seventy-five per cent of Britain is farmed, and only when farmers have a greater financial incentive to adopt wildlife-friendly farming systems can we hope to see a change for the better. The blame is not on farmers for the loss of biodiversity in the farmed landscape, but on the subsidy system that has effectively forced them to farm in the way they have. Fortunately, there are encouraging signs of a shift towards 'greener' farming. In late 1999, after intensive lobbying by The Wildlife Trusts and others, the Government announced a doubling of the agri-environment programme. However, there is a long way to go. The Common Agricultural Policy needs a radical overhaul. The Wildlife Trusts would like to see production subsidies phased out and a massive shift in support towards wildlife-friendly farming.

  The Wildlife Trusts are not only lobbying for change in agricultural policy, they also work with individual farmers at local level. In Devon, for example, the Devon Wildlife Trust has succeeded in persuading and helping more than 200 farmers to enter areas of culm grassland – a particularly valuable habitat – into Countryside Stewardship. The Essex Wildlife Trust has recently acquired a large arable farm at Abbotts Hall with the specific objective of demonstrating that commercial arable farming and wildlife can co-exist.

- *Marine:* It has been estimated that 50 per cent of the biodiversity in the UK lives under the sea. Yet for a country that has over 5,000 Sites of Special Scientific Interest (SSSI) on land and prides itself on its conservation credentials, our approach to the marine environment has been little short of a disgrace. Fish stocks have been allowed to crash; thousands of animals, from non-target fish species to porpoises, have been allowed to die each year as 'incidental bycatch'; seabeds have been hammered by heavy beam trawlers; and vital coastal habitats such as saltmarsh and mudflats have been eroded at an alarming rate.

  The Wildlife Trusts have targeted the marine environment as a priority for greater attention. The Dorset Wildlife Trust, for example, runs a voluntary marine nature reserve at Kimmeridge Bay. Several coastal Wildlife Trusts are now represented on their local sea fish

63

eries committees, promoting the conservation cause. Our Seaquest project in the south-west is designed to record and monitor marine life, and to promote public awareness by encouraging the public to get involved.

Crucially, however, changes are needed at the political level. Just as the Common Agricultural Policy has been a disaster for wildlife on farmland, so the Common Fisheries Policy has been a disaster for marine life. We need an 'ecosystem' approach to fisheries, whether offshore or inshore, that rewards sustainable practices. As Lord Donaldson recommended after the grounding of the *Braer* (but has never been implemented), we need a system of special protection for 'marine environmental high risk areas' – ecologically valuable sites where commercial activities are permitted only if special care is taken. Perhaps most important of all, we need a change from the current disjointed approach to the marine environment where different government departments are responsible for different parts of it. An integrated approach, with sustainability a central objective of marine policy, is essential.

- *Habitat restoration*: The Wildlife Trusts manage 2,300 nature reserves in the UK, but they are relatively small, isolated sites vulnerable to external influences. Small sites need to be linked and expanded so that much larger areas are managed for nature conservation purposes. This would not only have ecological benefits, but would provide better recreational and economic opportunities. The Wildlife Trusts are involved in bigger habitat restoration projects than ever before – from heathlands in Shropshire, to hay meadows in Wiltshire and salt marsh in Essex. However, a massive nationwide habitat restoration programme in town and country needs to be undertaken.

- *Think people:* Public support for the environment continues to grow, but we still need to get our message across to more people and more sectors of society, and to show that wildlife is relevant to them in their daily lives. Again, there are encouraging developments. The Sheffield Wildlife Trust, for example, is working in three of the most deprived urban communities in Britain – Manor, Castle and Wybourn – on a regeneration project that will create not only jobs and housing but wildlife-friendly green space to contribute to quality of life. In a different context, the Scottish Wildlife Trust is working on the Isle of Eigg in partnership with the local people and local authority to promote economic development for the islanders within an over-arching goal of nature conservation. But there is a long way to go, and The Wildlife Trusts believe that engaging and involving people throughout society is fundamental to a sustainable future.

Achieving these goals demands not simply technological improvements, but also significant changes in consumption by organizations and citizens – for example, much less use of fossil fuel-powered vehicles, much more efficient use of water and much less use of pesticides and nitrogen fertilizer by farmers. These changes involve shifts in behaviour, assumptions and aspirations that are deep-seated. There is no escaping the need for ethical debate about what matters most to us. There are clashes between the claims of people and animals to habitats, and there will be hard choices about which species we abandon to extinction and which ones we try hard to conserve.

65

But above all else, we need to reorient markets and economic policy frameworks to promote the great advances in resource productivity and conservation that we know can be made. We know what we need to do; we have the capacity to do it; but there is a wide 'sustainability gap' between policy aspirations and the economic signals given to producers and consumers. Bridging this gap is the crucial task facing Government and its partners in coming years, and urgent action needs to be taken.

Witness Box 5: World Wide Fund For Nature (WWF-UK)

The past three decades have witnessed an unprecedented destruction of the natural environment. WWF estimates that freshwater ecosystems have declined by 50 per cent, marine ecosystems have deteriorated by 30 per cent and forest cover worldwide has been reduced by 10 per cent. Global energy use has increased by 70 per cent, bringing with it the build up of greenhouse gases and unpredictable changing weather patterns. The build up of environmental problems has contributed to an unprecedented increase in environmental disasters and associated human costs. Soil degradation now affects some 1,900 million hectares of land and the livelihoods of more than 1 billion people. The global fisheries crisis threatens the primary protein source of 950 million people.

Present trends could be interpreted as indicating a high level of indifference on the part of the present generation towards future generations, and a lack of clear commitment to sustainable development. So is sustainable development a lost cause? WWF believes there are encouraging signs that these trends can be reversed. Governments and the industry sectors, challenged by civil society groups, are beginning to take the environment and sustainable development more seriously. But much more must be done:

- The UK Government deserves recognition for taking a lead role on the global stage in terms of action on climate change. It has made a commitment to reductions in domestic carbon dioxide emissions that surpass those of most of its European neighbours. It has also set a target for increasing the contribution of renewable energies – an area where the UK lags behind most of its EU partners. Additionally, it has begun to introduce a system of ecological tax reform, most recently through the implementation of a climate change levy applied to business. But this should not encourage complacency. The Government must implement the appropriate policies and measures as soon as possible to ensure that the targets are achieved and that steps are taken towards changing to a low carbon economy .

- The Government has also taken a lead in recognizing that sustainable development needs to be taken seriously if poverty is to be eliminated in the long term. To this end, an OECD International Development Target – the implementation of national strategies for sustainable development in all countries by 2005, so as to ensure that current trends in the loss of environmental resources are effectively reversed at both global and national levels by 2015 – has been adopted by the UK. The Department for International Development (DFID) is working with the European Commission (EC) in supporting best practice in the development of national strategies for sustainable development with developing-country partners. Such efforts to eradicate poverty while promoting sustainable development continue to be constrained by the level of development aid contributed by the UK Government: it has still not reached its committed target of 0.7 per cent of gross national product (GNP). WWF would like to see an increased commitment to the Global Environmental Facility to help developing countries that have taken on commitments to implement multilateral environmental agreements.
- Again in the global context, to ensure that trade and environmental policies are compatible, the UK Government must take a leading role in demanding reform of the World Trade Organization (WTO). Priorities identified by WWF include: sustainability impact assessments of existing and future trade agreements; ensuring that signatory countries to international environmental treaties can use reasonable trade restrictions to make those treaties effective; the promotion of environmentally and socially beneficial trade; and ensuring greater transparency, democracy and accountability in the decision-making process.
- Research by WWF shows that the interactions between foreign direct investment (FDI) and the environment are complex. The Westminster Government must play a more proactive role to ensure that UK companies working overseas adhere to the highest environmental and social standards. Support for FDI should be conditional on review of the social and environmental impacts, and projects should be amended or rejected if necessary. Incentives such as preferential access to aid contracts should be given to firms operating at high environmental standards and supporting clean technology transfer.

- The knowledge economy presents unprecedented opportunities for business to demonstrate greater social and environmental responsibility as part of the drive for competitiveness, for example, through innovation and transfer of clean technologies and a shift towards a service – rather than a product-focused economy. The innovative legislation that requires pension fund trustees to state the extent to which social, environmental and ethical considerations are taken into account in their investments is a major step forward in acknowledging the role that private-sector investment can play in promoting sustainable development.

- There are some UK leaders in the field of corporate social responsibility that report regularly and transparently on social and environmental issues. Statutory environmental and social reporting for the largest public and private companies would provide a level playing field and would reinvigorate consumer confidence in the role that business and industry plays in the global economy.

- Consumers are already making their own choices – based on accreditation systems such as those of the Forest Stewardship Council – to ensure that the natural resources on which we all depends are used in a sustainable manner for the benefit not only of people now, but of future generations and the planet. Already, nearly 20 million hectares of forest worldwide have been certified, due to demand from farsighted businesses and discerning consumers. The Government should support such market-driven voluntary measures as important tools for promoting the sustainable use of biological resources

- For decades, our marine environment has been largely ignored in terms of environmental management. Recently, the Government has taken a progressive stance in its actions at the international level, with legislation designed to clean up the North Sea and the North-East Atlantic. Nationally, an integrated approach to manage and restore the marine environment is needed urgently to tackle habitat damage, poor fisheries management and degradation from mineral extraction and shipping which are threatening the livelihoods of our coastal communities and the sealife on which they depend. Greater safeguards for our marine heritage should include the integration of ocean and coastal policies into a comprehensive regime for marine ecosystems. This should address protected areas, fisheries management, pollution reduction, coastal management and restoration, and the control of offshore activities.

- Freshwater ecosystems provide water and food, carry away waste and bring economic benefits through a range of activities from fisheries to small-scale hydropower. Floodplains naturally filter some forms of pollution and cushion the effects of floods, and their fertile alluvial soil provides the basis for agricultural activities. The UK Government should act quickly to adopt the EU Water Framework Directive, ensuring that whole river basin management is implemented, and measures are taken to actively promote the restoration of freshwater systems.

67

> • WWF is also calling for the control and, where necessary, phasing out or ban of known endocrine disrupting chemicals (EDCs). These toxic chemicals pose a hazard to wildlife populations worldwide and may be affecting human reproduction and susceptibility to disease. We know they are affecting intelligence and behaviour. The British Government is aware of the problem of endocrine disruption, as can be seen from the large volume of EDCs-based research it is carrying out. The Precautionary Principle dictates action to control exposures of wildlife and humans to EDCs rather than simply doing more research. Action must be taken now to protect future generations from the ever increasing threat of these chemicals. Pro-active steps to involve consumers and civil society groups in the decision-making process would ensure a transparent, democratic and inclusive outcome.
>
> Present trends in environmental degradation highlight the growing predicament that faces us today. Clearly environmental regulations need to be strengthened at both the national and international levels. The Government must continue to introduce progressive environmental policies, and to translate the existing 'language of sustainability' into tangible actions on the ground.

Towards Environmental Sustainability in the Economy

Against this background, what kind of gains do we need to make in resource productivity, and how do we make them? The scale of the efficiency gains we need to make depends on our overall environmental impact, which in turn depends on population size and consumption levels. We also have to take into account the inequalities in consumption within and between countries, in order to arrive at a fair distribution of the effort needed to make radical gains in resource productivity. There is no avoiding the issue of equity in assessing the changes we need to make:

• The growing population of the developing world, and especially the 1.2 billion in 'absolute' poverty, has an unanswerable claim to improve its living standards (see Chapter 4). If it does so on the Western model, many environments will be strained to the point of collapse. Similarly, the South and the ex-Communist economies of the North need help to modernize their economies on sustainable lines.

• Acceptance of limits to conventional production and consumption raises issues of equity – between the rich and low-income worlds, and between rich and poor in the developed world. We also need to take account of our responsibility to future generations, bequeathing good institutions and an environment capable of meeting their needs. We need new ways of distributing 'fair shares' of consumption: innovations such as more equitable systems for carbon dioxide emissions trading, and other ways to allocate shares in 'environmental space' – levels of consumption of energy and materials by households, organizations or countries.

- This underlines the message that environmental policies must be designed for improving the social and economic conditions and prospects of the poor, who are typically the most affected by pollution, health threats and damaged environments.[12]

[handwritten margin note: rather than 'women']

This implies that over the next generation very large gains need to be made in the efficiency of resource use in the West, with attendant shifts in production and consumption. What does this mean for the UK? A Friends of the Earth (FOE) analysis of the UK's resource use suggests that we are over-consuming key resources by between 15 and 100 per cent, and need to make major changes by 2050 in order to arrive at a fair share of the world's 'environmental space'.[13] From this we can derive estimates of reductions needed and targets for improvements in resource efficiency and waste minimization for the UK over the coming decades (see Figure 3.4).

Some environmentalists and most politicians and business leaders assume this must mean unpalatable 'sacrifices' for consumers, or radical regulations on industry that will have costs for competitiveness and jobs, or major investments in infrastructures such as public transport that will require tax increases. The received wisdom is that acting on the diagnosis of unsustainable environmental development will be unpopular and economically damaging.

Two replies can be made. First, although moving to environmentally sustainable development does involve costs to consumers and the wider economy, these are insignificant compared to the costs of remaining unsustainable. It is precisely 'business as usual' that will bring much greater sacrifices and costs than will radical changes in the next two decades to promote resource conservation and efficiency.

Second, the costs of making changes now will be outweighed by benefits and new opportunities. Far from involving

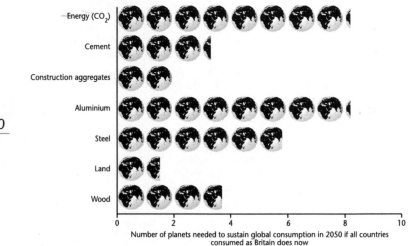

Figure 3.4 *UK Consumption of Resources*

Source: D McLaren et al/Friends of the Earth, *Tomorrow's World: Britain's Share in a Sustainable Future* (London: Earthscan, 1998)

net sacrifices in quality of life, sustainable development strategies can bring net gains, both economically and politically. These are of several kinds: new opportunities for business, job creation and technological development; improved quality of life and health from reduced pollution and congestion; and prevention of future environmental threats to well-being, economic stability and health. The point made in the first Real World book stands:

> 'sustainability is compatible with improved, not reduced living standards... Some expectations in life would no doubt have to change. But the claim is reasonably confident: a sustainable economy would make us better off, not worse.'[14]

How do we design policies for reversing unsustainable consumption trends in ways that reduce environmental damage while benefiting the poor and ensuring we gain the benefits noted above? How do we develop an economy which respects environmental limits and serves social aims and needs, fully integrating sustainable-development thinking in its operation?

The answers have been emerging from debate on the greening of the economy and technology.[15]

What they point to is first, immense scope for improving resource efficiency across the economy; second, many benefits to competitiveness and employment from comprehensive investment in 'cleaner production' and new forms of consumption; third, the possibility of new forms of growth and industrial innovation in the economy rather than of a 'steady state' or contraction under the impact of environmental measures. These opportunities amount to a programme of environmental modernization compatible with – and essential to the long-term viability of – the project of 'modernizing Britain'.[16]

Witness Box 6: Friends of the Earth (FOE)

After a rough start, New Labour's track record on environmental and sustainability issues is improving. They have begun assembling a credible eco-tax package, introduced a Countryside and Access Bill, and brought out a revised and improved UK Sustainable Development Plan. The Food Standards Agency is established, and the 20 per cent carbon dioxide reduction target remains as the core of a new climate strategy. Many positive noises are made about transport and agriculture, and some money is being found.

But political necessity, not belief or commitment, has been the driver. The Government, particularly No 10, has suffered damaging and demoralizing knocks for largely ignoring a long list of manifesto promises and public concerns – housing, transport, GMOs, nuclear power, farming, renewables, urban regeneration and wildlife. In each case, public pressure and evidence forced a policy change or reordered priority. Much still needs to be done, and there are other failures. The trouble is that the environment does not figure for the Prime Minister – at least not yet.

Sustainability is about enhancing people's lives, the economy and the environment together. It is an awkward term for a common-sense goal, which should be at the heart of every political economy. Mr Blair's backing for these three measures would ensure it were so in Britain:

1 Set clear and challenging medium- and long-term targets to reduce resource-use and pollution in every sector, as a cornerstone of economic and industrial strategy. Britain consumes and pollutes too much. Our 55 million people use up far more than their fair share of natural resources, at rates that ecosystems cannot tolerate. Neither aspect is sustainable, as other nations increasingly take up their shares of the biosphere's capacity, and more.

   FOE has calculated targets for a wide range of sectors, as the basis for outlining how to achieve the significant transformation of our political economy, which sustainable development requires. Strategic targets, with timetables and periodic reviews, would give companies, organized labour and communities three things that they want from the State: policy certainty, time to adapt and opportunity to influence.

2 Implement substantive green tax reforms across the economy. Making polluters and wasters pay for the damage they cause makes sense, and is essential to shape a sustainable market economy. But eco-tax reform is as much about incentives as penalties. That money could be recycled to good use: as tax breaks for environmentally virtuous company and household behaviour, or for innovation; as spending on essential public infrastructure and services, such as public transport, waste minimization and energy conservation; and as tax reductions on labour.

These measures would stimulate new markets, help both established and start-up firms, and generate jobs. Combined with the targets above, they would force technological and management innovation, greatly increase production and end-use efficiencies, and help modernize the economy.

3 Introduce statutory environmental rights for all people. We must also address our social or cultural economy. Passing laws and changing tax regimes is what Government can do. We need 25 million households to choose to live sustainably! Spending millions of pounds of public money on advertising that 'urges everyone to do their bit' won't work. Giving people real rights to back up their responsibilities just might. Every citizen should enjoy inalienable environmental rights to clean air, pure water, uncontaminated land, wholesome food and peace and quiet, guaranteed by the State. Other enabling rights – such as access to data on the state of the environment, convenient green services or private prosecution against environmental crimes – would give people the tools to lead sustainable lives and help Government and industry do the same.

The Environmental Opportunity: Resource Productivity and the Low Waste–High Value Economy

So what does the emerging vision of 'environmental modernization' offer? It argues that we need to decouple growth in the economy from growth in consumption of key resources, from growth in pollution and from growth in waste and congestion. It aims to recouple growth to gains in quality of life, focusing on increasing the flow of things we want from the economy (amenity, jobs, innovations) and cutting the flow of things we do not want to consume (pollution, time spent in traffic jams). In some cases this means a halt to growth and a decrease in output and jobs – for example, in fossil fuel-intensive energy generation, or in production of fossil fuel-powered vehicles. But these cuts in production and jobs would be offset, and potentially more than compensated, by increased growth in 'sustainable sectors' such as renewable energy generation (wind and solar energy); public transport; video-conferencing services; waste recycling; repair and reuse of products and organic food production.

In all of these areas there is immense potential for growth in activity and for increases in resource productivity. We could promote a tenfold improvement in resource efficiency over the next generation, opening up a vision of a low waste, low carbon, high value and high innovation economy (see Panel 4). The UK is experiencing a boom in demand for organic food, yet imports 70 per cent of its supply and directs little funding towards the thousands of farmers wishing to convert to organic production. It has huge potential for offshore wind power, yet fails to give incentives in the energy market for development of wind technology and renewables in general. It has rising volumes of waste, but provides few incentives for markets in recycled products and waste minimization technology. A huge potential for green growth in these areas is waiting to be harnessed.

73

Panel 4

Factor 10: Towards a 'Lasting Value' Economy

The rich world will have to make major gains in resource productivity in order to allow the developing countries to increase their growth rates and consumption, giving them more 'environmental space'. The famous book *Factor Four* argued that achieving a 75 per cent increase in the efficiency of energy and materials use in the West is feasible, through making use of new technologies, changes in production systems and new market incentives. But this represents just a start in reaping the rewards that can be gained from innovation strategies to maximize eco-efficiency in business. A tenfold increase (Factor 10) in energy and material efficiency is achievable over the next generation. Factor 10 means a 90 per cent reduction in energy and materials intensity is possible without loss of economic utility or damage to quality of life.

Factor 10 improvements in the ways in which we use energy, natural resources and other materials can flow from a wide range of innovations in technology, Government policy and market operations:

• Moving from 'end of pipe' pollution control technology to cleaner production systems that minimize energy and material use at all

stages of products' life-cycles, from design to final disposal.
- Adopting new designs for buildings, vehicles and factories to optimize energy efficiency and produce major savings in use of resources
- Reforming economic and fiscal policies to remove 'perverse subsidies' that give incentives for damaging practices in industry and agriculture, and to provide incentives for boosting resource productivity.
- Encouraging manufacturers and utilities to provide long-life products and sustainable services to consumers, rather than disposable products and units: for example, giving incentives to energy utilities to provide efficient and energy-saving services for warmth and lighting rather than simply to maximize sales of units of electricity.
- Harnessing the potential of new information and communication technologies to help make major gains in resource productivity.

The Factor 10 vision is thus one of an economy based on 'lasting value' – products and services which are sustainable and embody high value and durability. It creates a low-waste and low-carbon economy that uses high technology and innovation to create high value. It is technically feasible and could be realized within the next two to three decades. The barriers are not technological, but institutional:

- The resistance of organizations to radical changes in market frameworks that could involve investments with significant short-term costs.
- The attachment of interest groups to established subsidies.
- The need for Factor 10 innovations to be introduced on a sector- and system-wide basis, optimizing chains of production and consumption.

Sources: E von Weizsäcker, A B Lovins and L H Lovins, *Factor Four: Doubling Wealth, Halving Resource Use* (London: Earthscan, 1997); T Jackson, *Material Concerns: Pollution, Profit and Quality of Life* (London: Routledge, 1996); Factor 10 Club, *The Carnoules Declaration* (Wuppertal: Factor 10 Club, 1994)

The policies needed for environmental modernization are well understood. The shift towards the 'Lasting Value' economy of low waste and low carbon emissions, high value and high innovation can be promoted by progressively changing market frameworks and taxes to reward sustainable resource use and penalize waste, pollution and fossil fuel use. Specific measures include redirection of subsidies from damaging activities (such as many forms of intensive agriculture) towards new environmental industries (such as organic farming – and possibly environmentally beneficial forms of genetic engineering, such as for waste disposal by bacteria), or through 'ecological tax reform'. The latter is gaining favour among policy-makers in the UK and beyond. It involves shifting tax from labour and from non-polluting forms of consumption, towards fossil energy, waste and congestion. In short, it taxes 'bads' rather than 'goods'. Research strongly suggests that such tax reform, if well targeted and with revenues recycled to improve public services, could play a crucial role in changing behaviour by organizations and consumers, in creating new jobs, and in providing revenue for 'sustainable modernization' (see Panel 5).

Panel 5

Green Collar Jobs and Enterprises: Employment, Economic Development and the Environment

It is no accident that the countries with the largest 'environmental' business sectors are those with the most stringent environmental regulations – Japan, Germany, Sweden and the USA. In each case, waves of regulation have stimulated waves of innovation, and these countries dominate the world market for environmental protection technologies and services. This market is now worth some US$300 billion – bigger than the aerospace sector – and is set to grow substantially as major developing economies such as China and India industrialize further and need to 'green' their economic growth to avoid environmental degradation.

The potential for new jobs as well as new market opportunities is very great. Studies for the UK suggest that the more than 100,000 existing 'green collar' workers in environmental occupations could be joined by many thousands more, both in the private sector and the 'social economy' of community enterprises. Work by FOE indicates that investments in energy conservation and renewable energy could create some 130,000 jobs; some 120,000 net new jobs could come from a sustainable transport strategy; some 60,000 from a sustainable agriculture programme and up to 110,000 from waste minimization and recycling initiatives. A 'green' taxation package that would recycle eco-tax revenues into schemes to boost environmental markets and investment in sustainable transport and technology, could create some 400,000 jobs by 2010. Such projections are mirrored in many other studies in the UK, Europe and North America.

Sources: C Secrett, *Making Work: The Environment* (London: Employment Policy Institute, 1999); D McLaren et al/Friends of the Earth, *Tomorrow's World: Britain's Share in a Sustainable Future* (London: Earthscan, 1998); M Renner, 'Creating jobs, preserving the environment', in L R Brown et al (eds), *State of the World 2000* (London: Earthscan, 2000); R Murray, *Creating Wealth from Waste* (London: Demos, 1999)

Progress Towards Sustainable Environmental Policies

The opportunities for a better quality of life and new forms of innovation and growth from a programme of environmental modernization are many and substantial. This much is also agreed, in principle at least, on all sides by politicians, business leaders and NGOs. What progress have we seen since the launch of Real World in 1996, and what are the sustainability gaps that remain to be bridged?

There is good news to report at both the global and the national levels. UNEP highlights the following developments as advances that promise major benefits in future:[18]

- The increase in public concern and the rise in pressure from NGOs and other civil society organizations on businesses and governments to take steps to protect environments and reduce hazards to health from pollution.
- The reality of 'win–win' results in many cases from action by businesses to reduce pollution and improve resource efficiency – not only does this benefit the environment, it also produces economic benefits for companies as they are able to reduce the costs of waste.
- Considerable reductions in the developed world's emissions of many air pollutants.
- The increase in forest cover in parts of the developed world, despite many cases of unsustainable logging; and the development of certification schemes for sustainably managed timber.
- Local Agenda 21 initiatives that are stimulating local community action on sustainable development.
- The success of the Montreal Protocol in greatly reducing output of ozone-damaging emissions, with the result that the ozone layer should recover by mid-century.
- The development of a set of global environmental accords since 1992 that provide the basis for dealing with the most complex problems we face – climate disruption and loss of biodiversity.

Achievements in the UK and Europe

In the UK and in the EU there are positive developments to report. First, there are some encouraging signs of the integration of the environment 'at the heart of government', as promised by New Labour on its election. These include:

- Acceptance of the principle of hypothecation (earmarking) of environmental tax revenues for specific purposes. UK 'eco-taxes' now include the Landfill Tax and the Climate Change Levy.
- Establishment of the House of Commons Environmental Audit Committee.
- New power for local authorities to promote well-being, and requirement on them to produce Local Agenda 21 plans on sustainable development.
- Updating of the UK Sustainable Development Strategy, with new indicators of quality of life to help assess progress in meeting sustainable development targets.

Second, there are specific measures to welcome:

- Mechanisms for reviewing risks of genetic engineering and food safety.
- Moves to shift farming subsidies towards sustainable care of the countryside.
- Access to the Countryside and Wildlife Protection legislation, ensuring the right to roam in the countryside and enhancing protection for biodiversity and Sites of Special Scientific Interest (SSSIs).

Also, the UK has shown leadership in key areas of international policy. Within the EU, the UK is among the small group of countries committed to above-average cuts in greenhouse gas emissions by 2010, and has promised to reduce carbon emissions by 20 per cent from 1990 levels by the end of this decade. This goal also places the UK among the international leaders in facing up to climate change; the UK played an honourable role in promoting action by the EU and the USA at the Kyoto summit on climate change in 1997.

More generally, there are positive developments within the EU despite the evidence of continuing deterioration in much of the European environment.[19] The Treaty of Amsterdam, which governs the EU's activities and structure enshrines sustainable development as a principal goal.[20] The EU is also developing its first Sustainable Development Plan, going beyond the environmental action plans that have so far been the main driving force for policy.

Conclusion: Closing the Environmental Sustainability Gap

There is much here that makes progress towards meeting Real World's aspirations, and on which more imaginative and beneficial policies can be built. But far more remains to be done, and the sense of urgency, outrage and opportunity that should be driving debate and policy is miserably under-powered. NGOs, UNEP and the UK Government alike recognize that for all the achievements in integrating the environment into policy-making at local, national and global levels, we are still going too slowly. There is a wide – and still widening – sustainability gap that must be bridged if trends in pollution, loss of biodiversity, over-exploitation of resources and growth in carbon emissions are to be halted and reversed. UNEP makes the point bluntly:

> 'There used to be a long time horizon for undertaking major environmental policy initiatives. Now time for a rational, well planned transition to a sustainable system is running out fast. In some areas, it has already run out... Full scale emergencies now exist on a number of issues ... on balance, gains by better management and technology are still being outpaced by the environmental impacts of population and economic growth. As a result, policy actions that result in substantial environmental improvements are rare. The present course is unsustainable and postponing action is no longer an option. Inspired political leadership and intense co-operation across all regions and sectors will be needed to put both existing and new policy instruments to work.'[21]

The environmental sustainability gap is not being closed fast enough, because Government has yet to see the challenges it presents through the prism of sustainable development, and thus as a strategic opportunity for the economy and social cohesion, not as a threat. In the economic growth sectors of the 21st-century economy – solar and wind power, cleaner production

technology, waste minimization and recycling, habitat conservation, low energy/high efficiency buildings, organic and low
impact farming, zero-emission vehicles and other Factor 10-type
appliances – the UK risks falling ever further behind other countries, losing opportunities for jobs, enterprise, export markets
and leadership in new technologies and service industries.

The gaps between current achievement and what is needed
to halt and reverse unsustainable environmental trends include
the following:

- *Leadership:* Government needs to lead inclusive debate and
  promote education on the issues, solutions and targets for
  all sectors (including households) from the very top, opening up information to all and emphasizing the seriousness
  of the need for deep cuts in carbon emissions, and the
  opportunities that can flow from a strategy for a 'Lasting
  Value' economy as described earlier. Leadership also
  means pressing publicly and strongly for action to cut
  carbon emissions in the USA and the EU, and for measures
  to help developing countries embrace cleaner technologies,
  renewable energy and other strategies and tools to allow
  them to leapfrog environmentally destructive forms of
  economic growth, and safeguard biodiversity and vital
  resources such as fish stocks.
- *Economic signals to favour sustainable development:* We need
  more and better-targeted incentives and economic instru-
  ments to influence production and consumption. These
  should include eco-taxes – for example, on the carbon content of fuels, green field development, pesticides and waste
  disposal – with revenues recycled to support cleaner production, protect the less well-off, and allow cuts in labour taxes.
- *Integration of environmental and social sustainability:*
  Policies need to harness the potential of environmental
  action to promote social inclusion, through new job
  creation and investment in infrastructure. A key policy
  is the Government's welcome plan for the elimination of
  fuel poverty by 2010: this needs to be pursued through a
  programme of insulation, which will create many jobs.
- *Climate change:* The gap between the present 2010 targets
  and what is required by around 2030 is approximately a 50
  per cent reduction in carbon dioxide emissions. A powerful
  analysis and radical but achievable strategy is ready to
  hand in the 2000 report on energy and climate change

from the Royal Commission on Environmental Pollution, which notes that the UK's achievements so far in reducing carbon dioxide emissions have been largely 'fortuitous', and need to be based on a strong commitment to energy saving and renewables, a carbon tax and long-term targets for at least 60 per cent cuts in emissions by 2050.[22]

- *Transport:* There is a large gap between the unimpeachable analysis in the Government's Integrated Transport Strategy document and the continuing growth in road traffic and its emissions of carbon dioxide. We need targets for reduction in traffic and new recyclable taxes such as charges for congestion, following substantial investment in public transport and in much stronger measures to promote cycling and walking.
- *Agriculture:* There is a huge gap between public demand for organic foods and domestic supply (we import 70 per cent of organic produce); and between the scale of subsidy for intensive farming and the incentives for environmental stewardship of the countryside. The lack of a tax on pesticide and artificial fertilizer use means we lack tools to tackle the growing risks from chemical pollution in farming and food.
- *GM science and technology:* The dawning realization that GM crops could further undermine the sustainability of agriculture needs to be reflected in practical policy. There is a need for more measures to build up public confidence in the precautionary assessment of GM technologies; to tighten the management of trials, and to examine the implications of genetic engineering for intellectual property rights. Along with the issues raised about its independence and quality, there are also important questions to be asked about the impact of GM science on research and development spending: what are the opportunity costs, and what research and development could be pursued into far more environmentally sustainable techniques for better organic and less intensive conventional farming?
- *Planning:* There is widespread dissatisfaction with planning, which has failed to help prevent the intensification of economic and social divisions between regions and within cities. Citizens need to be reconnected to planning through measures to increase accountability, participation and access to information (see Chapter 6).[23] Sustainable devel-

opment requires more measures to make urban living more attractive, and to eliminate social exclusion in cities and countryside alike.[24]

- *Waste:* There is a gap between the recognition of the need for waste minimization and the existing policy of increasing incineration capacity because of the slow rate of increase in markets for recycled materials.[25] Failures to take waste reduction and recycling seriously enough put greater pressure on landfill and incineration, which create pollution problems. The National Waste Strategy is a major step forward, as it sets statutory targets for a 25 per cent recycling rate for household waste by 2005; but the UK lags well behind leading practice internationally in recycling and waste minimization.

- *Toxic chemicals:* There needs to be far tighter control of emissions from chemical plants, and rigorous implementation of environmental management standards in the chemicals industry so that cleaner production processes are developed further. There is also a need for more progress on public consultation and access to information on the risks and effects from chemicals production, use, disposal and incineration, and on the presence of risky chemicals in everyday products. Government should set a target for a major reduction in toxic chemical emissions by 2005.

Much can be done at the level of the UK Government and local authorities. But most environmental legislation is shaped by the EU. The gaps between the goal of environmental sustainability and EU policy remain wide. The EU lacks a common strategy for achieving its Kyoto targets and making deeper cuts in greenhouse emissions and faster progress towards Factor 10 eco-efficiency. We need an EU-wide carbon tax, with funds recycled to support sustainable development measures. The Government should continue to press for faster reform. There is a powerful case for promoting sustainable development as the overriding project for the EU's next phase of integration.[26]

The gaps are wide, and amount to an environmental sustainability gap that must be bridged over a period of two to three decades, starting now. Much has been achieved, but far more remains to be done. The key to promoting environmental sustainability is, first, to understand why the environment must be a priority and, second, to devise a strategy for restructuring markets and stimulating industries to move from carbon-intensive and wasteful production and consumption towards what we call the low carbon, high value economy. The tools are at hand; the benefits to the economy and to social inclusion are potentially huge; the environmental, economic and social degradation resulting from inaction is intolerable. Harnessing the potential of the 'lasting value' economy depends on Government at last seeing strong environmental policy as a strategic priority, the essential foundation for the modernization of the economy and for social progress, as well as for wise stewardship of our environment.

Poverty Amid Plenty:
Reducing Poverty and Inequalities

'Development that perpetuates today's inequalities is neither sustainable nor worth sustaining.'
United Nations Development Programme[1]

'Poverty is the ultimate threat to stability in a globalizing world. The widening gaps between rich and poor within nations, and the gulf between the most affluent and most impoverished nations, are morally outrageous, economically wasteful and potentially socially explosive.'
Michel Camdessus, former Director of the International Monetary Fund[2]

Introduction

While globalization and economic development have brought real gains for hundreds of millions, and the world has enough wealth to provide decent living conditions, work and food for all, many societies are growing more divided by inequalities of income and quality of life. In the midst of plenty, vast numbers of people throughout the world still live out their lives in appalling conditions of poverty. About 1.2 billion people are living in 'absolute' poverty – living on less than US$1 dollar per day, a figure which is used to reflect people's ability to afford a diet sufficient to meet minimal nutritional needs.[3] Even within the UK, more than 13 per cent of the population are defined as living in poverty, with the accepted definition of poverty here being those living on less than half the average income.[4]

This matters for progress towards sustainable development for all. The Brundtland Report drew attention to the connection between poverty and unsustainable trends in the economy and our use of the environment:

> '*Poverty is not only an evil in itself, but sustainable development requires meeting the basic needs of all and extending to all the opportunity to fulfil their aspirations for a better life. A world in which poverty is endemic will always be prone to ecological and other catastrophes ... The point is that the reduction of poverty itself is a precondition for environmentally sound development.*'[5]

Here we examine the ways in which existing economic policies and practices, despite their contribution to gains in wealth and living standards globally, have failed to eradicate the problems of deep poverty, and in some cases have made them worse. This chapter explores poverty in the UK as well as in the developing countries. This is not to suggest that the overall level of deprivation in the UK is comparable to the worst poverty of the developing world. But it underlines the point that while the degree and depth of poverty are very different, there are some important parallel causes and consequences. Globalizing capitalism has produced many winners – in some places, far more than it has produced losers – but it has also marginalized a significant minority of people in the developed countries and whole nations in the South.

The Lessons of Recent Development

The dominant 'neo-liberal' economic policy model of the last two decades was built on the idea that economic growth and the deregulation of markets create opportunities and wealth not only for the enterprising and gifted, but also, in time, for the poor. Wealth will 'trickle down' to the poorest, and inequalities matter little as long as all parts of society are able to experience economic growth and better themselves. The best anti-poverty measure, on this influential analysis, is to free societies for market-based competition and to let economic growth do its work.

This prescription has been applied all around the world in the last decade. The results are clear. While hundreds of millions have seen their real incomes rise, their opportunities improve and their quality of life get better, many have seen no advance and in some cases are actually worse off. In countries such as Russia, a raw capitalism has developed which, far from integrating the former USSR with the liberal capitalist democracies of the West, has been the worst possible advertisement for market forces because of the huge gaps between the new rich and the mass of impoverished

Witness Box 7: Save the Children

As we enter the first decade of the 21st century there is acute schizophrenia regarding children and young people in our global society. All but two of the nations of the world have ratified the UN Convention on the Rights of the Child, committing themselves to achieving the full spectrum of children's rights – civil, political, economic, cultural and social – through the 'maximum use of the available resources'. The vision of the Convention is gradually having an influence and children are increasingly seen as full human beings, rights-holders who can play an active part in the enjoyment of their rights. They are not – as they have so often been presented in the past – mere dependants, the property of their parents. Every child is seen as important, no matter what its abilities, origins or gender.

However, the Convention is operating in an environment that is extraordinarily hostile to its vision for children. The last decade has seen prolonged conflict and genocidal wars, and more than eight million children have lost their mothers or both parents as a result of HIV/Aids. Many countries in central and eastern Europe, the former Soviet Union and East Asia embarked on a painful transition towards capitalism, reducing public childcare, health and educational provision services in the process. Growth has undoubtedly occurred, but the macroeconomic policies forming the basis of international aid and trade have adverse distributional consequences.

Half the world's poor are now children and, as population grows, there are more children living in poverty than ever before. In the poorest 50 countries of the world, declines in infant and child mortality are slowing or have been reversed; children who survive infancy bear a huge burden of infectious diseases, malnutrition and disability, mostly from preventable causes; and maternal mortality and morbidity rates remain appalling. One hundred and thirty million children of primary-school age are not in school, and many who do attend are offered poor quality education. Girls, children with disabilities, and children from minority ethnic groups face obstacles to their development because of discrimination.

Conflict persists; 13 million children around the world, for example, are displaced within their own countries, losing their homes, security, land, livelihoods and possessions. Most displacement lasts for six years or more – a high proportion of a child's life. If children miss out on good nutrition, education, healthcare and play during their formative years the damage cannot easily be undone. Protecting the rights of children is part of the process of creating the conditions of peace.

The trends identified above must be reversed; resources must be made available. Children's issues must be made more visible and recognized as a collective responsibility of the international community.

Most importantly, tomorrow's challenges have to be met by today's children. To prepare them for this we must treat them as respected citizens, providing opportunities to learn leadership, democracy and collective responsibility, as children learn best by doing. The responsibility for this does not lie with any single institution; governments, civil society and business must work hand in hand if we are to create a world where children are truly seen and heard.

85

citizens. In the rich world, pockets of extreme deprivation persist, and the poorest face major barriers to 'inclusion' in society and economic life. In the developing world, income inequalities are widening just as they have in parts of the West. The reasons are complex, but an overall picture has emerged from the experience of recent globalization:

- *Winners take (almost) all:* The modern economy is based on swiftly developing, complex and expensive new technologies, and on high levels of skill and knowledge. In developing new markets, products, processes and skills there is a considerable advantage to those citizens, companies, regions, countries and governments that have already gained significant wealth, market share and know-how. To adapt a phrase: to those that already have, shall be given more. And in the global service markets – of sport, entertainment and financial management, for example – where there is intense competition to win the large prizes on offer, the people who can make the difference between coming first and second can attract huge rewards. Winners take all or most.[6] Inequalities of opportunity and outcome on a huge scale are inevitable, given the unequal distribution of the assets that make most difference to prosperity.
- *Trickle down doesn't:*[7] Experience has persuaded some policy-makers that the idea of a 'trickle down effect', by which wealth created by the successful reaches the poor via the mechanism of the market and local economic development, is badly flawed. This effect does not automatically create greater equality of opportunity and wealth, especially in the absence of market and institutional frameworks to improve the capacity of poor people and areas to gain access to opportunities and build up assets.
- *The poorest are superfluous to the modern economy:* The poor in the West are a minority, albeit a significant one, and are decisive neither to market development nor to political calculations. The least educated in a country such as the UK no longer find a place within industries that are increasingly about advanced technology, high quality service and continuous learning. Business and political leaders do not need to appeal to the poor to succeed, as demonstrated by retailers' abandonment of low-income areas across the UK. Meanwhile, the poor people of the world are numbered in the billions, but currently have little collective

political or economic weight. On a global scale, the poorest countries are marginal to the operation of the economy. If we wish to change this situation, we need to help the poorest countries and social groups gain and keep assets that will lift them out of poverty and dependency.

- *The global needs the local:* Local economies are increasingly affected by decisions taken at the international level, and global corporations and investors can move their capital from place to place. It is easy to see local economies as vulnerable and wholly dependent on the global system. But in reality they are intertwined, since the global market needs local producers, consumers and infrastructures, no matter how 'virtual' it becomes. A connected global economy that destabilizes or abandons national and regional economies on a large scale is self-defeating and unsustainable; and trade which depends on global transportation of goods, many of which could be produced and exchanged on a regional basis, is environmentally unsustainable. It is in the interest of sustainable globalization for there to be more resilient and diverse local economies worldwide.

- *Institutions matter:* Global bodies such as the World Bank now acknowledge the crucial importance of good governance, education and public services such as healthcare, and honest legal agencies in underpinning the work of markets and enterprise. Where governance is bad, conflict rife, trust in institutions and law lacking, there will be no progress for the poorest. The experience of developing and post-Communist countries where there is widespread corruption and conflict underlines the point. But it also applies to the developed world. In the ghettoes of the USA and in the worst-off estates of the UK, the poorest people do not simply experience a lack of money and employment. They also lack access to good quality education, healthcare, housing and transport. In North and South alike, the vital role of good education is now recognized: without it, economic development for the poor is blocked. Across the world, policy-makers have failed to invest enough in the institutions of good education and governance which everyone, and especially the poor, need in order to thrive. This is a powerful reason for the failure to bridge the widening gap between winners and losers in the globalizing economy, both in the developed and developing countries.

The Impact and Extent of Poverty

Definitions of poverty are always problematic, and there are criticisms of both the absolute measures (such as US$1 dollar per day) and relative measures (such as half average incomes). There is also a real and understandable resistance among those people classified in these ways to be lumped together and dealt with as a homogenous group labeled as 'poor', as if that characteristic alone defined them.[8]

88

The experience of poverty is easier to understand than bald statistics. In much of the developing world, it is about lack of food and water, living in insanitary and dangerous environments, being exposed to violence, crime, harsh working conditions and malnutrition (Figure 4.1). It is about the hardships of rural subsistence and the risks of being at the bottom of society and the economy in the fast-growing big cities of the South. It is about the exposure of the poorest to the ravages of diseases – such as the epidemic of HIV/Aids now dragging down life expectancy in many African countries – and to regular environmental crises such as floods.

Poverty in the developing world is sometimes viewed in the West as somehow inevitable, connected to the rise in population in the South and the pressure on resources (see Panel 6).

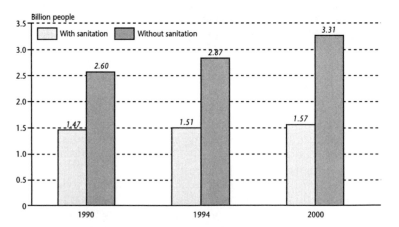

Figure 4.1 *Population With and Without Sanitation, All Developing Countries*

Source: UNEP, *Global Environment Outlook 2000*, Earthscan, London, 1999

Panel 6

Population Trends

During the autumn of 1999, a Millennial milestone was reached – the six billionth human being was born. In May 2000, the arrival of the billionth citizen of India was announced. The upper bound of UN demographic projections forecasts a global population of nearly 12 billion by 2050, and the median projection indicates growth by mid-century to some 8.9 billion. Growth has been concentrated in the developing world, notably in Africa, while populations are stable or declining in Europe and Japan. But the peak of population growth seems to have passed: the high point was 1989, when an additional 87 million people were added. Now, two out of five people worldwide live in countries where fertility has dropped to replacement level. Various factors explain the slowdown in overall population growth:

- The 'demographic transition' – the tendency of family size to fall as living standards increase, women gain more economic and social independence, contraception becomes available and urban populations grow at the expense of the countryside. This transition, widely observed in the industrialized world, is beginning to affect much of the developing world.

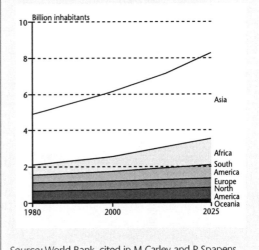

Source: World Bank, cited in M Carley and P Spapens, *Sharing the World: Sustainable Living and Global Equity in the 21st Century* (London: Earthscan, 1998)

- Support for the outcomes of the International Conference on Population and Development (ICPD) in 1994. This recognized women's low status and its negative impact on development, and led to objectives being set in areas of education, mortality reduction and reproductive health, with an emphasis on providing information and services for young people. Elements of the ICPD Programme of Action included increased access to family planning services and information, more reliable and widely available contraceptives, better education, and economic opportunities for the poorest. The Fourth World Women's Conference in 1995 set the scene for better rights for women in terms of sexual and reproductive rights, social, economic and civil rights.

- The impact of HIV/Aids infection on mortality rates in Africa.

Overall, long-standing concerns about 'over-population' per se have been modified. It seems that the Earth can support the current population and absorb more growth, while at the same time we can live sustainably and protect biodiversity even if our numbers rise. The issue is not so much one of absolute numbers, although these do matter, but of the kind of consumption in which we engage. So attention is shifting from global population size towards the inequalities and excesses that characterize particular populations globally and within regions and states, and towards further measures to improve economic and social rights and status for women and boost education for young people in developing countries.

Sources: UN, *World Population Prospects: The 1998 Revision* (New York: United Nations, December 1998); L R Brown et al, *Vital Signs 1999–2000* (London: Earthscan, 2000)

But successes in development in parts of the South, and the wealth available worldwide to eliminate deep poverty, give the lie to this perception. Tackling poverty is the key to reducing population pressures where they exist in developing countries.

In the UK, poverty is rarely about exposure to risks of the kind faced by poor people in the developing world. But this relative well-being should not blind us to the reality of the disadvantages generated by poverty in the UK. Many people in the UK who lack work, access to decent transport, and the skills needed to enter and remain in jobs, find themselves cut off from a meaningful life, from social networks and from family ties. Relative to the poorest of the planet, most of Britain's poor are well off; but that does not diminish the barriers they face to meaningful participation in our society, and does not make any more acceptable the deprivation experienced by those living in homes that are unfit as a result of being damp or infested, with no nearby sources of cheap wholesome food, or those with little or no chance of access to good schools or higher education or training.

For the poorest in the rich world, poverty can mean 'social exclusion' – inability to play a full part in social and economic life. For many, it means living with pollution and crime in a degraded environment. Living in impoverished conditions is bad enough, but it is the lack of options, the apparent impossibility of escaping these circumstances, that creates the real horrors of poverty.

Witness Box 8: Population Concern

Population Concern is a charity working with local partner organizations in less developed countries to improve the quality of life worldwide. This is achieved by providing accessible information, education and services relating to sexual and reproductive healthcare for all, with a special focus on young people. This allows people to make choices about childbearing and to protect themselves against infections, including the HIV/Aids virus. Population Concern believes that this is necessary to bring about sustainable development.

Women play a vital role in development, especially in the developing world. They give birth, look after their children, look after the family home, provide food for the family, work on the family's land and try to earn money by selling food, crafts or some other product. It is therefore important that women are in good health. They make up half the world's population and make very positive contributions to their families and to the communities in which they live. However, they also make up 70 per cent of the 1.3 billion people living in extreme poverty; every year 600,000 of them die due to pregnancy-related causes, and many millions more suffer infection or injury, which is unlikely to be treated. This situation needs to be addressed.

In 1999, however, DFID introduced guidelines for its new Civil Society Challenge Fund which stated that organizations working on sexual and reproductive health programmes would be able to apply for only 50 per cent funding, instead of the previous 100 per cent. Lobbying by organizations affected by this decision has resulted in the funding decrease being staggered – 85 per cent in the first year, 70 per cent in the second, down to 50 per cent in the third year. Even so, these organizations are left wondering where the extra cash will come from. It is not easy to raise money for sexual and reproductive health programmes. Many people do not agree with the provision of such services, and yet they are absolutely essential if sustainable development is to be achieved.

Governments alone cannot provide these services, yet increasingly Northern NGOs and civil society organizations (CSOs) appear to be sidelined. It is important that Government recognizes the significant contributions that Northern NGOs and CSOs can make. In many developing countries they provide services which otherwise would not exist, like health and education. They bring their expertise and knowledge and can help to build the capacity of local organizations, resulting in more efficient and effective organizations. In addition, because they work at community level they are able to identify problems and solutions and are aware of any sensitive issues.

Another area that negatively impacts on sustainable development is the HIV/Aids epidemic. With half of all new HIV infections being to young people aged 15–24 years, it is extremely important that HIV prevention education is integrated into health services aimed at young people. Recent studies in Africa show that girls aged 15–19 years are

91

five to six times more likely to be HIV-positive than boys their own age, probably partly resulting from older men coercing teenage girls to have sex, and the 'sugar-daddy' syndrome, where older men buy sexual favours. Therefore HIV-prevention education should not only be about condom use. It should also be about creating an environment where young women can assert themselves and say 'No', and where they can recognize that there are no long-term benefits in such relationships. In addition, men and boys must learn to respect young women.

The issues discussed above are fundamental to sustainable development – adequate funding, recognition of NGO/CSO support and HIV-prevention programmes for young people. This is not impossible, but it will not be achieved without political will.

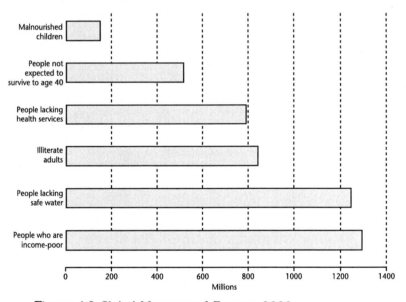

Figure 4.2 *Global Measures of Poverty, 2000*
Source: UNDP, cited in UNEP, *Global Environment Outlook 2000* (London: Earthscan, 1999)

Why Poverty and Inequalities Matter

Should affluent people care about the plight of the worst-off at home and abroad? Yes, for reasons both of ethical principle and long-term self-interest. As Ross McKibbin writes:

> 'There are two reasons why we should worry about
> poverty. The first is one of simple morality: it is wrong
> in a rich society for many to be poor... The second is
> what the Edwardians called 'efficiency'.
> No society in which many are poor can achieve its
> potential, economic or cultural.[9]

The damage done by poverty is evident. But do we need to worry about inequalities per se? The trend over the last 20 years among policy-makers and politicians has been to downplay inequality as an issue of relevance to the economy. But although inequality has not been a potent political topic for years in the West, we may be reaching a threshold beyond which such tolerance of widening gaps between rich and poor cannot be sustained.

93

International agencies are now making this point. At the annual meeting of the World Bank and International Monetary Fund (IMF) in Prague in September 2000, the Bank's head, James Wolfensohn, expressed sympathy for many of the arguments of the protesters outside the conference, and said, 'We live in a world scarred by inequality. Something is wrong when the richest 20% of the global population receive more than 80% of the global income'. The UNDP *Human Development Report* for 2000 argues that the inequalities between the rich of the North and the poorest of the South are 'by orders of magnitude out of proportion to anything experienced before'. The report described the millennial pattern of inequality as so dramatic and dangerous that the situation of the poorest amounts to a violation of human rights. Political and civil liberties need to go hand in hand with economic and social rights, without which people are in no position to exercise their human rights and fulfil responsibilities. This is an important extension of the argument that development depends on good governance and respect for rights, and recognizes that extreme inequalities can undermine both.

But the argument against tolerance of widening inequalities does not rest simply on an ethical basis. There is a practical argument, rooted in the long-term self-interest of all, including the rich: extremes of inequality are damaging not only to those who are poor but also to the wider society.[10] Inequality affects the success of anti-poverty strategies and overall economic growth in two main ways.[11] First, countries with deep inequality may grow more slowly because, in unequal societies, poor people's productivity is limited because they have less access to credit or assets, and may suffer from ill health or lack of skills. At the same time, richer people may use their power to increase the benefits they receive, even if they lead to economic inefficiencies.[12] Second, the greater the inequality, the weaker will be the poverty-reducing effect of growth, because a smaller share will go to the poor.

Social cohesion is undermined by excesses of wealth and poverty and 'there is growing evidence that narrowing income inequality in a society adds to the overall social quality of life ... In societies where the income distribution is narrow, there is greater social cohesion, less violence and crime'.[13] Very unequal societies are unhealthy ones, running up huge 'defensive expenditures' to pay for unemployment benefit, the costs of ill health, the effects of crime, environmental damage and family breakdown.

Extreme inequalities threaten the whole economy in the long term, as a large proportion of society loses any connection with the assets and organizations that generate wealth. The American business thinker Jeff Gates has noted the impact of 'two-tier' market economies on social cohesion and people's stake in the wider system. Increasing exclusion of the poor from employment, ownership of assets and decent incomes leads to more dependence on state benefits and more fiscal strains on government. Widening gaps between rich and poor in the developing and ex-Communist worlds fuel discontent with capitalism and democracy. As Gates remarks, 'Two-tier societies and two-tier marketplaces are not the fertile soil in which robust democracies take root'.[14]

At the global level, the limits to rising inequality between rich and poor nations and within them are also being tested by environmental change. There are limits to growth in consumption of fossil fuels. We know that we need drastic cuts in the use of fossil fuels if we are to avoid climate disruption that would harm the well-off as well as the poor. But cuts cannot be demanded equally of the poor and the rich nations, or of everyone within them. If the rich world is to secure the cooperation of the poorer countries on climate strategy, it must make much deeper cuts in fossil fuel emissions, and help the developing world to raise living standards. And if within the rich countries there are to be caps on certain forms of consumption – such as use of petrol-powered cars and of fossil fuels for heating homes

– then attention immediately focuses on issues of equity. If we are all in the same environmental boat, and in relation to global warming we definitely are, then the rich need the cooperation of the poor, and policies need to give equitable outcomes. Thus there is an element of self-interest of the rich world to assist the developing countries – first, to grow their economies using the most efficient technologies available and adopting renewable energy systems; and second, to improve education for the poor, increase their economic opportunities and provide access to sexual and reproductive healthcare information and services. Such measures can not only raise living standards and quality of life, but also help promote smaller families as a norm.

Making Progress in Reducing Poverty and Inequality

How has the picture changed since the establishment of Real World? There are hopeful signs of a movement towards more sustainable development. The West has accepted the principle of debt reduction and forgiveness for the poorest debtor countries. The World Bank has led moves among the big global economic agencies to rethink development aid strategies in the light of protests and critiques from NGOs in the North and the South and from communities and governments in the developing world. Strategic thinking on aid and development is now beginning to leave behind a crude emphasis on market deregulation and is focusing far more on the need for intelligent regulation and for market-based policies to be underpinned by policies for 'good governance' – providing support for human rights, democratic institutions, the rule of law, sound health and education systems, above all for the poor and for girls and women, and measures to protect the environment and manage resources sustainably. Little of this is yet in evidence on the ground in the policies of the global economic agencies, but it is a cause for optimism that such a change might follow their recognition of the limits to their recent policies for restructuring developing countries' economies.

Tackling poverty and inequality is now a policy priority throughout much of the industrialized world (see Panel 8, Chapter 5). There is a common element to programmes to reduce poverty globally and in a rich country such as the UK. The emphasis is on improving the capacity of the poorest people to help themselves, primarily by improving education and training, and by improving the infrastructure (health, transport, schools) on which poor people depend for basic improvements to their quality of life and their future prospects. These approaches are designed to improve the well-being and economic independence of poor people, and to combat their 'exclusion' from society and the economy.

As discussed in the next chapter, there is a growing understanding among the major industrialized countries that the global trading system underpinned by the WTO is neither 'free', fair to the developing world, nor compatible with international accords on environmental protection. There is a fast-growing movement to develop 'ethical' trade and investment, with new 'fair trade' enterprises emerging from innovative work linking NGOs, crop producers and corporations. More transnational corporations are acknowledging the need for, and the long-term benefits from, contributing to improving the conditions of the poor and investing in the social and environmental resources that underpin all economies.

In the UK, the New Labour Government has introduced initiatives to analyse the factors behind 'social exclusion' and develop better policies for the regeneration of deprived areas – including a new system of regional development and a strategy for 'neighbourhood renewal' in the worst-off communities. It has taken steps to improve the incomes and living standards of the poor, introducing a minimum wage and tax credits for the poorest working families, and investing in the improvement of public services. It has also taken a lead in promoting debt relief for the poorest countries and in supporting 'good governance'.

So, there is positive change to report. However, there are vital ethical and political questions to be asked in the light of the dramatic widening of inequality gaps around the world, and in the face of the persistently grim statistics on poverty: a system that condemns 1.2 billion people to extreme poverty while others become richer by the day can no longer be considered a success. So far, the positive developments of the past few years in policy approaches are simply not being implemented fast enough to meet the needs of the poorest countries and citizens worldwide.

What about progress in reducing poverty at home? Below, we consider the state of poverty and inequality in the UK. While progress is being made, there is a great distance still to go before the UK overcomes the worst of its problems of poverty and social exclusion.

Witness Box 9: Church Action on Poverty (CAP)

Debt on our Doorstep

Jubilee 2000 has achieved much success in drawing the world's attention to the unpayable debts of the 'two-thirds' world, but individuals and communities in the UK are struggling with debt too. According to the Child Poverty Action Group and the National Association of Citizens Advice Bureaux, personal debt is now reaching unsustainable levels, with some 900,000 individuals seeking help with debt from local Citizens Advice Bureaux in 1999. For the poorest in society, the burden of debt is exacerbated by financial exclusion – a lack of access to sources of affordable credit and other financial services.

Some 1 in 5 households (9 million people) have no building society or bank account, while 1.5 million households in Britain (7 per cent) do not use financial services at all. Yet it is estimated that running a household without access to a basic bank account costs on average £260 a year – £5 per week. Many people on low incomes are frequently unable to meet the cost of essential items and occasional life crises and turn to money-lenders in times of need.

Yet current legislation offers vulnerable customers virtually no protection against unscrupulous or extortionate – but perfectly legal – money-lenders, charging interest rates in excess of 150 per cent to low-income customers with few if any alternative sources of credit. The 1974 Consumer Credit Act does, in theory, cover 'extortionate credit', but the Office of Fair Trading has admitted the measure is ineffective and successful prosecutions are very rare. While statutory interest rate ceilings are common within Europe and apply in most American states, the Government has to date refused to consider introducing a legal maximum in the UK.

Despite the woeful inadequacies of the DSS's own Social Fund, and the fact that the Fund is now itself a major contributory factor to the growth of personal debt, the Government has not yet given any indication that it is prepared to act to reform or replace it.

'Debt on our Doorstep' – a network for fair finance of more than 20 key voluntary organizations and community groups – was launched in April 2000. Members include Barnardo's, Child Poverty Action Group, Children's Society, Church Action on Poverty, the Fawcett Society, Help the Aged, Money Advice Association, National Local Government Forum Against Poverty, New Economics Foundation, Oxfam, Tearfund and the YMCA. Debt on our Doorstep is campaigning for urgent action and reform in four key areas:

1 Reduction and eradication of irresponsible and extortionate lending.
2 Reforming and/or replacement of the social fund.
3 Promotion of socially responsible service provision by high street banks.
4 Promotion of credit unions and other community finance initiatives.

Establishing Minimum Income Standards

The basic question, 'What are benefits supposed to cover?' has not been answered since the system was introduced in 1948. Since then there has been no attempt to set rates according to some agreed standard of what they should, and could, actually cover.

A study by the Family Budget Unit, *Low Cost but Acceptable*, set out to define a standard of living and level of income 'below which good health, social integration and satisfactory standards of child development are at risk'. This showed that benefits for an out-of-work couple with two children aged 10 and 4 years fall £39 per week below this 'low cost but acceptable level'. The benefits received by a single-parent with children of the same ages fall short by £27 per week.

CAP, with other voluntary sector agencies, is now campaigning for the development of agreed minimum income standards which would be taken into account when setting benefit levels, minimum income guarantees and minimum wage levels.

Bringing Britain Together: Putting People in Poverty at the Centre

In recent years, in the work done by CAP with people in poverty, one theme that consistently crops up is the way in which poor people feel 'invisible'. The people most directly affected are effectively excluded from the debate about how to tackle poverty. Yet we know that many of the so-called solutions to poverty and exclusion of the past failed because they did not take the experiences and views of those most directly affected into account.

The third test of the Government's commitment to tackling poverty is in the area of participation. This is clearly an area in which the Government has made some headway in the past two years, not least through the establishment of the Social Exclusion Unit. In drawing up the National Strategy for Neighbourhood Renewal, the Unit has attempted to listen to the widespread concerns of local communities about the failure of previous Government initiatives. Achieving the real and active participation of people and communities who directly experience poverty and exclusion will be key to the success of the National Strategy (and its equivalents in Wales and Scotland).

The Government still has a huge way to go in recognizing the expertise and insights that people in poverty can bring across the spectrum of policy-making. For unless people in poverty are at the table, any attempt at 'joined up' policy-making will remain wide of the mark.

Poverty and Inequality in the UK: New Approaches to Social Exclusion

In spite of a flourishing economy, high levels of economic growth and increasing affluence for many people in the UK, poverty and inequality remain major problems (see Panel 7).

The UK is one of the most unequal countries in the industrialized world, with earnings inequality having increased more in recent years than in any other OECD country.[15] In the UK, average incomes grew by about 40 per cent between 1979 and 1994/95, but this growth was not equally shared: the richest 10 per cent of the population saw their incomes grow by 60–68 per cent; the poorest 10 per cent saw their incomes fall by 8 per cent (after housing costs).[16]

Panel 7

Poverty and Inequality in the UK

The UK is among the bottom five industrialized countries in the UN Human Poverty Index (1997 data). This index is based on the percentage of people not expected to survive to age 60 (9.8 per cent in the UK); adult functional illiteracy (21.8 per cent); percentage of people living below the poverty line – ie 50 per cent of median personal income – (13.5 per cent); and long-term unemployment rate – ie more than 12 months (3.3 per cent).

Poverty in the UK has increased since the 1980s, with 24 per cent of households living in poverty in 1999, compared to 14 per cent in 1983.

- Child poverty and the problems of families with children appear particularly intractable.
- The number of children living in relative poverty has more than tripled since the 1960s: one-third of all children (over 4.3 million) lived in households with below half the average income in 1995/96, up from just 10 per cent (1.3 million) in 1968.
- Between 17 and 19 per cent of children live in households with no workers; this figure has remained steady between autumn 1996 and spring 1999.
- Women and cultural minorities in the UK continue to experience worse than average impacts from inequality. For example:
  - In April 1999, the average salary for men was £23,000; around 42% higher than that for women.
  - In spring 1999, unemployment rates for men were twice as high for those from black or Pakistani/Bangladeshi groups as for those from white or Indian groups.

Sources: UNDP, *Human Development Report 1999* (New York: OUP, 1999); Joseph Rowntree Foundation (1998a), *Income and Wealth: The latest evidence*, by John Hills; Joseph Rowntree Foundation (1998b), *Income Gap Remains Wide Despite Mid-1990s Fall in Inequality*; Joseph Rowntree Foundation, *Child Development and Family Income*, by P Gregg, S Harkness and S Machin (York: York Publishing Services, 1999); Office for National Statistics, *Social Inequalities* (London: ONS, 2000); Dorling, Daniel, *The Widening Gap*, (Bristol: University of Bristol, 2000); Joseph Rowntree Foundation, *Poverty and Social Exclusion in Great Britain* (York: Joseph Rowntree Foundation, 2000).

In the late 1990s there was falling unemployment, an end to the growth in numbers of people claiming income support and slower growth in average incomes. These changes, and a declining proportion of pensioners entirely dependent on state benefits, all contributed to the slowing of the rate of growth in inequality.[17] These changes are welcome, but there is still a very long way to go to reach a more equitable society. Recent research shows that, although there is some mobility out of poverty, 'people drop back after an initial escape and others stick at the bottom'.[18] And regional inequalities in the UK remain wide.

Current levels of poverty alongside excessive wealth have helped create a deep and growing fear of crime and lawlessness that is particularly corrosive. Social divisions and lack of contact between rich and poor lead to increased demonization of certain groups (including certain cultural minorities such as asylum- seekers). The perception that crime is endemic deeply affects public morale, individual well-being and the quality of social life.

Witness Box 10: Black Environment Network

Ethnic Environmental Participation

The Cultural Gap

Government should strategically promote multi-culturalism within all sectors in the context of sustainable development, in order to build a socio-cultural framework within which the full participation of ethnic groups can take place – a multi-cultural society within which each cultural group finds its rightful place, to be nurtured at the same time as playing a full contributing role.

Significant ethnic communities are settled in Britain because of the engagement of their countries of origin with Britain. They tend to be concentrated within the inner cities, but each is bound to every British person, even in the remotest parts of the countryside, through a common, multi-cultural British history.

'Equal Opportunities' is very shallowly understood. A deeper understanding within each sector needs to be put into place.

The Resources Gap

Government should structurally express its commitment to the diverse ethnic communities within the UK by setting appropriate spending and programme targets across the framework for sustainable development. This means:

- Recognizing the specific forms of deprivation and the necessary accelerated development of ethnic groups.
- Responding to the nature and scale of the needs of ethnic groups by multiplying population numbers with deprivation factors.
- Attending specifically to enabling the consolidation and expansion of the infrastructure of ethnic groups.
- Attending to the details of structures of mechanisms that aim to release resources to ethnic groups, for example, setting aside resources in grant funds specifically for ethnic groups, with criteria that are relevant to those groups.

The Commitment Gap
Government should take a lead in promoting the inclusion of the needs of socially excluded groups in the policies and strategies of the public, private and voluntary sectors. This includes programmes for ethnic groups, in order that monetary resources and programmes of activities may be released.

Such commitment also means:

- Setting targets for working with ethnic groups.
- Undertaking programmed organizational culture change to enable its personnel at all levels to gain the awareness and skills to work effectively with ethnic groups.

101

The New Labour Government has made it a priority to reduce social exclusion and poverty. Improvements include changes to welfare benefits, such as the working families tax credit; increased income support and child benefit; the Sure Start programme for educational support of children in vulnerable families, and the proposed child tax credit from 2001. For those in low paid jobs, the minimum wage, tax incentives and other measures are beginning to have positive impacts, although the levels set remain low. The New Deal programme for the young and long-term unemployed people and others has brought gains for young people in particular.

Much of the Government's anti-poverty strategy has been focused on encouraging people on benefits to gain the skills to enable them to find employment ('welfare to work'). These programmes have provided individual advice and support; greater opportunities for education and training (including through the New Deal), and tax and other incentives to reduce the difficulties of moving from benefits to paid work. Evaluation of programmes such as the New Deal suggests that they are effective for many of the less disadvantaged people using them, but that the worst-off individuals and areas need much more comprehensive assistance and long-term investment, since they are the least equipped for thriving in the mainstream economy.[19]

UK Government policy has also recognized that reducing the harms done by social exclusion, and by the huge variations between areas of the UK in quality of public services, must be a priority for any government aiming to promote social cohesion.[20] The Government's Comprehensive Spending Review in July 2000 set out plans for increased spending on regeneration, established the New Deal programmes as permanent initiatives and set targets for poverty reduction. For example:

- improved employment rates in the 30 worst-off local authority districts;
- much reduced crime rates in deprived areas;
- all social housing to meet standards of decency by 2010;
- the energy efficiency of 600,000 homes to be improved by 2004, targeting households vulnerable to 'fuel poverty';
- £500 million extra funding for regeneration work by the Regional Development Agencies.

If sustained investment is made in programmes such as the New Deals for employment and community regeneration, then a great advance could be made in overcoming poverty and social exclusion. New Deal schemes have been successful in finding jobs for many young people at a time of economic growth and high demand for labour. However, the real test of anti-exclusion programmes is how far they can help people to earn a decent living during economic downturns, and help disadvantaged groups and communities weather difficult times and thrive. Programmes such as the New Deal have the potential to make a connection between economic growth and gains in well-being for deprived communities – a link that would otherwise be lacking.

There are wider concerns. To ensure that the 'poverty gap' is being closed, Government needs to be able to show how its initiatives on social exclusion and support for the poor fit with its wider strategy of sustainable development and its vision of globalization and a modernized economy. So far there has been little integration between Government's programmes on social inclusion and environmental sustainability, despite the evidence that strong measures for the latter can generate jobs and revenues to help overcome exclusion (see Chapter 3). It is vital that measures to combat social exclusion do not simply help the dis-

Witness Box 11: Community Action Network (CAN)

Developing New Ideas and Lobbying Government and Industry

The voluntary sector as a whole in the UK is stagnating. Despite increasing individual wealth, giving is steadily declining. Support from Government, especially local government, is declining and central government is increasingly focusing its resources on state-run services. However, as the following case studies illustrate, there is a great deal of potential to change this in the following ways:

Enterprise
While many community organizations are developing trading activities as an extension of their work – providing employment, generating revenue, etc – the results are often poor. CAN believes there is tremendous potential for increasing greatly the quality and quantity of community enterprise activities. There are huge opportunities for producing and marketing products and services, for organizations to trade with and learn from each other, and for exposure to excellence and good practice.

Level Playing Field: Running Services
Many social entrepreneurs are part of local excluded communities. This means that they are often very well placed to enable services to be run by excluded communities, especially in education, health, training and employment. However, there are a number of very considerable barriers. There is often no mechanism for local organizations to bid to run services. Where there are mechanisms, the bureaucracy involved frequently means that it is impractical and uneconomic for them to do so. In addition, there are often real issues of quality and consistency. The UK Government spends billions on statutory services. Currently less than 0.01 per cent of such services are run by local community organizations. CAN's long-term target is to increase this figure to 1 per cent, which will create the beginnings of a mixed local economy. CAN is approaching this on two fronts:

1 Where there is the potential to bid for funds – for example regeneration funding – CAN is bringing together groups of members as a consortium to keep the bidding costs to a minimum It is also addressing issues of quality.
2 Lobbying Government to open competition for provision of local services to local organizations, such as schools, health centres and colleges, in order to create a level playing field, especially when the local provision has been of a poor quality for many years.

Communities in Business
Through its commercial arm, CAN is working with a range of leading multinationals. 'Communities in Business' starts from the simple premise that business needs to understand the community into which it sells, and that 'virtuous circles' can be created whereby marginalized communities

> become directly involved in the business, increase sales and improve the public profile of the company, as well as providing local jobs and injecting resources into local economies. CAN provides the opportunity for local communities to tap into its commercial arm and access business links.
>
> CAN believes that the future is about creating a new entrepreneurial culture that would empower individuals to bring about real change. Such a culture would focus on the individual as a catalyst of change; encourage social entrepreneurial initiatives to grow around the energy of individuals, rather than systems or structures; take seriously the new opportunities presented by the partnership agenda and the IT revolution; and demand of all politicians, and those in the chattering classes, that they climb down from their ivory towers and immerse themselves in the practical realities of some of their poorest communities. It is amid some of our greatest social problems, in the disconnections between people and structures, business and the social sector, that CAN believes the clues to a new future are to be found. CAN aims to promote a new practical way of building that future – what the British Prime Minister calls the Third Way.

advantaged to compete in a system that is inherently unstable and unsustainable. At present, policies on exclusion tend to reinforce the sense of division and lack of common cause between the affluent and those losing out in the modern economy. In future, policy measures need to focus on a strategic reorientation of the economy that unites all parts of society, rich and poor, in a common long-term purpose.

There has also been little recognition that, as noted earlier, a strong global economy needs to be connected to strong and diverse local economies and employment. The rapid development of new technologies, and the erosion of full-time permanent jobs as more work becomes organized on 'flexible', often less secure lines, make it vital for policy to improve people's skills and employability, as well as to secure increased commitment from employers to equal opportunities policies and fair treatment of workers displaced as technologies and markets change. The probability that there will continue to be sharp downturns in the economic cycle makes it essential to devise policies that foster diversity and resilience in local and regional economies, and that reduce their reliance on traditionally dominant products and sectors. As in farming, monocultures are unhealthy in the local economy.

Against this background, employment as we currently understand it may not provide a complete answer to poverty.

Witness Box 12: UK Public Health Association (PHA)

The UK Public Health Association is a voluntary organization, made up of individual and organizational members across all nations and regions of the UK. Our aim is to be an advocate of healthy public policy, working with and for people throughout this country.

At a time when Government is devolving its structures, even if hesitantly, it is crucial to us that we can truly represent people from all parts of the UK. It is equally crucial that we can genuinely communicate, to all levels of decision-makers, the lived experiences of people in local communities.

We are concerned about health – far wider than the NHS. This means we want to see an environment that promotes good health; we want employment and education opportunities for all, and we want social and emotional support for individuals and communities. We want to see governments paying greater attention to the well-being of their populations, in a holistic way, supporting their whole health. In particular we believe this means it is vital to tackle inequalities. Health – for all – requires a shift of wealth and income from those who have to those who have not. Simply speaking, we need a fairer society in order to create a healthier society.

We are concerned about the health of the public. Public means not just individual. And not private. We want to see governments willing to pay for the services needed to sustain people, not to divert them into the hands of those who exist to make private profits. We want to see higher standards of public services, not to see them as second-class or residual for those who cannot afford anything better. The funding, production, supply, distribution and regulation of vaccines against life-threatening illness such as TB cannot be left to the vagaries of the free market. The control of poor working conditions cannot be left to the individual self-restraint of the private employer. The removal of toxic substances from our air, water, food and communities cannot be left to the goodwill of every 'consumer'. Indeed, 'consumer protection' (in economic terms) has been advanced by legislation. Public protection, from hazards facing us, and public promotion, in positive ways to improve our health, require public Government action.

Not everyone is going to be able to find 'flexible' work in the new digital sectors of the knowledge economy. Given the direction of globalization and technological development and their implications for jobs, greater value needs to be placed, by Government and other policy-makers, on voluntary as well as paid work and employment, on caring as well as profitable work,[21] and on work that helps to provide essential social benefits, including environmental action. Informal work that improves overall quality of life and greatly reduces the costs of social security to the state deserve recognition through benefits and support for new forms of 'social economy' such as cooperatives, small mutual organizations and networks in which people can barter services and goods (such as 'time–money' initiatives developed in the UK and North America).[22] This leads us to the connections between anti-poverty strategies and policies for community development based on 'sustainable livelihoods'.

Sustainable Livelihoods: Closing the Poverty Gap

The concept of sustainable livelihoods links policies for social inclusion and reducing poverty to programmes for environmental and economic sustainability. It recognizes that progress towards ending poverty will not be secured if it relies simply on present economic structures and cycles, dominated by a globalizing trade system and transnational corporations, and by over-dependence by countries and regions on particular sectors or companies. Without structural change to the rules and systems of the wider economy, communities and whole regions are vulnerable to turbulence in the global system, and the poor are most at risk. The idea of sustainable livelihoods is based on the idea that globalization needs not only to be reformed (see Chapter 5), but also complemented by more local economic diversity to make local and regional economies worldwide more resilient and resourceful. Strategies to promote this are increasingly recognized as having a vital role to play in combating poverty and social exclusion in neighbourhoods and local economies, and in using environmental regeneration to create jobs, develop skills and enterprises, and raise confidence.

Community initiatives can range in scale from low cost, low technology approaches[23] to major partnerships for integrated conservation and development that may focus on mainstream economic activities such as agriculture, fishing, tourism and education,[24] energy production[25] or financial support. In the South, micro-credit schemes are delivering financial support to some of the poorest individuals struggling to make a living. In the North, community credit unions are providing low cost savings and loan accounts for people without bank accounts and unable to borrow money. In some European countries (Ireland, for example), credit unions are an accepted part of mainstream financial service options, and they may be about to expand in the UK.[26] LETS (Local Exchange Trading Systems) are also being established in greater numbers in low-income areas in the UK, providing a mechanism whereby people can barter their time and skills outside the money economy[27] (although the tax and benefits position of those engaged in LETS schemes remains unresolved). The UK Government has already recognized the importance of community finance initiatives by announcing a £30 million 'phoenix fund' for them in the March 2000 Budget.[28]

Community businesses and small-scale economic activity around community centres straddle the mainstream and non-mainstream arenas of the economy, and can provide some small incomes as well as opportunities to engage with local community activities and with other people in a way that mixes social and economic priorities. Bulk-buying schemes, community caring projects and the provision of welfare rights advice can all create opportunities for work and economic activity even in the poorest communities. Such innovative schemes can also provide people with ways back into mainstream employment by developing their skills and confidence through experience of collective civic activity, developing new skills, creating a sense of achievement and empowerment through helping to meet local needs. But these community-based approaches need to be incorporated much more fully into the mainstream economy if they are to make any long-term contribution to sustainable local economies.

Much greater support and investment is also needed in small and medium sized enterprises, both in the private and community sectors, to develop and strengthen locally-based economic opportunities and secure more jobs. Small and medium sized enterprises that are locally based, locally controlled, and have an understanding of local opportunities and pressures can contribute substantially to the creation of a more robust, secure and diverse economy.

For all their strengths, these local approaches are not a panacea. They must be accompanied by changes in the rules and operations of the globalizing economy within which local economies are embedded. Without reforms to this broader economic system – which shift it towards sustainable development goals and measurements of progress – local economic development and community building, and national programmes to end poverty and social exclusion, will continue to be fragile.

This leads us to look at the big picture of trade, globalization, aid and investment: what reforms are needed to make the global economy work more fairly and sustainably, in the interests of the poor and the environment as well as the affluent world? This is the focus of the next chapter.

A New Economic Order? Making Globalization Fair and Sustainable

'The time has ... come for a radical rethinking of
policies and responsibilities ... It is now time to take
a long hard look at the international trading system'
UNCTAD[1]

'The danger is that globalization can come to mean
only the free flow of goods and finance, the open
access to markets, the breaking down of barriers to
trade and commerce. The concern for the common
good ... is in danger of being lost in the current
understanding of a global world.'
Nelson Mandela[2]

Introduction: Towards Sustainable Globalization

The inequalities and depth of poverty considered in Chapter 4
show the unbalanced and dangerous nature of the current form
of economic development across the world. While growth continues to be the engine that increases incomes for millions, the benefits have not been distributed fairly. As a result, inequalities are
being accentuated and unacceptable damage is being inflicted on
the public goods – environment, social capital and cohesion – on
which everyone, rich and poor, ultimately depends. The answer is
not to abandon growth and globalization: even if this were possible, it would deny to the world's poor the chance to improve their
economic prospects and quality of life. Globalization of economic
life is a fact: the challenge is to make it environmentally sustainable, socially equitable and far better governed.

The existing international economic order, represented by
the institutions of the WTO, the World Bank, the IMF and so on,
has come under furious attack from NGOs and developing countries for its failure to help overcome the grossly uneven pattern
of development. The success story of the last decade is that

many policy-makers in the developed countries and global economic agencies have come to share the diagnosis that the system of global economic governance is not accountable and democratic enough; it lacks the means to regulate competition, investment and corporate behaviour; it is unfair in its treatment of developing countries in terms of trade, and it fails to ensure that global economic policy is integrated with international accords on the environment and social protection. The sustainability gap is measured by the distance we have yet to travel before this diagnosis of what is wrong is turned into effective institutional reform and innovation.

Any reforms must be underpinned by better ideas about what should count as 'free trade', 'growth' and 'liberalization of markets'. These terms have become associated with the existing, inequitable and unsustainable order, and some of its critics take the view that all of these concepts therefore need to be abandoned. But in order to improve the prospects and conditions of the world's poor, trade, economic growth and access to markets are all essential. What we need are new criteria to specify what kind of trade, growth and market liberalization – and on whose terms – are compatible with fairness for the developing world, environmental sustainability and long-term economic and social security.

Developing such criteria needs to be part of a wider reform of the global economic institutions, so that they help promote a sustainable model of globalization. This demands, as we discuss below, the development of rules to govern the operation of transnational corporations; the reform of the international trade system; new approaches to debt relief and aid; new targets and measures of progress for international development; and new trust between North and South. This means a radical departure from globalization as we know it: but the beginnings of such a shift are now apparent even among the global economic agencies and corporations. Real World urges faster and more determined progress towards implementing the long-term, phased programme of reform that policy-makers and development campaigners alike know is needed.

Globalization as We Know It

Economic globalization encompasses a number of developments of the post-1945 period that have accelerated and inten-

---

Panel 8

Growing Global Poverty and Inequality

Some 1.2 billion people throughout the world are living in absolute poverty – that is, living on less than US$1 per day. This represents one-fifth of the world's population. The same number do not have access to clean water. About 840 million in the world are malnourished. In recent years, millions of people have moved out of absolute poverty, but in some regions poverty has worsened. For example:

- In sub-Saharan Africa, the population living on less than US$1 per day increased by about 20 per cent between 1990 and 1996, and there is no evidence of any substantial improvement.
- In the 'transition economies' of Eastern Europe and Central Asia poverty has soared: in 1989 about 14 million people were living below a poverty line of US$4 per day (considered comparable to US$1 per day in developing countries); by mid-1996 the figure had risen to 147 million, or one person in three.

Sex discrimination is still alarmingly prevalent, and plays a major part in trapping women in poverty. There are 60 per cent more illiterate women than men. The number of rural women in poverty has risen by 50 per cent to 565 million in the last 20 years. By December 1998, 163 countries had ratified the 1979 Convention on the Elimination of Discrimination Against Women (CEDAW). Others, including the USA, had not.

The gaps between rich and poor – countries and people – have increased dramatically:

- The richest 20 per cent have 86 per cent of world GDP; the middle 60 per cent have 13 per cent, and the poorest 20 per cent have 1 per cent.
- The assets of the three richest people in the world were more than the combined GNP of the 48 least developed countries, and their 600 million people. The net worth of the world's richest 200 people increased from US$440 billion to more than US$1 trillion in just four years (from 1994 to 1998). By 1999 their combined wealth (US$1.13 trillion) was nearly ten times that of the total income of the least developed countries.
- Poverty now affects future potential for economic development as, for example, new technology advances. For example, to buy a computer would cost the average Bangladeshi more than eight years' income; it would cost the average American one month's income.

Sources: United Nations, OECD, World Bank and IMF (2000) *A Better World for All*; UNDP, *Human Development Report 1999* (Oxford: OUP, 1999); UNDP, *Human Development Report 2000* (Oxford: OUP, 2000); DFID, *Economic Well-Being: International Development Target Strategy Paper* (London: DFID, 1999); United Nations, *Global Economic Prospects* (New York: UN, 2000); Nick Mabey, *Poverty Elimination and the Environment* (Godalming: WWF UK, 1998).

sified in recent years. These include the global spread of industrial production; the development of intricate linkages between national economies through growth in trade and developments in communications and transport; and the global reach, through mass media, of images of both Western consumer culture and human suffering caused by wars and environmental disasters.[3]

Much globalization has been as a result of economic policy regimes in the West, and the extension of neo-liberal prescriptions for economic management around the developing world. These processes began in the 1980s. During the 1990s they went further, but also began to generate turbulence and local crises. Gross world product expanded from US$31.6 trillion in 1990 to more than US$39 trillion in 1998, with global growth of over 4 per cent in 1994. However, growth rates were very uneven, with deep inequalities between the OECD countries and the poorest developing countries. As Clare Short, UK Secretary of State for International Development, has said:

> *'Global integration and interdependence are a reality...*
> *The challenge of our age is to manage this inter-*
> *dependence in a way that is equitable and environ-*
> *mentally sustainable, that maximizes the benefits of*
> *interdependence and minimizes its costs'.*[5]

Major programmes of international investment, loans and development assistance (overseas aid) have accompanied the rapid expansion of global trade and the economy. These programmes have complex links: development assistance can carry conditions for structural adjustment that can lead to opening new markets for trade and opportunities for investment. These issues and their connections are considered in more detail below.

Witness Box 13: Christian Aid

Debt

For many of the world's poorest countries, external debt is now at a level where it is effectively unpayable. In Tanzania, for example, debt service payments amount to more than Government spending on health and education combined. This drain of resources has resulted in dramatic cuts in spending on social services, which directly impacts on the lives of the poorest people. Children are denied an education, families are denied clean water, babies are denied proper healthcare.

Unpayable debt is also damaging the long-term prospects for sustainable development and poverty eradication. Debt discourages investment and increases inequality. Christian Aid believes that debt repayment should not be put ahead of the lives and livelihoods of the poor. Unpayable debts should be cancelled now.

Trade
All countries and people trade, whether it is barter between two people in a remote village, or international trade in oil worth billions of dollars each year. Trade between developing and developed countries is worth much more than aid flows. The UK Government gives around £3 billion (some US$4.5 billion) in aid each year, but trade between the UK and developing countries is worth about 100 times that. Making trade work for poor communities requires two things – a representative organization to manage international trade, and trade rules that put the interests of the poor above those of large corporations.

What Kind of Trade Organization?
The world needs an effective organization to manage international trade, but so far the WTO has not played that role. It is dominated too much by the interests of a few countries and large corporations, and cannot make rules that make trade fairer for everybody. Two essential things need to change in the WTO:

1 Developing countries need to increase their capacity to negotiate and to participate in the WTO. All WTO members should make binding commitments to contribute to a common fund to support the activities of developing countries in the WTO.
2 The way decisions are made in the WTO needs to be changed. Small meetings excluding most members are no way to get fair decisions. WTO members need to ensure that all countries are represented at all talks.

What Kind of Trade Rules?
Trade can only contribute to development if the benefits to trade are spread among the majority of the world's population, rather than concentrated in the hands of a few individuals and corporations. The rules made in the WTO should attempt to reconcile the interests of people and of corporations. Governments have always regulated at the national level to control restrictive business practices, protect consumers and distribute wealth from rich to poor. As economic activity becomes increasingly globalized, we need to look at how we can regulate business activity at the international level. The WTO will be an important part of any such attempt.

Any new agreements in the WTO should be about making trade fairer, rather than having liberalization as the main goal. Two important parts of any set of trade rules should be that they:

1 ensure that governments retain powers to act to guarantee that the activities of both domestic companies and foreign investors are beneficial to their populations; and

113

2 establish institutions to control the activities of trans-national corporations (TNCs) at a global level where appropriate, including regulating on global anti-competitive practices and restrictive business practices.

Poverty

Poverty is the lack of opportunity to fulfil essential human capabilities. It is multi-dimensional; insufficient income is only one among many dimensions of human deprivation. Despite progress in reducing poverty, there are still 1.3 billion extremely poor people in the world. This is poverty amid plenty: the income gap between the poorest and richest people is enormous and increasing. Poverty is a violation of rights and of human dignity.

Poverty is caused by unequal power relations within and among countries. Structural causes of poverty ensure an adverse redistribution from the poor to the rich: the debt service burden, unfair terms of trade and trade rules that favour rich companies based in the North, and the lack of resources for investment. Market incentives ensure that the benefits of technology and globalization accrue to the rich. Present systems of governance are ill-equipped to address these causes; there are no accountability systems to regulate transnational corporations and only imperfect accountability for the IMF, the World Bank and the WTO.

Among attempted solutions, economic growth has enjoyed the greatest support. But even a 'pro-poor' growth has failed to overcome poverty because it does not challenge the unequal distribution of resources. In fact, macroeconomic reform and fiscal stringency have required governments to withdraw resources from poor people.

Christian Aid believes that the poor need:

- Empowerment to overcome powerlessness.
- Redistribution to overcome inequality.
- Global governance to overcome the adverse effects of globalization.

The poor need to own the development process. Solutions lie in increasing people's participation in decision-making, strengthening the capabilities of poor people, and broadening their asset base to achieve sustainable livelihoods. Redistribution of assets is needed at the household, national and global levels. Redistribution liberates the rich as well as the poor. Debt relief, aid and macroeconomic policy are practical ways to achieve redistribution and the International Development Targets of halving extreme poverty by 2015.

Systems of global governance need to embrace the rules and institutions necessary for regulation of transnational corporations and global financial markets. Redistribution can be assisted through direct taxation at national level and new global taxes such as that proposed on currency conversion. If we are ready to accept the necessary institutional and personal changes, the eradication of poverty and inequality is within our reach.

Trade and Investment

The globalization of trade is among the most powerful driving forces of the modern world. What is new is the pace and nature of global trade, driven by technology (especially communications technology and the internet). Trade can take place faster than ever, and for 24 hours a day, every day. International investment, too, has changed and grown dramatically. FDI expanded six-fold in the 1990s, to more than US$400 billion in 1997 – seven times the level in the 1970s.[6] This growth was partly because of increases in short-term capital flows, and partly as a result of new technologies and the global production systems operated by transnational corporations.

Conventional trade continues as countries export and import food, raw materials and manufactured products around the world, but there have been dramatic changes to the nature of some of the services and products traded. There is substantial growth in what are variously described as 'soft', 'virtual' or 'thin air' products and services:[7] insurance, banking, telecommunications, marketing, 'futures' of commodities, currencies, patents, internet services and software. However, some of these transactions – such as currency speculation and unregulated capital flows (as a result of capital account liberalization) – can be destabilizing to national economies, generate no productive investment for the long term, and for all their 'weightless' quality have real material impacts on economies and lives.

Trade is also facilitated by export credit agencies supported by national governments. These agencies and the guarantees they provide are a powerful force in many cases for unsustainable development, damaging to communities and to the environment. The controversy over the UK Government's plan to back, through export credits, work by contractors on the Ilisu dam in Turkey, in the face of strong protests over its social and environmental impacts, underlines the political as well as the economic and environmental costs of trade policy.

International trade and investment will remain an essential element of most national economies, and will have a major role in ensuring a stronger role for developing countries in the global economy. However, while trade is one of the essential transactions of human society, it is often portrayed as a purely economic activity. Western governments and international economic agencies have seen the political relationships, social impacts and environmental consequences of trade as subsidiary to the economic imperatives but, thanks in large part to the impact of critiques from NGOs and developing countries, they now increasingly recognize these factors as vital to long-term economic success.

Meanwhile, there is greater understanding of the inequalities that underpin global trade and investment. OECD countries have only 19 per cent of the world's population, yet they receive 58 per cent of FDI and control 71 per cent of global trade in goods and services.[8] Trade 'liberalization' has created most opportunities for those with substantial existing assets:[9] the top 20 per cent of the world's people in the richest countries enjoy 82 per cent of the expanding export trade, and 68 per cent of foreign investment; the bottom 20 per cent get barely more than 1 per cent.[10]

At its best, foreign investment, through the location of companies and the provision of loans and other financial services, can provide otherwise scarce jobs and capital. It can act as a conduit for transferring skills and technologies and build links with local economies (for example, by sourcing components and services locally). At its worst, it can undermine human rights by providing support for oppressive regimes, eroding land rights and undermining basic employment rights (for instance on wages, working conditions and unionization), because of downward pressure on costs and moves towards deregulation. Poor quality investment can also make little or no contribution through taxes to local economies as governments keen to attract inward investment in competition with other countries often adopt low tax regimes.[11]

Witness Box 14: Oxfam

Sustainability can only be achieved if the extraordinary wealth generated in the world is shared more equitably. The Government could play a lead role in achieving this by responding to the global education crisis, tackling new types of conflict and working for a fairer distribution of the benefits of the global economy.

Education
Education is a human right, yet 125 million primary-school aged children are out of school. Millions more drop out before becoming literate. This education deficit limits economic growth, and undermines efforts to improve public health and to build thriving democracies.

The World Education Forum in Dakar, Senegal in April 2000 reaffirmed the international commitment to achieving universal primary education, and bound countries to 'launching with immediate effect' a global initiative which will guarantee that 'no countries seriously committed to education for all will be thwarted in their achievements of this goal by a lack of resources'.

Although the Dakar Framework for Action represents a small positive step forward, there is still a real question mark over whether the political will exists internationally to turn words into action. Oxfam believes that the Government is in a unique position to drive forward the 'education for all' agenda. We urge the Prime Minister to make his rallying cry 'Education, education, education' apply to all the world's children.

Conflict

Much recent conflict has been within states and often over natural resources. Civilians, who are the main victims of these wars, are too often left unprotected by the world community. Meanwhile, humanitarian aid, the last vestige of support for victims of wars and natural disasters, has been declining.

We need better-targeted international policies to help reduce the risks of future violence, and a more proactive international effort to protect civilians when wars do break out. There has been a stark contrast between arguably successful efforts to stem violence in Timor and Kosovo and the largely forgotten wars of Sudan, Angola, or the Democratic Republic of Congo.

Oxfam is pushing for a consistent and robust response to future conflicts from Security Council members. There is also a need for greater control over the distribution of arms. Britain, as the world's second largest arms exporter, must take a lead. The Government should introduce tough legislation to tackle the loopholes in brokering, licensed production and end-use of arms.

Trade

Trade can be a powerful tool in combating poverty. Unfortunately the benefits of global trade are unfairly distributed. The 48 poorest countries have seen their share of world exports decline by almost half over the past two decades, to a paltry 0.4 per cent.

Following implementation of the Uruguay Round agreements, the average tariff on imports from the least-developed countries into industrialized countries will be 30 per cent higher than the average tariff on imports from other industrialized countries. Poor countries have opened up their markets under IMF structural adjustment programmes, while rich countries have jealously guarded access to their markets. Rich countries continue to dump heavily subsidized agricultural exports, destroying the livelihoods of poor farmers.

Radical institutional reform is required to transform the WTO into a transparent organization that takes decisions with the full participation of poor countries, and that allows poor countries to benefit from integration into the global economy.

The Government must take the lead in persuading its EU and US colleagues to eliminate subsidies for agricultural over-production and export, to redesign intellectual property rules, and to improve market access for poor countries, especially for processed goods. Only in this way will global trade rules facilitate poverty reduction and sustainability.

The Pressure for Reform

The East Asian crash in 1997–98 underlined the turbulence of the new global economy and the speed with which capital can flow out of vulnerable countries, causing shock waves across the world. It gave added impetus to calls for the development of an already rapidly expanding system of global institutions, systems and rules to regulate trade operations. While there is strong support among NGOs and other campaigners for a robust system of rules and regulations to govern global trade and investment, the existing rules – and the creation and enforcement of these rules by non-elected, non-accountable and often secretive global bodies – are increasingly being challenged. The movement against the existing international trade and investment rules and institutions gained its first major success with the abandonment by OECD governments of the proposed Multilateral Agreement on Investment (MAI) in 1998 – the result of a concerted campaign by NGOs and other bodies. The MAI was targeted because it was devised by the OECD with virtually no attempt to open the process to debate and scrutiny, to include developing countries or to reconcile it with global accords on environmental and social protection.[12]

The next self-inflicted disaster for the global economic agencies was the collapse of the world trade negotiations in Seattle in November 1999, as a result of poor preparation and of action by individual governments as well as pressure from campaigning NGOs. This created an opportunity for far-reaching reforms to international trade and investment policy to make it more appropriate to human needs, cultural diversity and environmental security. What had been portrayed as the inevitable and inexorable spread of globalization in its current form had been challenged as a project that could be responded to politically.[13] This has sparked off a renewed debate on new mechanisms to manage globalization so that the benefits are distributed more equitably and the process becomes sustainable.

The rapidly growing policy-making power and influence of international institutions and transnational corporations has emerged as one of the most significant developments in global politics. Corporations and the key international institutions are not subject to any effective democratic controls, despite their enormous power and influence in directing the expansion of global trade and investment. The most influential body on trade, the WTO, has aimed to reduce customs duties on all kinds of goods (to reduce barriers to imports), and to regulate what are described as non-tariff barriers to trade, which can include environmental, health and safety regulations.

Panel 9

OECD Targets for International Development

In 1996, the countries of the OECD, which includes all the main Western countries that contribute to overseas development assistance, committed themselves to a 'partnership with developing and transition countries', the success of which would be measured against key targets from UN summits. Since then, the World Bank and the IMF have also agreed to coordinate their development efforts behind the targets. These targets are outlined below.

Economic Well-Being

- A reduction by one-half in the proportion of people living in extreme poverty by 2015.

Human Development

- Universal primary education in all countries by 2015.
- Demonstrated progress towards gender equality and the empowerment of women by eliminating gender disparity in primary and secondary education by 2005.
- A reduction by two-thirds in the mortality rates for infants and children under age five, and a reduction by three-quarters in maternal mortality, all by 2015.
- Access through the primary healthcare system to reproductive health services for all individuals of appropriate ages as soon as possible, and no later than 2015.

Environmental Sustainability and Regeneration

- The implementation of national strategies for sustainable development in all countries by 2005, to ensure that current trends in the loss of environmental resources are effectively reversed at both global and national levels by 2015.

These targets are compatible with the development of national sustainability strategies that focus on promoting economic well-being for all, environmental protection and equitable social development.

Source: DFID, *Eliminating World Poverty: A Challenge for the 21st Century.* White Paper on international development (London: Department for International Development, 1997)

Trade and Investment: Institutional Issues

The round of WTO talks that some governments wanted to begin at Seattle in 1999 were designed to agree new measures that would further reduce the ability of individual governments (and groupings such as the EU) to control imports, price controls and much else. The proposed expansion of the supposedly 'free' market in the new rounds of trade talks would have drastically reduced the role of individual democratic states, and increased the WTO's decision-making power.

The Seattle conference foundered not only because of protests from campaigners, but mainly because of deep divisions between countries. Current agreements on trade and investment are unfair: they demand liberalization from developing countries to increase imports (even where that may not be appropriate given their national priorities for development), allow industrialized countries to continue protectionist policies that restrict imports, and provide little or no regulation of the activities of transnational companies.[14] There is growing pressure from some governments (especially in the South), national and international NGOs and grassroots organizations around the world to reform the WTO and the trade systems it oversees, although there is still debate over the extent of the reforms that will ultimately be required.[15] While there are many views in the NGO movement on the details of reform, there is agreement across Northern and Southern NGOs on the direction it needs to take.

There is consensus that, at the very least, the operations of the WTO need to be much more open and transparent, and that there must be mechanisms to allow decisions to be questioned and changed. A new rules-based trading system is needed, and all countries must be empowered to take part fully in the decision-making process. There is also a strong argument that, where there is a clash, multilateral environmental agreements should take precedence over trade rules.

There are some proposals for developing international legal aid to improve the bargaining position of (particularly poor) countries in WTO disputes, and for the establishment of policy forums to enable poor countries to formulate and defend their views, and to participate effectively in the decisions that affect them (the UK Government is funding a legal centre in Geneva to contribute to capacity building for poor countries). The more radical critics of the WTO, including hundreds of NGOs from 49 countries (to date), have launched the Boston Coalition, with specific demands for a scaling down of the powers and authority of the WTO, and for a new system of trade rules based on the principles of democratic control of resources, ecological sustainability, equity, cooperation and precaution.[16]

Late in 1999, in advance of the Seattle conference, 1,500 NGOs from 90 countries signed a joint statement against the WTO's proposed extension of trade rules, including the patent rules under a planned review (and extension) of intellectual property rights. The NGOs identified a whole series of fundamental concerns, including: the importance of preserving biodiversity rather than manipulating nature purely for commercial gain; the ethics of Western corporations taking out patents on genes and seeds; the importance of ensuring access to health care and drugs (which would otherwise be priced beyond the reach of many countries); the need to respect other forms of ownership (including shared ownership and free access); and the need to prevent a widening gap between industrialized and developing countries as technology advances.

This joint statement was a major advance for global cooperation between NGOs, with significant implications for democracy and civic participation (see Chapter 6). It also represents the widespread concern in rich and poor countries about the direction of globalization and the power of unaccountable global institutions – a concern that is hard to express through national and local democratic processes.

Witness Box 15: Quaker Peace and Social Witness (QPSW)

Since 1996 the Religious Society of Friends has concentrated on three main areas relating to (international) sustainable development:

1 *Trade-Related Aspects of Intellectual Property Rights (TRIPS)*. The main objective in this work has been to attempt to provide assistance to raise the capacity of the developing nations to engage with the complex debates around TRIPS, biodiversity and food security. This work has been done mainly at the international level at our Geneva office, and partly in London in conjunction with other British NGOs.

2 *Work on the policies of the IMF*. This work has mostly been done in London, in cooperation with other NGOs involved with the International Finance Network. The aim has been to develop relationships with the key institutions: UK Treasury, Bank of England, DFID, IMF and others to then seek to influence the policy debate in

the direction of sustainable development. The principal aim has been to work on the financial architecture, as Jubilee 2000 has done an excellent job on the debt question. It is the policies needed to deal with the volatility of capital flows to developing nations that we have been most interested in being involved with. The involvement of the private sector in the avoidance and resolution of financial crises has been a major focus.

To this end we have had extensive contacts with the private sector banks and other financial institutions. This work has also been carried out in Washington in relation to the IMF, and in New York in relation to the Financing for Development Conference of the UN (Quaker UN office in New York).

3 *Ethical Trade, Labour Standards and codes of conduct as a development tool.* We have joined the Ethical Trading Initiative (ETI) as we believe that the model it is developing has serious potential to be a development tool because it involves all the key stakeholders rather than just being a top-down model as many codes are. The work on this policy area has been done extensively in London and in Geneva at the International Labour Office (ILO). We aim to provide work at the policy level both in the North and in developing nations where we have developed relationships with relevant organizations.

We see all the three areas mentioned above as being inter-related and linked parts of one whole attempt to work for sustainable development. Three key policies needed to close the sustainability gap are:

1 More power to the UN, together with serious democratization of the organization to give the poorer and poorest nations much more of a real say. This would help to balance the huge power of the Bretton Woods organizations and the WTO. Real democratization of the international institutions is essential if they are to be accepted by the world outside Europe and the USA. Reform not revolution.
2 Serious engagement with the private sector as private sector flows are much the biggest source of capital in the world. This engagement has to happen at all levels.
3 Serious resources for education and health to the poorer and poorest nations to raise their capacity to engage much more on parity in the context of a globalized economy.

The forthcoming DFID White Paper on globalization should deal with financing for development in a serious way; in other words there should be a real attempt by the UK Government to push the UN Financing for Development Conference up the international political agenda. Specifically, this will mean continuing to play an important role in the IMF, and to seek to assist the developing nations to cope with the vast capital flows in and out of their countries. The UK could be a force for good if it seeks to influence the US administration in the direction of sustainable development. Leadership from the UK Government could seriously assist getting many of the bigger London based private-sector institutions involved in the debate, and hopefully lead to some action.

> Intransigence on the part of the private sector is a major problem, as is the attitude of the US Congress on anything international. US politics will remain crucial on international questions for the foreseeable future.
>
> The levels of real poverty in the poorest nations is the best way of assessing progress.

Corporate Influence on Trade and Investment

There is also growing concern about the concentration of trade and ownership of assets among corporations and industrialized countries. Some transnational companies now have sales that are greater than the GDP of certain countries: for example, in 1997, General Motors and Ford each received more income in sales alone than the GDP of Norway, Saudi Arabia, South Africa or Greece.[17] Access to technological progress is reduced because it becomes priced out of reach for poor people and poor countries as a result of market control by these near-monopolies: 97 per cent of patents worldwide are held by the industrialized countries. The same lack of balance is reflected in the increasingly controversial biotechnology industry: the top five biotechnology companies, which are based in the USA and Europe, control more than 95 per cent of gene transfer patents.

Some leading companies are beginning to adopt a more ethical business agenda and to take sustainable development seriously as a guiding principle for corporate strategy.[18] Some of the best involve cooperation between companies, and with NGOs, to establish systems that ensure implementation and include the essential element of independent verification, such as the Ethical Trading Initiative[19] and the Forest Stewardship Council. The retail sales of fairly traded goods are now worth more than US$250 million in Europe alone.[20] Although these schemes are currently very small in relation to the overall global economy, they are growing and they underline the point made in Chapter 2 – that sustainable development approaches open up alternative routes to global integration and richer choices about the nature of modernization, going beyond the prescriptions of the global economic agencies.

Some corporations are taking steps to establish their own codes of conduct and guidelines for good practice, and to develop strategies on sustainable development and corporate responsibility. At their best, voluntary codes can guide companies towards good practice and set standards for others to follow. At their worst, however, voluntary codes are no more than public relations exercises.[21] Many of the most responsible companies are not averse to statutory regulations, seeing them as providing a level playing field so that competitors have to conform and face similar costs. They also recognize that companies' reputations have been increasingly affected by their performance in social and environmental management, alongside the more traditional economic performance and the development of desirable products at the right price.

However, corporate and sectoral codes vary widely, and most lack independent verification. Campaigners continue to call for international regulatory measures to underpin and drive better practice among corporations – such as withholding export credit guarantees from companies that flout the OECD Guidelines for Multinational Enterprises (a voluntary guide to corporate conduct agreed by OECD governments in 2000). The campaign for better regulation of transnational companies is not an anti-business measure; it reflects the need for the social and environmental values upheld by democratic governments and the most responsible businesses, and reflected in global accords, to be applied to international enterprise overall. The transnational business community has seen its rights enhanced enormously as globalization has proceeded since the 1980s; it is time that the rights of corporate powers were matched with their responsibilities. If the language of 'rights plus responsibilities' is good enough for the poor citizens and countries of the world, it is good enough for all transnational corporations, not just the enlightened minority of companies taking sustainable development seriously.

This points to the need for measures to close the gap between declarations by global agencies and corporations about sustainable development, and the reality of limited progress towards a fairer trading system. Sustainable development emphasizes fair trade, not more trade as a good in itself. It also stresses that global trade needs to go hand in hand with a renewed emphasis on local and regional economic diversity and trade, in order to reduce environmental impacts and the risk of over-dependence on sectors and crops. These principles can be used to establish a framework for a global expansion of trade with many of the benefits, and far fewer of the disadvantages (particularly for poorer people) of the current system.

Witness Box 16: World Development Movement (WDM)

The major challenge faced by the world today is surely the widening gap between the haves and the have-nots in our society and internationally. History has never seen such gross inequity as 800 million people without enough food to eat, and a similar number who eat too much; half of the world's people living on less than £1.30 (US$2) per day; and four families controlling as much wealth as 280 million people. The rich are still getting richer while the poor are exploited, marginalized and getting even poorer.

The World Development Movement (WDM) was established to campaign against the causes of poverty and achieve justice for the world's poor. WDM believes that action has to start at home, through fundamental changes to the policies of rich world governments, businesses and international agencies.

We live in a world where companies have globalized at an alarming rate. Mergers and acquisitions have concentrated economic power in virtually every industry and sphere of human activity. The world's top 500 multinationals control most of the world's trade, investment and patents. Governments have progressively given more rights to these companies to operate unimpeded across the world, without regulating for the public good.

Among all the utopian talk about globalization are the harsh facts of life for most of the world. The past 25 years have promised much and delivered little for the poorest countries. Prices for the major commodities exported from the developing world have fallen by two-thirds, as the supply chains have been dominated by a handful of multinationals. Developing countries are prevented from exporting textiles, shoes and agricultural products because of import barriers imposed by the rich countries. Most foreign investment comes in the form of acquisitions: big foreign companies buy up smaller local companies with resulting job losses. Young money traders in the City of London speculate on currencies, the IMF steps in to protect them and the burden of adjustment is forced on workers and the poor. Rich countries and companies use their powerful influence to sell weapons, cigarettes, dangerous pesticides and Western culture.

WDM and other campaigners have been calling for a rethink, rather than a continued rush down the path of blind liberalization. In the wake of the collapse of the proposed Multilateral Agreement on Investment (MAI) and the Seattle trade talks, we have an opportunity to formulate new rules for the global economy – to put poverty eradication, sustainable development and the promotion of human rights at the heart of a coherent international system. Trade and investment rules must have a purpose – not liberalization as an end goal, but the promotion of equitable and sustainable development.

Our target is to get the elements of a new international system on to the agenda:

- Strong and enforceable rules to implement internationally agreed

standards for labour (such as the core standards of the ILO); the environment (based on the 1992 Earth Summit Principles); human rights (Universal Declaration of Human Rights) and development.
- An international mechanism to enforce these standards on international companies, since they are the main actors in the global economy, and to prohibit monopolies and cartels, tax avoidance and other restrictive business practices. These rules are vital to provide a level playing field for those companies that are serious about adopting ethical practices.
- Coherent international policies that will encourage democratic decision-making in all countries, including the right to make decisions on their development path, rather than following the dictates of the IMF or World Bank. The emphasis must be placed on building capacity and accountability for decision-making through strong civil society movements, instead of reducing the role of government.

Aid

Aid for development from rich to poor countries has often been tied to security or commercial interests in the developed world, or given purely for disaster relief. It has also been more of a gesture than a strategic tool for promoting genuine progress in the South. Overall aid from OECD countries to developing countries fell to an all time low in 1999, and almost all countries in the North continue to fail to reach the UN target of 0.7 per cent of GNP. The UK Government has led a reversal of these trends and increased official development assistance by more than almost any other country (to US$3,433 million in 1997). However, aid from the UK has still fallen as a proportion of GNP (from 0.28 per cent in 1998 to 0.23 per cent in 1999), and it remains far below the level of development assistance given by Norway (0.86 per cent), Sweden (0.79 per cent), The Netherlands (0.81 per cent) and Denmark (0.97 per cent). But the Government has firm plans to increase aid to 0.3 per cent of GNP in 2001.[22]

The ethical public pronouncements of donors are further undermined by the targeting of aid to certain countries: the largest recipients of aid from OECD countries in 1999 were Israel, China and Indonesia – none of which are in the poorest category of human development according to the UNDP. In addition, the share of aid going to low income countries fell from 45 per cent in 1991 to 28 per cent in 1996, while basic education and health services count for less than 5 per cent of the overall aid effort.[23]

However, aid policy has been changing as donors have come to recognize that trade and market growth could be undermined by growing poverty and inequality within and between countries. Aid has become much more sophisticated in recent years, partly as a result of the long-term involvement of international as well as local NGOs. They have been among those working to ensure an increasing emphasis on adequate nutrition; safe water supplies; better medical services; more and better schooling for children; cheap transport; adequate shelter; continuing employment and secure livelihoods; and productive, remunerative and satisfying jobs. There has been a shift in the structure of aid arrangements too, away from project-focused aid to policy dialogue, sectoral investment programmes (such as education and health) and strategic partnerships between donors, recipient countries and NGOs.

The social and political needs of communities are also increasingly recognized: people seek freedom of movement and speech; liberation from oppression, violence and exploitation; security from persecution and arbitrary arrest; a satisfying family life; the freedom to express religious and cultural values; adequate leisure time; a sense of purpose in life and work; the opportunity to participate in the activities of civil society, and to gain a sense of belonging to a community – all of which may be as highly valued as income.[24] An improved distribution of income and assets has also become a priority, including proposals for land tenure reform, and comprehensive pro-poor public expenditure and taxation policies.[25] The establishment of the UK Department for International Development (DFID), and its support for ambitious targets and many of the principles and priorities of Real World member organizations, is an important sign of progress in this area.

International Debt

The growing burden of debt owed by developing countries to global institutions, governments and individual banks in the industrialized countries is a key factor undermining the ability of the debtor countries to engage more fully and fairly in global trade and improve economic and social conditions within their own boundaries.

The debt problem began from an apparently successful phase in the economies of developing countries. In the early 1970s, many developing countries were benefiting from a rise in commodity prices. This was also a period of vast lending. Newly industrialized countries in the developing world were encouraged to borrow heavily by Western banks (themselves awash with cash from oil price rises) and, as interest rates were so low, the borrowers could simply wait and let the debt be reduced by inflation. Between 1970 and 1980, the long-term foreign debt of Latin America and the Caribbean alone rose from US$27.6 billion to US$187.3 billion – a 600 per cent increase. From 1980 onwards there were huge increases in interest rates and falls in commodity prices. The monocultural cash crops that had been introduced into developing countries, often replacing subsistence farming, were hit hard. This removed these countries' main source of foreign exchange – needed to service debts, which were at the same time rising as interest accumulated.

Most poor country debt is owed to rich country governments and to official organizations such as the World Bank and the IMF. These have imposed repayment and rescheduling schemes damaging to local economies, communities and the environ-

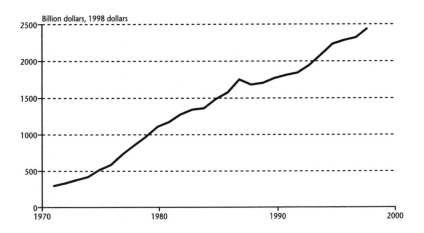

Figure 5.1 *External Debt of Developing Countries, 1971–98*
Source: World Bank, cited in L R Brown et al, *Vital Signs 2000–2001* (London: Earthscan, 2000)

ment – thus making it still harder for the aid recipients to develop strongly and sustainably and escape from the burden of debt. The debt burden has become a potent symbol of the imbalance and injustice in the global economy.

A major step forward in debt relief was taken in June 1999, when the Cologne Debt Initiative was agreed at the G8 Summit, promising to provide US$100 billion of debt relief for up to 36 of the poorest highly indebted countries. The UK Government played a major role in championing the cause of debt relief in the negotiations of the Cologne agreement, as did the international NGO coalition Jubilee 2000 campaign. This highly effective campaign started in 1993 and used postcards to government, demonstrations, high profile celebrity involvement and a petition with 17 million signatures. A World Bank member suggested that 'the pledges that Blair and Clinton have made would not have happened without the Jubilee 2000 campaign. It is one of the most effective global lobbying campaigns I have ever seen.'[26]

However, disenchantment swiftly set in. By mid-2000 frustration was growing among NGOs and developing countries at the slowness of the implementation of the Cologne agreements by the richest countries. Just US$10 billion had been offered since Cologne in debt write-offs, and the USA, now with a US$200 billion budget surplus, had failed to deliver even its promised US$600 million for the World Bank/IMF trust fund established to cover their share of debt relief. Only the UK among the G7 countries had delivered 100 per cent debt relief for any eligible poor country by the time of the 2000 G8 Summit in Okinawa. This lavish event, which cost some US$500 million to stage, failed to give the debt relief process renewed impetus as the world's leaders simply rehashed their warm words of the previous year while offering the poor yet more grandiose pledges and targets, this time on healthcare and information technology.

Moreover, the details of the debt reduction scheme have yet to be worked out, including who has to pay what. Even the amount of money available to cover the scheme is uncertain, as contributions are needed from other countries to a Millennium Fund, which has a target of US$2 billion (the UK has pledged US$171 million). In the meantime, rises in interest rates have compounded problems: in Latin America, for example, in spite of repaying US$740 billion between 1982 and 1996, the debt has increased from US$300 billion in 1982 to US$607 billion in 2000.[27] Even as drafted, the debt relief scheme would leave many countries still spending more on servicing their debts than on their health and education services combined, and much remains to be done. Debt relief is being linked increasingly to specific programmes for poverty reduction, so that the poor are more likely to gain some direct benefits from these promising developments. But further debt relief is needed and, in the case of the poorest countries, full debt cancellation is required to free the resources needed for poverty eradication. Debt reduction has the potential to provide a dramatic boost to the economies of poor countries, but progress is both shamefully slow and partial.

Proposals have also been made for changes in the ways that debt relief is handled within debtor countries, in order to reduce corruption and increase democratic controls and civil society involvement.[28] National debt relief committees in each country have been proposed, to oversee a national fund that holds the resources from debt relief. These consultations could ensure that the harsh economic conditions imposed by the IMF under Structural Adjustment Programmes are replaced by pro-poor, sustainable policies. Yet the IMF retains the veto over government policies, continuing to insist on privatization, trade liberalization and fewer regulations on foreign investors. The core problem was identified by the former Chief Economist at the World Bank, Joseph Stiglitz:

> '*I was often asked how smart – even brilliant – people could have created such bad policies. One reason is that these smart people were not using smart economics. Time and again, I was dismayed at how out-of-date, and how out of tune with reality, the models Washington economists employed were.*'[29]

What the Rich World Owes the Poor: The Idea of Ecological Debt

A new dimension in the search for solutions to the problem of debt and deep poverty is provided by the idea that the North should repay the ecological debt owed by the industrialized world to the South. This ecological debt is based on assessments of the damage to the environment of the South as a result of past exploitation by the North, including extraction of raw materials, pollution and destruction of natural areas[30] from oil, timber, gold, diamond and other extraction of materials, and the introduction of new agricultural practices for cash crops.

The idea of ecological debt covers not just damage to the Southern environment, but also the effects on the atmosphere and the whole planet's 'absorption capacity' by long-standing and continuing emissions (such as carbon dioxide) by the North. The rich world has contributed most to global environmental problems, while the poor countries are most vulnerable to the effects – especially of climate disruption. In these terms, climate disruption is an issue of environmental injustice that can only be rectified by recognition of the 'carbon debt' owed by the North to the South.[31] This debt could be paid by the North through cancellation of developing country debts and through large-scale programmes to invest in sustainable development (technology, infrastructure, environmental restoration, healthcare, etc) in the developing countries.

The imperative for dealing with financial and ecological debts does not only come from the need to acknowledge the rich world's ethical responsibilities to the South. The North has a great deal to gain by continuing trade and cultural exchange with the South. At the most practical level, developing countries are potentially major markets for products from the industrialized world, but it is clear that these markets will not reach anything like their full potential until the debt issue is resolved. Moreover, the rich world needs the developing countries to grow their economies sustainably in the future: the North cannot avoid the ecological damage that will be done if the South follows it down the path of unsustainable, carbon-intensive growth. If the rich world wants sustainable development in the South, it must help pay for it.

A major blockage to resolving the debt question in all its dimensions is developing countries' justifiable lack of trust in the political willpower of their rich trading partners, who have consistently maintained their own barriers to products from the South while demanding liberalization in the developing world and failing to tackle debt and unfair trade rules. Genuine reform of the global economic agencies and generous concessions by the rich world in debt forgiveness and new trade negotiations are essential to rebuilding trust. But the process of reform needs the wider perspective of a common cause – the imperative for the whole world of sustainable development – to make it coher-

---

Panel 10

UK Public Opinion on the Principles of Global Trade

The UK public have strong and clear views on the principles of global trade, according to an opinion poll carried out by MORI for *The Ecologist* in February 2000. Public opinion on the subject is rarely sought, and the results were surprising: a large majority reject the values that underpin the WTO and the global economic system.

Question 1
Thinking about trade between different countries, to what extent do you support or oppose national governments being able to protect the interests of companies in their countries (for example by offering tax advantages or setting up import barriers) against those of multinational companies?

Support   55%
Oppose   12%
Neither/don't know/no opinion   33%

Question 2
The Government has laws and regulations to protect a number of different areas of society such as the environment, employment conditions and human health. If a conflict develops between the interests of multinational companies and these areas, what do you think, in principle, the Government should do? Should it protect or not protect the following against the interests of multinational companies (that is, the companies that operate widely in a number of countries)?

a The Environment		b Employment Conditions	
Protect	90%	Protect	89%
Not protect	1%	Not protect	2%
Depends/don't know	9%	Depends/don't know	9%

c Human Health	
Protect	92%
Not protect	1%
Depends/don't know	7%

Question 3
To what extent do you agree or disagree that governments should be allowed to restrict the import of goods that they believe may be damaging to the health of the population?

Protect   89%
Not protect   5%
Depends/don't know   6%

These findings indicate a distinct division between the Government and public on world trade issues.

MORI interviewed a nationally representative sample of 982 adults, between 17 and 21 February 2000. Data was weighted to reflect national population profile.

Source: The Ecologist, vol 30 no 3, May 2000

ent and just. The idea of a global 'debt swap', exchanging Southern financial debt for Northern 'ecological debt', and funding for a coordinated programme of investment in sustainable development, is a powerful proposal for genuine progress.

Global Justice: Closing the Development Gap

Tackling poverty and inequality in an age of globalization requires new political priorities. The Government has made some welcome progress, both within the UK with policies on social exclusion and neighbourhood renewal, and in international development. The international community, too, has taken some important steps in setting targets to reduce global poverty substantially by 2015; in acknowledging the need for debt relief for the poorest countries, and in recognizing the need for fundamental reforms of the global economic agencies, above all of the WTO. However, much faster and more imaginative reform is vital to turn the new acknowledgement of the need for reform of global economic governance and policies on aid, debt and trade into reality. We know that reform needs to help improve and extend the key global public goods – a healthy environment, education, public health, good democratic governance. What is needed now is determined action to turn agreed international targets, declarations of intent and promises into reality.

We need a new compact between the rich and poor worlds to establish a fair framework for a sustainable model of globalization and targeted growth. Such changes demand new approaches to policy goals and measurement of progress. However, so far the final step towards linking meaningful indicators with firm targets and a shared vision of the future that can be agreed and implemented by democratically accountable institutions has not been taken.

Closing the development gap requires a long-term commitment by the rich world and the global agencies to match their lofty rhetoric about a new deal for the world's poor with resources and generous cooperation in programmes to improve governance, infrastructures, public health, education, take-up of new technologies and prevention and resolution of conflicts (see Chapter 7). It demands vigorous pursuit of the UN targets for international human development, improving education and health standards significantly by 2015. It means accelerating the process of debt relief for the most indebted countries and

133

improving the scale and quality of development aid. It means moving urgently to reform the WTO, IMF and World Bank so that they work together and with governments, NGOs and business to regulate transnational corporations and global trade, and to design and implement programmes that support sustainable development for all – especially helping the poorest countries to connect to a global economy which is being steered towards greater fairness, environmental stewardship and higher quality of life.

Good Governance: Strengthening Democracy and Civil Society

'The greatest challenge posed by globalization is that of good governance in the broadest sense... Good governance is perhaps the single most important factor in eradicating poverty and promoting development. By good governance is meant creating well-functioning and accountable institutions – political, judicial and administrative – that citizens regard as legitimate, through which they participate in decisions which affect their lives, and by which they are empowered.'
Kofi Annan, Secretary-General of the United Nations[1]

'What is needed is not a rejection of the positive role of the market mechanism in generating income and wealth, but the important recognition that the market mechanism has to work in a world of many institutions. We need the power and protection ... provided by democratic practice, civil and human rights, a free and open media... The fact that no famine has ever occurred in a democratic country (even in very poor ones) is only one rudimentary illustration of this connection.'
Amartya Sen[2]

Introduction: Sustainability Needs Strong Democracy

The New Labour Government came to power promising a long-overdue reform of British democracy from the national to the local level. This programme has been piecemeal and remains incomplete, but has been a welcome and necessary response to mounting evidence, highlighted in the first Real World book, that public disillusionment with politics has been growing and confidence in the core institutions of democracy and the state declining. This is a part of policy and political life often derided as being the concern only of the 'chattering classes', a side-show compared to the big issues of public spending and economic management. But this is far from the truth. The health of democratic process is fundamentally important to free societies, and also to prospects for achieving the transition to sustainable development explored in this book.

The quality of democracy at all levels from the local to the global matters in its own right as a fundamental feature of an open society and as a public good. But it is also vital for progress towards sustainable development, for four reasons. First, the choices we face on production and consumption are complex and involve challenges to deep-rooted behaviour and attitudes. Movement away from unsustainable 'business as usual' can only be based on consent, democratically given. So we need a democratic system that promotes rich debate about the state we are in and our long-term options. This means a thorough renewal of the institutions that have seen public trust and enthusiasm leak away over the years, in order to re-engage citizens with politics. It also means devising much better systems for civic and moral education, so that everyone is equipped with the 'moral fluency' to participate in debate, argue issues and make informed choices.[3]

Second, we need a renewal of trust between citizens and Government because, quite simply, sustainable development needs good government: it cannot be delivered solely through individual choices, business innovation and voluntary action. Sustainable development requires a huge and complex long-term negotiation of change; trade-offs between private choices and public goods; changes to market frameworks; and strategic investment in public services and new technologies. All this requires an effective, legitimate and trusted state. The transition to a sustainable economy demands the improvement of public services; long-term strategic planning; public indicators of progress; and careful regulation and design of market frameworks – which inescapably demands leadership and action that only confident, legitimate government can supply. Improving the efficiency, accountability, reputation and innovative capacity of the public sector as a whole is a key task, but this needs to be accompanied by efforts to make Government itself, from the national to the local levels, better respected, more responsive and open, and better able to handle long-term issues. Citizens suspicious of Government will not engage in the debates and changes in consumption we need to have; Government which

Witness Box 17: bassac

bassac supports a national network of independent community organizations. Its members work in an organic, multi-purpose way with others in partnership, working with, and supporting people to help solve problems. In this way each member develops unique solutions to the specific circumstances of their neighbourhood.

Community-Based Regeneration and New Labour
Regeneration has been a theme of Government policy for decades, and the value of involving the local community has often been recognized. During the last 20 years there have been numerous programmes to develop and sustain deprived areas of Britain, and the focus on community initiatives and consultation has improved. Yet however strong the rhetoric, the practice has been patchy at best.

Drawing together professionals and local people has proved an obstacle for many regeneration projects. As a result, either the investment has been far less successful than it might have been, or the imposition of plans from outside has produced local resistance. Local ownership of regeneration initiatives is key to their long-term sustainability.

In practice, the New Labour Government has changed the style and nature of the debate substantially during its first years in office. However, the impact of these words on deprived local communities has yet to be felt. Seen as the friends of the voluntary spirit, New Labour has made many positive moves, but the practical implementation of these words still requires sustained effort.

Much is expected of the National Strategy for Neighbourhood Renewal. Whether it lives up to its billing as a means of driving up the standard of renewal efforts, and of coordinating the process at Government level, remains to be seen.

Focus for Action

- *Sustained funding for capacity building:* Few civil servants' or local government officers' careers are influenced by their record in involving the community. Still less do MPs or local councillors gain from establishing a culture of grassroots accountability. One key difference could be made by sustained funding of community capacity building – letting the people of some of the most deprived communities in the land have access to realistic levels of resources. The assumption of much talk about capacity-building is that a few courses or a day or two of a consultant's time will change the course of local involvement. The reality is that long-term investment in the infrastructure of local democracy is the only way to make partnerships work effectively.
- *Multi-dimensional, integrated partnerships:* Partnerships between private, public and voluntary organizations are seen as vital to regeneration. They provide opportunities to share information, build trust and generate enough momentum to attract outside interest. Many

suspect that the presence of community organizations in such partnerships only meets a funding criteria for the programme – be it a single regeneration budget, employment, education or health. Widespread cynicism among community groups is the result. The development of trust and the overcoming of mutual suspicion has yet to mature enough to sustain the stresses of important funding decisions. Development agencies and community groups are often left out of the key decisions, and local partnerships are lead by the public sector with some involvement of the private sector.

- *Open and accountable structures for neighbourhood governance:* Only when local areas gain their own structures of influence will the impact of local democracy on ordinary lives be realized. The inadequacies of the present discredited means of governing local rural areas – parish councils – are matched by the lack of a viable structure to order urban 'villages'. Both need a common form to reflect the changes in regional and local government. Both require a clear pathway to simple and routine participation at grassroots level. Local government must become more responsive to the people it governs; peoples' expectations of politicians and officers alike will no longer stand for occasional consultation exercises.

- *Multi-purpose models of intervention – promotion and dissemination:* Over more than a century, and in diverse settings, the concept of community action delivered from multi-dimensional agencies has prospered and shown its worth. The origins of the Settlement movement lie in the rounded response to the needs of Victorian slums. Today's community-development focus sustains a vision of self-reliant communities meeting each other's diverse needs in innovative ways. One-stop shops for services give people the opportunity to have their needs met without standing out from the crowd. Bringing together all ages and ethnic groups, able-bodied and disabled, men, women and children under (literally) one roof gives hope for an integrated and sustainable future.

lacks the confidence to lead and challenge the electorate as well as listen to it, will not have the political courage to take tough decisions and initiate complex debates on the choices ahead.

Third, sustainable development calls for a renewal of local democracy. We know that national and global frameworks and strategies for sustainability can only sketch the direction and principles for action. As the Agenda 21 statement from the 1992 Earth Summit underlined, effective measures for sustainable development must to a large extent be devised and implemented through democratic local government and partnerships at the local level between communities, public agencies and business. The demoralized state of much local government in the UK is thus not only of concern because it points to a weakening of democracy and trust in local civic life, but also because it suggests that a vital force for action on sustainable development is at a low ebb. Renewal of local democracy in a centralized state such as the UK requires Government to trust local governance far more; to let councils and their partners take more risks and innovate in the pursuit of national targets. Otherwise we will not see the experimentation and enterprise essential to tackling complex 'joined up' problems of social exclusion, environmental health and economic development at the local level.

139

Fourth, the nature of the present phase of globalization emphasizes the need for democratic accountability and deliberation to be extended to the international level, and for global institutions and corporations to be more open, democratic and accountable. The greatest challenge for democratic governments is to find ways to foster a global democratic culture and process, so that the international agencies that shape strategies on development work better, more accountably and in the interests of environmental sustainability and well-being for all.

This chapter looks at progress in democratic governance and the persistent 'democracy gaps' that block sustainable development. We consider the need to restore trust and vitality to democratic processes in the UK, and in the West in general; the need for better mechanisms to engage citizens and organizations in richer debates about the challenges of sustainable development; and the need for new democratic processes at the global level.

Restoring Trust and Energy to Democracy

Opinion polls and election turnouts consistently point to a deep disaffection with the process of democratic politics in the UK (see Panel 11). Trust in politicians and institutions has declined substantially over recent decades, not only in Britain but in many parts of the OECD world. Ironically, as the democratic world has finally triumphed over its authoritarian rivals, and as many developing countries are adopting or striving for democracy, many voters in the rich countries seem to be losing faith and interest in the democratic process.

In many cases this might seem to be a reflection of apathy and indifference, not an outright rejection of politics and politicians. It is also connected, surely – especially in the USA – to a

---

Panel 11

The Declining Vote

In the UK, voter turnout at elections is low and declining dramatically, especially at local elections. In May 2000, turnout at local elections in England was a mere 28–29 per cent, compared to 41.5 per cent at the same point of the electoral cycle four years previously. Even at the very high profile and controversial elections for London's first elected mayor and a new Greater London Assembly in May 2000, the turnout was only 33 per cent.

Declining participation is an international phenomenon, but voter turnout at sub-national level is much lower in England than in many other European countries – for instance Denmark (turnout 80 per cent), Germany (72 per cent) and France (68 per cent). None of these countries has compulsory voting. At national levels, their rates are even higher, with Denmark at 86 per cent and Germany at 82 per cent, compared to 72 per cent at the last UK General Election. The UK European elections in 1999 saw voter turnout sink to its lowest level yet – 23 per cent. The UK appears to be following the trends in the USA, where voter turnout at elections in 1998 was only 36 per cent.

Sources: DETR, Turnout at Local Elections: Influences on Levels of Voter Registration and Electoral Participation (London: DETR, 2000); Andrew Phillips, 'The rising tide of "sod them" politics', The Observer, 7 May 2000; UNDP, Human Development Report 1999 (New York: Oxford University Press, 1999); figures from the Electoral Reform Society, June 2000

---

long period of rising affluence and a convergence of priorities and economic outlooks between the main parties. 'They're all the same', an old complaint, has some truth now that parties of the centre-Left have made so many concessions to the New Right in terms of economic management, if not in terms of social objectives and values. Prosperity and the apparent lack of dependence of so many people on key state services also make a difference: for many affluent citizens, what Government does simply does not seem to touch their lives in any important ways. Apathy and indifference might be expected in times of unprecedented peace and plenty. But the absence of plenty also pushes people into apathy: on the thousands of 'excluded' housing estates and depressed neighbourhoods long stranded on the margins of policy, it is hardly surprising that faith in politics has dwindled or vanished.

However, it is too easy to interpret public disaffection and low electoral turnouts as a reflection of a loss of interest in political issues. Rather, it is also likely that the decline in trust and respect for politicians and mainstream politics reflects a deep frustration that the system is failing to deal with the big issues that make most difference to people's lives and to their hopes for their children. As Michael Jacobs noted in the first Real World book:

> *'The environmental crisis and the new threats to international security, the changes to the global economic order … these barely figure in national political debate … The failure of the political system to address the problems of the real world breeds in most people simply apathy and disillusionment.'*[4]

141

The failure of mainstream politics to engage with issues that matter deeply to people in local communities and in terms of wider values and global change has fuelled direct action and the rise in support for NGOs and other civil society organizations. Many people have not abandoned democratic politics; rather they are pursuing it through what seem to be more effective and meaningful mechanisms than those of representative democracy. In particular, the emergence of unfamiliar risks and new technologies that could have far-reaching environmental impacts – GM crops provide the classic case – has highlighted the mismatch between the concerns and perceptions of many citizens, and the view of policy priorities and risk assessments from Whitehall and Westminster. Controversies keep revealing that experts' reassurances are not always to be trusted, and that policy-makers have failed to communicate and manage uncertainty in scientific issues.

The conventional democratic process has often failed to anticipate such issues; to respond to them in timely ways; to genuinely listen to public concerns and confusions; and to open up information, and learn from the debates aroused. (Little seemed to have been learned in Whitehall from the BSE scandal as policy-makers found themselves stumbling to catch up with the arguments over GM crops.) The 'radar' of mainstream politicians and democratic processes is too often faulty where new risks, technologies and complex ethical issues are concerned.

This analysis gains support from the upsurge in energetic protests in recent years on issues that received scant interest or inadequate scrutiny from Parliament, Government and public debate. The fuel tax protests in 2000 reflected wholly inadequate national debate and public education by Government about the costs of road use, indirect taxation and the use of tax revenues. The Countryside Alliance's protests in 1998 helped to put on the

---

Witness Box 18: Charter88

In less than three years, New Labour has altered for ever the way our country is governed. A staggering 20 constitutional bills have ensured a list of changes which ten years ago would have been dismissed as inconceivable: the regular use of referenda; the creation of new national parliaments and assemblies; the Human Rights Act; the removal of voting rights from most hereditary peers; independence for the Bank of England; the Freedom of Information Bill; legislation on party funding; civil service reform; new voting systems for mayors; and the establishment of Regional Development Agencies.

The Government claims its reforms will improve and extend democracy. Charter88 agrees. But there are two major problems:

1 The Government's reforms do not hang together. It has broken all the principles that guided the old constitution, except for centralization, without replacing them with new ones. The reforms have a dynamic of their own and have already begun to work against one another, especially with respect to the various national questions, including the English question, that were previously smothered within the UK.

2 The reforms have been presented as something 'being done' to us. Despite all the change there is no renewed sense of public ownership of the political process. To continue in this vein would be to shackle the reforms' potential. Reform of our constitution must belong to the people and not be regarded as the preserve of any one single political party.

Two key elements for the future of democratic reform flow from this analysis. The first is for the Government to have the courage of its convictions and to complete the urgent reform of key institutions:

• *a fully democratic replacement for the House of Lords* – not the largely appointed House recommended by the Royal Commission;
• *a referendum on a proportional system of voting for the House of Commons* – not on an unproportional system like the Alternative Vote;
• *devolution for the English regions*, where there is a clear desire for it.

The second key element is the creation of a Citizens' Constitution. This is a development of Charter88's call for a written constitution. We believe this is necessary now more than ever before, not least to define the relationship and powers of the individual and the state, and to resolve the potentially damaging inconsistencies thrown up by piecemeal reform.

However, the call for a Citizens' Constitution is not meant in a narrow technical sense. In the UK today any notion of citizenship must be broad. It must guarantee that the rights of minorities will be protected from the majority. It must ensure equal access to decision-making for all. It must confront and remove the barriers to engagement in the democratic, cultural and social life of the various communities that exist in the UK. It is these barriers that stand between individuals and full citizenship. A citizen must be someone who has the chance to participate – who is empowered to act.

The Citizens' Constitution should be much more than words on paper. It should set out the rules by which we make and change the rules, and it should give us the basic law and fundamental rights that together provide a framework within which our society will live and prosper. But a Citizens' Constitution will in part be defined by the manner of its creation. This will establish the way it is lived. A Citizens' Constitution must be created by the citizens whose rights, powers, freedom and duties it will outline. In short, for the citizens to possess a constitution they need to have built it themselves.

Therefore Charter88 would like to see:

- the Government initiate an open, participatory process in which as many people as possible have the chance to take part, and which will lead to a new Citizens' Constitution; and
- the Citizens' Constitution ratified in a referendum by 2010.

143

agenda many rural citizens' concerns about being marginalized by New Labour. The protests against road-building in the 1990s helped put an end to the expansion of the road network and contributed to the major change in transport policy thinking heralded in Labour's White Paper on transport. The protests against GM foods – linking NGOs, retailers and consumers – wrong-footed Government and effectively forced a radical rethink of policy on testing and acceptance of GM crops. The MAI (see Chapter 5, page 118) was abandoned by the OECD after an international campaign led by NGOs: governments and parliaments had failed utterly to subject the flawed proposals to adequate scrutiny. The Jubilee 2000 campaign, with NGOs mobilizing millions of citizens in support, also energized debate and action on an issue that elected governments in the rich world seemed unable to tackle seriously.

While it is sometimes cheering to see effective action outside the normal democratic channels which engages citizens, sparks debate and leads to progress in policy towards sustainable development, we cannot be happy with the underlying cause – the lack of vitality in representative democracy, and the failure of much of the mass media to take seriously the big issues. The tools and energies of 'direct democracy' are a vital complement to representative processes, but cannot replace them. It is essential that the pressure for more participatory democracy is accompanied

by measures to renew formal representative democratic processes and institutions, and to find new ways to give a voice to citizens that connect them to the mainstream system of democracy.

New Labour's Reforms

New Labour came to power acknowledging the need to foster
public trust in government and to reform the UK's constitution.
The Government has launched a policy of modernizing local
democracy, through the introduction of an elected mayor in
London, and through measures to improve local public services
and the decision-making processes in local authorities. It has
established elected parliaments and assemblies in Scotland,
Wales and Northern Ireland, and could eventually commit itself
to elected regional assemblies in England. We also have a partly
reformed House of Lords. Finally, there are moves to encourage
more grassroots participation in neighbourhoods and consultation by local authorities, and also measures to devolve some
budgets and responsibilities from town halls to community
forums or neighbourhood councils. These moves are welcome
as signals of Government's commitment to modernizing democracy, and its acknowledgement of the problems of public trust
and engagement.

But this programme, while bold in many ways and a welcome change in British politics, has yet to prove itself capable of
re-energizing the system and halting the slide in public trust and
interest in formal politics. First, New Labour's programme of
reform for representative mechanisms has been selective and
disconnected, and there is still no sign of a thorough debate and
the promised referendum on reform to the national voting system for general elections. Second, New Labour has yet to
embrace the potential of participatory processes, which could
harness the civic energies and commitment on display in so
many recent protests and campaigning movements.

Electoral reform has been substantial and unprecedented,
but promises of reform for elections to Westminster are not
being followed up as quickly as reformers had hoped.
Democratic devolution has not been applied to the English
regions – a source of rising discontent among politicians and
business leaders, especially in the North of England. The House
of Lords has been partially reformed, but radical options for an
elected upper chamber have been rejected. The Government

Witness Box 19: The Electoral Reform Society

Our constitutional arrangements, including the voting system, have been in place since the 19th century. Although there has been much political and social change since then, little of it has been reflected in our democratic processes – to the detriment of the electorate, and of candidates, parties and representative democracy generally in the UK. Turnout has been decreasing amid general disillusionment with a political system that no longer seems relevant to people's lives, and a voting system that allows too many people's votes to be wasted.

In the last few years, however, there have been several positive developments. The New Labour Government, elected in 1997, has made constitutional changes that many believed they would not see during their lifetime. We have seen:

- a report from the Independent Commission on the Voting System recommending a new, more proportional system for General Elections which would do a great deal to improve voter choice;
- devolution to new institutions in Scotland, Wales, London and, potentially, Northern Ireland, and proportional voting systems introduced to elect them;
- legislation (currently underway) to create an independent Electoral Commission that will have a wide-ranging remit on electoral matters, including 'a duty to promote awareness of electoral and democratic systems'.

While the Electoral Reform Society warmly welcomes these developments, we must not forget that much remains to be done:

- The Government committed itself to holding a referendum to let the electorate decide whether it wants to retain the current system, or to opt for change. As yet, no date has been fixed for such a referendum. Pressure must be maintained to hold the Government to this manifesto commitment.
- A Working Party set up by the Scottish Parliament will make recommendations for a more proportional voting system for local government in Scotland – a system that will do much to end single-party domination of councils, and to make politicians more accountable to their electorate. There will be considerable vested party-political interest to be overcome before these recommendations are accepted.
- Citizenship Education is to become a compulsory subject. It is crucial that we ensure the inclusion of a component that will help pupils to understand society's democratic structures, and enable them to use these structures to influence the society in which they live.

Each of these measures would help to achieve government which, at all levels, is more representative of the electorate and more accountable to it.

145

faces accusations of being over-centralist, cramping local and regional autonomy and scope for innovation with excessive red tape and complex funding and evaluation systems. The modernization programme in local government has so far focused on 'best value' in procuring services, and on organizational change within councils, not on the renewal of the democratic link between citizen and local government, or the decentralization of responsibility and resources to regional and local governance on a scale that will genuinely transform the system and allow regions and localities to develop strong policies for sustainable development.

This partially reformed landscape lies alongside a largely unexplored world of participatory democracy and increased accountability for business and other organizations, including NGOs. New Labour has yet to explore the scope for meeting demand for better debate and more local empowerment of citizens, through innovations in participation and the opening up of information from Government, business and other key agencies, in order to better inform democratic debates and to reinforce bonds of accountability and trust between citizens and decision-makers.

Towards New Forms of Empowerment: Participation and Access to Information

Sustainable development requires a revitalized political process to engage local citizens and other interests in debating and acting cooperatively on the social, economic and environmental imperatives ahead. A key failure of Government, national and local, has been lack of engagement in open debates about the future of local communities as globalization, new technologies and industrial change have increasingly affected them. There remains a strong sense in both national and local government that 'we know what is best', and that any increased public involvement must be limited and controlled. Therefore, in addition to a fundamental reform of existing democratic structures, new democratic institutions may be needed to bridge the gap between traditional representative democracy and a more participatory politics. Such reforms will be much needed if local government is to be able to respond to New Labour's modernizing agenda.

Within local and national government there has been a growing emphasis on consultation with citizens. Consultation exercises have become widespread in recent years, particularly at local level, but there have been more large-scale consultations, on issues ranging from local government's scope to promote homosexuality (through a privately funded referendum in Scotland) to a UK Government survey on future priorities for the NHS (12 million questionnaires for the whole of the UK). National Government's own 5,000-strong Citizens' Panel, established as part of the Better Government initiative, is a welcome development. So too are the inclusion of lay members, consumers and ethicists, as well as scientists and industrialists, in the new Human Genetics Commission and the Agriculture and Environment Biotechnology Commission, and proposals for new citizens' commissions to act as watchdogs on the commercial use of new technologies.[5]

147

While any increase in dialogue between national or local Government and the public is to be welcomed, there are serious concerns that some of these exercises may be designed more for PR purposes than to engage with the views of citizens. Unless great care is taken with future consultation exercises, to ensure that people feel their views carry some weight, and that they see action flowing from initiatives designed to strengthen and improve overall democratic processes, then the same cynicism and apathy could develop in relation to these exercises as currently exists in voting behaviour, and in attitudes to Government's favoured forms of 'consultation' – the ubiquitous focus group and private poll.

The progress of the UK Freedom of Information Bill reflects the uncertainty in Government about greater openness and transparency. The initial proposal for such a Bill was very warmly welcomed, as was the first unofficial draft. The actual draft that appeared for consultation provided greatly reduced rights to information than had been expected and drew howls of protest from those involved in earlier consultations. However, the UK Government is under pressure from the EU and the UN in this field. The EU Convention on Human Rights – which is about to come into force – will require Government to provide more information to the public about its policies and activities. In addition, the UK is one of the signatories to the UN Economic Commission for Europe (ECE)'s Convention on Access to Information, Public Participation in Decision-Making and Access

Witness Box 20: Town and Country Planning Association (TCPA)

Planning for People as Well as Places

Planning must look outward for its purpose, towards citizens and their world. Sustainable development provides an explicit new focus on managing change for the better to benefit everyone. Improved, more inclusive processes are needed, to shape change to get us where we want to be, and to provide a toolkit which will enable planners and others to put strategies and plans into action. Seven steps can be taken which will assist:

1 *A duty to promote sustainable development:* For local authorities and other agencies responsible for planning, implementing or investing in public services, infrastructure and development. Putting sustainable development on a par with education, health, transport and other key services.

2 *Visions and strategies for sustainable development:* At various levels and generated through collaborative, deliberative processes involving all stakeholders; to identify community needs and opportunities and suggest ways of making things happen. New systems are also needed to monitor progress towards objectives. Are we getting there? If not, what changes do we have to make?

3 *Community planning at all levels:* From a spatial sustainable development strategy for the UK, to neighbourhood action plans and development control, new frameworks and tools are needed to facilitate the making of political choices at various levels in the development process. Democracy and subsidiarity are key tests in this hierarchy, which should emphasize the shift away from the waste of natural resources, to conservation and replenishment.

4 *Partnership trusts:* Independent, but fully accountable organizations involving the public, private and not-for-profit sectors should be created, to bring forward sustainable development in areas where a wide range of parties need to be engaged. Formal mechanisms would be needed to ensure public scrutiny and democratic accountability.

5 *Rewards rather than penalties:* To encourage environmentally sustainable development and practices. Too often in planning, the emphasis is on the negative.

6 *Capturing betterment:* A more transparent system than planning gain, to enable the community to benefit more fully from the uplift in land values created by development planning.

7 *Mutual learning for participation:* Education for citizenship and participation for all, to encourage full stakeholder involvement in town and country planning for sustainable development.

Source: TCPA, *Your Place and Mine: Reinventing Planning* (TCPA, October 1999), designed as the framework for policy action for the TCPA in the first decade of the new Millennium.

to Justice in Environmental Matters – the Aarhus Convention – signed in June 1998.[6] While the Convention deals only with environmental information, it has been incorporated (in principle) into the UK's 1999 Strategy on Sustainable Development.[7] Increasing public access to information about public policy and government processes could make a major contribution to rebuilding public trust and goodwill. It would be unfortunate if Government missed the opportunity to make these changes enthusiastically, rather than being seen to accept pressure grudgingly from external sources.

149

Public rights to information form one element in the complex relationships between rights and responsibilities and between citizens and democratic institutions. Building trust between people and Government requires much greater respect, openness and responsiveness on both sides, and this implies increased rights for citizens to participate more fully in the decisions that affect their lives – rights that need to be balanced by a growing sense of collective responsibility for the impacts of those decisions. Much of the debate on sustainable development focuses on increased responsibilities for individuals, companies and governments. But there remains much to be done in increasing people's basic human rights – including environmental rights and justice[8] – and in increasing their awareness of those rights and how to use them responsibly.

There are those who argue that human rights are a Western invention and that the traditions of other cultures should be respected. While respect for different cultures is a valid and important goal, cultural relativism is no excuse for weakening universal human rights. The Charter of the United Nations and the Universal Declaration of Human Rights (UDHR) provide a set of core values: respect for life, liberty, justice, equality, tolerance, mutual respect and integrity. These basic values, and the principle of balancing people's rights and responsibilities (see also Chapter 2), provide solid foundations for programmes of sustainable development.

Greater rights for public participation in policy development and implementation will need a substantial investment in education and learning. Government plans to introduce education for citizenship and for sustainable development into the national curriculum will provide a basis for children to explore these ideas in school. However, the biggest challenge for educationalists is the proposition that education for sustainable development cannot simply be added on to existing learning, but requires a systemic change to the learning process and priorities for education. We need a revolution in education, to link moral and civic rights and responsibilities with sustainable development – starting at school but continuing throughout people's lives.[9] New attitudes to educational priorities and lifelong learning will be critical if people are to gain the knowledge, skills and 'moral fluency' they need to participate in debates about a shared sustainable future.

'Community' and the Renewal of Democracy

The 'democracy gap' in part reflects a disconnection between national and local government on the one hand, and local communities on the other hand. Disaffection with national politics has not fuelled more interest in local councils: people evidently feel they and their community are detached from both. To remedy this, a stronger focus on 'community' as a new location for civic rights and responsibilities has been supported and encouraged by the UK Government. For example, the New Deal for Communities is establishing long-term mechanisms for regenerating some of the most disadvantaged neighbourhoods in the country, with strong mechanisms for community control. Local government is charged with developing new forms of community planning for long term well-being; and, at national level, the Active Communities Unit, based in the Home Office, is promoting volunteering and community action.

The concept of community provides a focus for political action at a different level of social relationships, somewhere between individuals and families and the more distant 'society'. After all, it is often communities that implement policy, and that have the power to maintain or subvert programmes of change. In policy terms, this suggests the need for initiatives and institutions through which people would have more control over power and resources at local level, and over the decisions that affect their lives – not just the most disadvantaged people for whom more 'community empowerment' is too often prescribed as an answer to poverty and exclusion, but everyone. These initiatives are likely to include innovations such as Citizens' Juries to explore complex issues; mechanisms for public involvement in local planning; and integration of the new national school curriculum in civic and moral education (to be introduced in

2002) with practical processes of deliberation and debate at local level that can involve school students.[10]

To make a reality of democratic renewal at the local level, we need initiatives that genuinely address the issues people care most about; that can improve public understanding of policy dilemmas and options; and that offer a measure of real control over budgets, land use planning and decisions about priorities for spending on local regeneration in deprived areas. Government is edging towards such a vision with its plans for a strategy for neighbourhood renewal. We emphasize that this idea, while promising, needs to be joined up effectively to modernized processes in local government and to wider programmes for sustainable development and public consultation; otherwise there is a risk that we will see a mass of fragmented micro-experiments in community participation which are 'ghettoized'. 'Community participation' is a policy goal that requires investment and commitment if it is to provide the key link between the most local, neighbourly connections and a revitalized democracy.

Strengthening Democracy and Participation at the International Level

Healthy democracies and the politics of sustainable development need a vibrant culture of local governance, and this must be based not only on improved efficiency in local authorities, but on better processes for community participation in the decisions that matter most to citizens about the places in which they live. However, while such downward devolution from the national level is essential, in the light of globalization we also require more 'upward devolution'. There is an urgent need for better international and global institutions and more experiments in developing supranational democratic communities. The EU and the emerging networks of NGOs and internet-linked campaigners on environment and development across the world indicate the potential for formal democratic processes and looser forms of participation and shared agenda-building to work at the international level.

National governments are not redundant, and will remain the key political mechanism for implementing change, including agreements made at the global level. But there is a need to complement them with stronger international bodies. There are three clear gaps in the framework of international and global institutions.[11] The first is a gap between global and national governance. Policy issues are often global in nature, but policy-making is still mainly national in focus and scope. Where global institutions do exist, they lack public trust and credibility. For some issues (such as environmental protection and international crime) there may need to be new institutions. For example, the UN suggests a world environment agency and an international criminal court.[12]

A reformed global architecture of institutions is needed to reduce financial insecurity; protect people during crises and periods of adjustment; control global crime; protect cultural diversity; preserve the environment; promote fair trade especially for poorer countries; reduce debt and improve aid; and narrow technology gaps.[13] In particular, some form of global body may be needed to establish, monitor and help national governments enforce binding global rules to ensure the accountability of multinational corporations and their adherence to globally agreed principles of performance on human development (labour standards and human rights); economic efficiency (fair trade and competitive markets), and environmental sustainability (to avoid degradation and pollution), and to debate openly with civil society and governments. Greater balance is needed to ensure that decisions are taken at the appropriate level; that the principle of subsidiarity applies, and that those who make decisions are accountable.

The second is a democratic deficit. The global institutions, especially economic agencies such as the WTO, lack adequate democratic accountability.[14] This is also true of the international and regional networks of governance – above all, the EU, the G8 Summit process, and the OECD. Existing structures need to be reformed, and new institutions established, to ensure they are democratically accountable, open to public scrutiny, and willing to explain not only the decisions that are made, but also how and why those decisions are made. New mechanisms will be needed to provide information openly, fully and at low or no cost so that national governments, elected representatives, NGOs and others can monitor developments. Representative democratic institutions and participatory mechanisms can all then be expected to play a fuller role in international and global decisions. As part of these developments, NGOs as well as corporations and global agencies should be expected to embrace open reporting and accountability on their operations and impacts.

The third is a participation gap. Although national and local politics are increasingly about partnerships across sectors and debates across civil society and the media, as well as contests between parties, most international cooperation and action is still inter-governmental. Greater openness is needed in forums such as the G8 Summit and the WTO, bringing in NGOs, business representatives and other actors from civil society to ensure that the different parties to global discussions develop a better understanding of each other's cultures, so that when they do meet, their discussions – and potential agreements – are not undermined by avoidable mistrust and misunderstandings.

153

Conclusion: Closing the Democracy Gaps

A revitalized democracy at national and local levels is an essential public good in its own right. In the light of globalization, a programme of reform of international institutions to improve their accountability and introduce more democracy and openness into their decision-making and deliberation is vital. Both are fundamental to making progress towards sustainable development: sustainability demands strong democracy and richer processes for planning and debating the choices that face us as citizens, consumers and producers.

How can we close the democracy gaps we have identified? The New Labour Government has made encouraging progress in constitutional reform. But more needs to be done to restore the vitality of local governance and to experiment with new mechanisms for participatory democracy – such as Citizens' Juries and citizens' commissions to debate environmental risks and the implications of new technologies – and to connect these fruitfully to a revitalized and updated system of representative democracy, with a voting system in which people feel that their vote can make a difference.

Downward devolution to the local level is essential to renewing connections between citizens and politics. So is effective and open national government. But equally important is the need for upward devolution to the supranational and global levels of governance, which we need to guide and manage globalization, and which demand more accountability and democratic legitimacy. A key task for the UK Government and its partners in the EU will be to improve the democratic culture of the EU; and to press their international partners in the OECD and UN to experiment with more open, accountable and diverse processes for democratic debate and decision-making in the global economic agencies.

The fundamental driver of sustainable development must be democratic debate – decisions reached through open discussion, consensus based on shared goals and trust. Sustainable development needs representative democracy that is trusted and vibrant, and new forms of participatory democracy to complement it that can inspire greater engagement by citizens in creating a better world. The prospect before us will only improve if citizens are involved in shaping change and can take their share of the responsibility for the problems and the solutions ahead. Such a transformation will require leadership and vision, and a constant review of the aims, strategies and tactics needed for sustainable development – a dynamic process that can only be successful through methods that link technical experts, politicians and policy-makers with much deeper and wider public involvement.

From Conflicts to Security: Wars, Refugees, Disasters and Sustainable Development

'How are those of us lucky enough to live in zones of relative safety to assist those in the zones of danger to recreate viable states? How do we intervene without making things worse, either by introducing new weapons or, more subtly, by assisting populations to prolong the conflict?'
Michael Ignatieff[1]

'Whatever the colour of your skin, whatever god you worship, whatever hideous wrong you or your ancestors may have done me or my ancestors, each single person on this earth has more or less identical requirements when it comes to air to breathe, water to drink and food to eat. What could be more fundamental ground to meet on than that?'
Sara Parkin[2]

Conflicts, Security and Sustainability

In Chapters 4 and 5, we explored the economic, social and environmental instability and impoverishment endured by the losers in the process of globalization and 'structural adjustment' to market forces and industrial competition. The poorest countries suffer both from economic problems – such as low commodity prices for their exports, inadequate infrastructure, and insensitive and inappropriate economic policy interventions and trade rules imposed by the West – and political failures, above all from the corruption and repressive policies of so many of their leaders and their rivals. One process feeds the other. Economic failure increases the risks of conflict and repression. And the latter drives out skilled people and investors, and generates 'aid fatigue' in the richer countries.

This leads to the recognition that security issues, human rights and sustainable development are connected. Unsustainable development in the economy, social structure and environment raises the risks of conflicts within and between states, and of failures of governance that destabilize whole states. It also creates the conditions for large-scale migrations, which in turn can be a cause of tensions and conflict. This chapter looks at the connections and considers ways in which conflict prevention and security can be advanced by better strategies for sustainable development.

These issues have become more salient since the end of the Cold War, and with the rise of environmental concerns. The Cold War can be seen in retrospect as a period in which tensions between the superpowers both contained and inflamed conflicts. Many 'proxy wars' were fought out, and many repressive regimes maintained, for reasons of superpower strategy. While the end of the Cold War removed the rationale for the superpowers' support of repressive client regimes in the developing world and Eastern Europe, it did not bring a new 'world order' which could prevent long-stoked up or suppressed conflicts from continuing or erupting.

The result has been a sharp division between a post-Cold War 'order' in the South and ex-Communist world – the states and classes that overall are benefiting from globalization, democratization and rapid economic development – and a 'disordered' realm of states that have fallen apart or are on the verge of doing so. These are among the poorest, least industrialized countries, where globalization as currently organized is producing few winners, and where local failures of governance, repression and corruption combine with the legacy of Cold War conflicts and arms trading to create what have been called 'zones of chaos'. The images of inhumanity of the 1990s have not been dominated by conflicts between states, although major wars have been fought (NATO versus Serbia, Allies versus Iraq, and Ethiopia versus Eritrea). Rather, they have been largely about the disintegration of states into prolonged civil war and factional terrorism, as in Afghanistan, Angola, Colombia, Congo Liberia, Sierra Leone, Somalia, Sudan, Yugoslavia, and, most appallingly in the scale of killing, Rwanda.

In the countries now enduring civil strife the rule of law has largely vanished, or governments operate in a state of permanent siege; either way, civilians suffer wretchedly as factions kill, loot and maim, and as livelihoods and whole economies are wrecked. Deep poverty breeds more instability and conflict, which in turn diverts precious resources to arms and destruction, and thus poor countries become nailed to the bottom of all the development indices. Meanwhile, in North and South, regardless of economic status, countries continue to spend huge sums and incur vast opportunity costs on their armies and weapons, even though overall expenditures have fallen since the end of the Cold War. (Panel 12 outlines developments in recent years and the trends in military spending.)

157

Panel 12

Wars, Poverty and Unsustainable Development

The number of armed conflicts around the world fell in the 1990s, as did the number of nuclear warheads and the size of the world's armies. Military spending declined overall, with a decline in arms production. The so-called 'peace dividend' from the end of the Cold War in 1989–91 has been a reality. World military spending in 1997 was some US$740 billion, having fallen by an average of 4.5 per cent per year over the previous decade. The proportion of GDP spent on arms and armies also declined.

But the positive trends in security and conflict reduction were matched by negative ones. The proliferation of nuclear weapons remains a potent risk, and in recent years fear of proliferation has been heightened by tensions between India and Pakistan – both now possess nuclear arsenals. UN peacekeeping expenditure and personnel declined steeply in the 1990s, largely as a result of reluctance in the USA to support the UN. However, the budget for 1999–2000 shows an increase in UN peacekeeping resources.

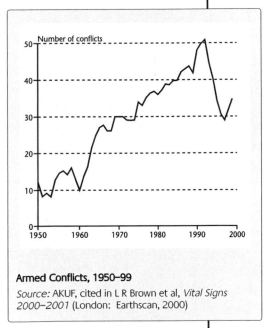

Armed Conflicts, 1950–99

Source: AKUF, cited in L R Brown et al, *Vital Signs 2000–2001* (London: Earthscan, 2000)

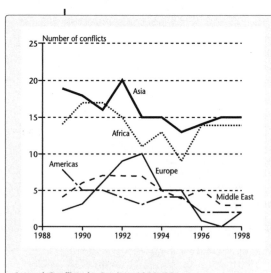

Armed Conflicts by Region, 1989–98

Source: Uppsala University, cited in L R Brown et al, *Vital Signs 2000–2001* (London: Earthscan, 2000)

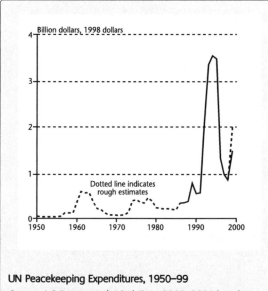

UN Peacekeeping Expenditures, 1950–99

Source: L R Brown et al, *Vital Signs 2000–2001* (London: Earthscan, 2000)

Arms spending is still extremely high, especially in the USA; military spending has risen recently in Asia and the Middle East; and in 2000 Russia announced a substantial increase in military budgets to revive its declining armed forces.

Conflicts create huge problems: refugee movements; famines; disease; extra vulnerability to shocks such as droughts; destruction of economic, environmental and social resources; waste of finances on arms and continuation of war; and increased dependency of countries on external support and intervention. Refugee movements are also a result of war, and can in turn spark turmoil in the areas to which displaced people flee.

The poor tend to suffer most from conflicts, and security policy and conflict prevention are thus key issues for development and anti-poverty strategies worldwide. A major fear for the future must be that unsustainable development; clashes over access to resources; environmental degradation and disasters (for example, resulting from climate disruption or water shortages) will in turn become a trigger for warfare within and between states.

Sources: L Brown et al, *Vital Signs 1999–2000* (London: Earthscan, 1999); L Brown et al, *Vital Signs 1997–1998* (London: Earthscan, 1997); UNEP, *Global Environment Outlook 2000* (London: Earthscan, 1999)

It is important to avoid falling into two traps when thinking about the post-Cold War world. One is the temptation to take an over-pessimistic or apocalyptic view of the many conflicts underway or in prospect, and to assume that there is nothing that can be done. The other is the temptation in the West to become complacent, viewing remote conflicts and arms races in the developing world as insignificant and unlikely to affect the developed countries. Compared to the risk of nuclear war between the USA and USSR, and the major wars of the pre-1989 period, the conflicts plaguing Africa now seem relatively small in scale, even though the suffering they unleash is as bad as anything we have done to ourselves in the past. The number of wars around the world has declined, and military spending has also fallen (see Panel 12) along with the volume of arms trading as the superpower stand-off has come to an end. However, the risk of nuclear war has not vanished, and if anything the dangers of proliferation and regional nuclear war have risen, as shown by the tensions between India and Pakistan, which have diverted huge sums into their nuclear programmes despite the scale of the poverty in both countries.

The estimated value of arms deliveries in 1998 was US$55,756 million.[3] Total global military expenditure was estimated for 1997 at US$740,000 million – a huge sum despite the annual average fall of 4.5 per cent in spending in the period 1988–97.[4] We also have the immense 'legacy' costs of Cold War and hot wars alike – the gross pollution from nuclear weaponry dumps and factories; the landmines littered across countries such as Cambodia; and the costs of rebuilding wrecked infrastructures in 'post-conflict' societies.

Like the perverse economic subsidies that underpin so much unsustainable production and consumption, the enormous scale of military spending between and within countries represents an opportunity cost that makes a mockery of protestations by governments that they cannot afford increased spending on sustainable development initiatives to benefit the poor and their environments. The 'military-industrial complex' present in so many countries diverts money, skilled people and innovative energies away from productive and sustainable research and development. It plays a major role in preventing human and environmental progress and warping development. In particular, the push to develop nuclear and chemical weapons has helped to create 'civilian' industries whose activities can have equally grim environmental consequences.

Witness Box 21: Campaign Against the Arms Trade (CAAT)

Arms are the ultimate unproductive commodity. If they are used they destroy; if they are not they still consume resources that could otherwise help alleviate poverty and promote sustainable development. It is imperative, therefore, that the UK reduces its military exports and works towards the elimination of them. CAAT believes that three keys steps towards this are an end to Government support for arms exports; tough new export controls; and real help for UK industry to move away from military production.

1 *End Government support for arms exports:* The Government actively promotes arms sales overseas through the Defence Export Services Organization (DESO). With offices in 12 overseas countries as well as in London, and approximately 600 employees, the DESO provides a level of assistance enjoyed by no other sector of UK industry.

   Although only about 3 per cent of all exports are military, on average they account for around a quarter of those underwritten by the Government's Export Credits Guarantee Department. These export guarantees allow arms companies to export their wares without taking the risk that they will not be paid.

   The Government must shut the DESO, and end export credits for military goods.

2 *Tough new export controls:* The current export controls were introduced as a wartime emergency measure in 1939 and are generally agreed to be inappropriate to the situation today. At present a UK company can grant a licence to an overseas company for the local production of its weaponry without having to comply with any UK regulations. Similarly, except in a few special circumstances, there are no controls on UK companies which broker arms deals. Known examples of this include making the arrangements for selling Bulgarian weaponry to Rwanda.

   Arms exports are shrouded in secrecy, as information on them is considered to be commercially sensitive. Applications for export licences are not published in advance of a decision so there is no opportunity for proper public and parliamentary debate on them.

   It is imperative that new export control legislation, incorporating controls on licensed production and brokerage, as well as providing for greater transparency, is introduced without delay.

3 *Help for industry to move away from military production:* As promised in its election manifesto, the New Labour Government has set up a Defence Diversification Agency (DDA). However, it is not what most people anticipated. It is within the Ministry of Defence's Defence Evaluation and Research Agency, has a minuscule budget, and is as concerned with bringing civil technology into military goods as vice versa.

> *The DDA should be relocated within the Department of Trade and Industry (DTI), and given proper resources to enable it to make a major contribution to the demilitarization of the UK economy. A fund should be created to support diversification strategies by, for instance, making low interest loans, financing product development, guaranteeing creditors during the process of diversification, and, where necessary, paying for retraining.*

The amount spent in 1999 by the Mugabe Government in Zimbabwe on its involvement in the Congo civil war was some US$70 million per month – 70 times the amount spent on the prevention of HIV/Aids, which affects one-quarter of the adult population.[5] The estimated annual cost of providing quality reproductive health services to all those who need them in the developing world is US$17 billion – a trivial sum to the rich world, compared to its total spending on the military. A global fund of some US$150 billion per year for sustainable development would be enough to put an end to absolute poverty, invest in sanitation and public health, and fund large-scale programmes for environmental protection and restoration, education, housing and family planning. Again, set against the sums spent on arms and the military now and during the Cold War, the amount is paltry. As Michael Jacobs has said, 'Whatever figures we choose, the problem is not money. It is political will'.[6]

The divisions of the new world order are starkly exposed by the security issues and conflicts that now dominate the international scene. As Michael Ignatieff has written:

> *'If we put together the two narratives – globalization and chaos – it becomes apparent that we are not being offered a picture of the world that makes sense. At the very least, we have a fractured image: Tokyo, Singapore, Taipei, Paris, London, Rome, New York, Los Angeles are being wired together in a twenty-four hour global trading economy. But vast sections of the world – central Africa, parts of Latin America, central Asia – are simply drifting out of the global economy altogether into a subrational zone of semi-permanent violence.'[7]*

The changes since the end of the Cold War point towards a more complex concept of what counts as 'international security'.[8] The reduction in the risks of major wars, and the rise of conflicts rooted in poverty, in clashes over access to resources such as water and oil, in environmental degradation and ethnic divisions, have focused attention on non-military factors in conflict prevention and resolution. Globalization means more interdependence of states in relation to economic, environmental and social security: the risks to stability may not come from military action, but from crises whose effects spill over boundaries. These include environmental crises (such as water shortages); expulsion of refugees; large movements of economic migrants; and cultural conflicts (such as religious and ethnic tensions). This points to the need, as a priority, for preventive strategies, focusing on non-military policies to tackle the environmental, economic and social causes of conflict in both North and South, and on measures to curb the proliferation of weapons of mass destruction. There is also an argument that, as a last resort, there will be a need for military intervention for peace-keeping purposes by the UN.[9]

Millennial Conflicts

The end of the Cold War and the nature of the conflicts that have recently developed or re-emerged encourages a sense of disengagement in the rich world. This is rooted in various reasons – economic, psychological and political. First, the conflicts that have dominated the 1990s, with the exception of the Gulf War, have not been wars that have significantly threatened Western economic interests.

Second, the conflicts often go unreported unless an atrocity, famine or other incident serves to attract media interest, at which point they might become 'real' in the eyes of Western policy-makers and publics, if only fleetingly. Many of the civil wars are complex and have obscure origins and motivations, even to the participants and suffering civilians, and are thus hard to understand in the rest of the world. Few, at the start of the Millennium, could begin to find a sane reason for war between Ethiopia and Eritrea, or to untangle the Congo's wars. Many conflicts are rooted in criminality and it is hard to identify a 'winning side' worthy of support: in many regions government and organized crime shade imperceptibly into one another. So a psychological barrier exists, reinforcing what Ignatieff calls the 'seductiveness of moral disgust', which permits the rich world to dismiss the zones of chaos as irredeemable and somehow 'fated'.[10]

Witness Box 22: Medact

Challenging Social and Environmental Barriers to Health

Medact is an organization of health professionals challenging social and environmental barriers to health worldwide. We highlight the health impacts of violent conflict, poverty and environmental degradation, and act with others to eradicate them. The key issues for Government are:

- *Nuclear disarmament:* This continues to be a very important issue, with 20,000 nuclear weapons still in service, many at states of high alert. Given the new geopolitical circumstances following the fall of the Berlin wall, accidental nuclear war may now be more, rather than less likely. Our analysis of the health consequences of the development, production, possession and potential use of these weapons is thus unfortunately still topical.

  UK health professionals are working with others in the Abolition 2000 coalition to ensure that the momentum for nuclear weapons abolition is maintained. We strongly promote the adoption of a nuclear weapons convention (NWC), an example of which IPPNW (International Physicians Against Nuclear War, of which Medact is the UK affiliate) has drawn up. A measure of our success will be the speed with which such a convention is adopted.

  We are also continuing our dialogue with decision-makers, and each year have fruitful discussions with many decision-makers in both nuclear and non-nuclear weapons states.

- *Economic policy and health:* Increasingly clear to us is the impact of economic policy on health, of which debt and debt relief are an important subset. Many health professionals consider the consequences of economic globalization as bad for the health of billions of people, recognizing that the changes associated with this process have provoked further impoverishment of the already poor, and more environmental degradation. The World Health Organization (WHO), among others, now accepts that economic growth that is not used to ease the impact of social and environmental injustice is bad for our health.

  Medact is working with others to clarify the links between economic globalization, environmental decay, increasing disparity in wealth between the rich and the poor and our global health. We will continue to publish and disseminate material identifying the health-related problems. To facilitate this process we have written a model medical-student curriculum, identifying the key barriers to global health, the links between them and possible solutions to them.

  We recognize that refugees are victims of the same range of injustices as blight the health of so many people. Thus helping in the rehabilitation of refugee health professionals is another tangible marker of our success.

- *Psychological processes underlying violent conflict*: Ultimately it is the mindset of all of us, as individuals and members of our communities, that determines our actions. Health professionals have an important role in explaining (in so far as we can) the roots of conflict. We can then use this knowledge to ensure the widespread use of mediation rather than violence to resolve conflict. Medact supports work on mediation, playing a practical role in the former Yugoslavia.

- *Defining health:* If we are to achieve health benefit through the evolution of environmental and social justice, health, as broadly defined, should be central to policy-making at all levels. Health professionals working in organizations such as Medact need to emphasize the links between weapons of war, environmental and social problems, economic policy and health. This is best done by developing a broad and agreed description of health that illustrates the interrelatedness of these issues. Medact is contributing to the development of such a description of health.

- *The voice of health professionals:* Medact believes that the voice of health professionals working through the many agencies with which we are all involved can greatly increase the possibility of getting health central to policy-making. An important part of our work is in informing, engaging and mobilizing as many health professionals as we possibly can.

  A marker of our success will therefore be an increase in both the numbers and age distribution of our members. In this context, we are particularly encouraged by the numbers of young health professionals who are now joining us.

Third, there are powerful political constraints against intervention by 'peacekeeping' forces from the UN or other sources. The record of peacekeeping missions has not been encouraging, and the country with the military and financial capacity to make most difference – the USA – has been especially reluctant to commit troops and money since the disaster of its intervention in Somalia. Intervention far away in confused and obscure conflicts is hard to justify to a sceptical media and to the public.

The practical problems of making a positive difference by intervening, rather than merely muddying the waters still more, are accompanied by deep political controversy as to the ethics of intervention. What are the criteria that should govern intervention? If we claim a justification rooted in universal humanitarian concerns, aiming to prevent or mitigate suffering, and fight against genocidal campaigns as in Rwanda, then do we not have a duty to intervene everywhere? If we keep out of

Chechnya while invading Kosovo and bombing Belgrade, are we hypocrites? The criteria in use are vague and pragmatic: the West and the UN go into zones of chaos and conflict when it seems that there might be a fair chance of 'winning', with minimal casualties and media sensation, and when there is no risk of serious tension with major powers such as Russia and China. Such criteria can easily be painted by opponents as a feeble rationale, courting failure. As the former BBC correspondent Martin Bell MP said of the UK's intervention in Sierra Leone in May 2000, you either have to go 'all the way in or stay all the way out.'

An anti-intervention stance is shared by people on the Right and the Left alike. Many on the Right see no self-interest or universal principle at stake in the wars and miseries of the 'zones of chaos', and regard peacekeeping missions as ill-organized and misconceived: it can be better to let opponents fight it out than to try to hold the ring. And many on the Left resist UN or Western intervention on the grounds that it can do no good, stirs up memories of colonialism, and is a poor substitute for economic and social justice promoted through reforms in the global system of trade and aid. Both perspectives have much political support. There is also obvious truth in the argument that ill-conceived interventions can make matters worse. Intervention can provide new rationales for carrying on a conflict.

Finally, there is the potent objection that the world of 'chaos zones' is not 'controllable' by people of goodwill sitting in the UN, even if that organization were reformed and provided with the support it deserves from its members.[11] Conflict has irrational as well as rational dimensions: if antagonists do not want to keep the peace, then peacekeeping forces cannot succeed unless willing and able to impose a 'result' by force. Wars such as the tribal conflicts in Afghanistan and Somalia have roots in clan interests and loyalties which do not admit negotiated, consensual settlements enforced by a state mechanism; in these countries, the state does not exist.

Reasons for Preventive Policy and Humanitarian Intervention: The Moral Imperative

Against these points, however, reasons can be advanced for positive action by the rich world to develop policies to prevent conflicts as far as possible, and to make a range of humanitarian interventions, including military ones as a last resort. The case for such action is based first on humanitarian principles; second, on arguments from Western responsibility for the consequences of colonial rule; third, on arguments from long-term self-interest on the part of the rich democracies.

The first argument is a simple one. Wars and repression violate human rights, cause mass suffering, and inspire in many people a humanitarian desire to help the victims, put a halt to conflict and help foster conditions that will bring long-term peace and security. If we believe in the universality of human rights and the need to uphold international law on warfare and protection of rights, then we cannot ignore conflicts and assaults on humane values.

The second argument for positive action in the face of conflict in the developing world draws on history. Western powers have contributed to the sources of war by dividing up their colonies in the South into artificial nation states that have often proved unviable ethnically and economically, and by failing to provide the development aid that would have put ex-colonies on a sustainable path and reinforced good government. Instead, Cold War pressures and ill-conceived aid policies led to Western powers propping up corrupt regimes, as did the USSR, and to irresponsible arms sales that have fuelled wars. This is not to absolve Southern governments of guilt for the crimes many have committed and still commit against their own people. It is simply to note that the rich world has to bear some measure of responsibility, based on universal principles and also on the history of colonialism in the South, and should make reparation in the form of investment in sustainable development and preventive security strategies for the poorest countries.

The third element in the case for positive action is the argument from long-term self-interest for the developed world. The sources of conflict are not only the legacy of colonialism and the power struggles of repressive governments and factions. As we have underlined in earlier chapters, the problems of global poverty and environmental degradation will, if they get worse, increasingly pose a threat to economic and social stability within and between nations. In short, unsustainable development is a threat to international security. As Michael Jacobs warned in the first Real World book, failing to take this seriously does not simply risk greater instability in the South, but also could fuel tendencies in parts of the rich world towards isolationism, protectionism and xenophobia:

> 'These phenomena represent a response to insecurity
> that can only fail; by ignoring the causes of the prob-
> lems they promise simply further conflict and social
> tension. The alternative approach is ... a gradual,
> agreed, managed shift in international economic rela-
> tions to tackle the sources, not just the symptoms, of
> conflict and migration.'[12]

167

We return to these issues later. The essential point is that the threats to international order are no longer mainly military ones. They are rooted in the deep poverty of many in the South and in unsustainable exploitation of vital resources. This points us towards a new concept of what counts as international security, and towards strategies for security that start from conflict prevention and the promotion of sustainable development.

Putting Conflict Prevention First

In recent years debates on security and conflict have been dominated by the arguments for and against peacekeeping missions by the UN and wars waged by Western powers to punish repression and invasions by dictatorships (Iraq, Serbia). The human costs and risks, the ethical complexities and the scope for making matters even worse, all underline the need to see war waged on humanitarian grounds as a last resort in a hierarchy of action to deal with conflict. This hierarchy puts conflict prevention at the top of the agenda:

- *Prevention:* curbing the arms trade; promotion of equitable economic development and good democratic governance; anticipation of conflicts and measures for consensus-building in and between countries.
- *Mediation and mitigation:* measures to broker a negotiated peace between warring parties; humanitarian assistance to victims of war; non-military assistance in peace-keeping and reconstruction after conflicts, aiming to prevent recurrence of war.
- Military involvement for peacekeeping after conflicts have ended.
- Military intervention for imposition of order and protection of civilians.

Witness Box 23: National Peace Council

The National Peace Council is concerned to contribute to a debate on how we should redefine 'security' in Britain, Europe, and the world. We may agree with military analysts that the main global threats to security include the proliferation of weapons of mass destruction; deep global socio-economic divisions, and protracted environmental limitations on socio-economic development. But we disagree fundamentally about how to respond. It is our basic contention that what is required are political and economic responses, not military ones.

British foreign and security policy needs to be based on an assessment of Britain's current and future needs, not on memories of a glorious past. A country with an average income below that of the EU, situated in one of the safest parts of Europe, no longer needs to spend proportionately more on the military than most of its allies. Britain must now join in the general trend throughout Europe to reduce military budgets and stop playing junior partner to US ambitions to achieve full-spectrum dominance.

Meanwhile, the primary role of security organizations must now be conflict prevention. This requires a shift in the relative importance of the European institutions. The Organization for Security and Co-operation in Europe (OSCE) is the only body with a mandate to deal with European security in economic, legal and political – as well as military – terms, and the Government should begin to press quietly for incremental enhancements of the OSCE's role.

Specifically, we feel the following security issues need to be addressed urgently by the next government:

- The nuclear weapons system to which Britain has belonged since the early 1950s is becoming more unstable. Britain is well placed to take the lead in negotiations for a nuclear weapons convention, which now has the support of the majority of other states, including many of our allies. In the absence of such negotiations, Britain should take further steps to lessen its doctrinal and operational dependence on nuclear weapons, and to distance itself from the US 'son of Star Wars' programme and other nuclear weapon developments that further undermine the non-proliferation regime.
- British foreign policy has embraced the concept of preventive diplomacy, but is allocating few resources to developing the mechanisms that are needed. The promotion of conflict impact assessments to determine appropriate aid and trade policies in relation to conflict areas is essential, as are other new approaches to effective intervention, including NGO partnerships and the use of new technologies to bypass political stumbling blocks.
- On peace-keeping, Britain could work within the UN system to create a national coordinating body to bring together a range of civilian agencies and expertise for contributions to peacekeeping missions; create a national training centre; and establish rules of

engagement for both civilian and military peacekeeping personnel, while the latter are involved.

- Britain needs a policy of defence procurement reform that over time changes the present system from British/defence specialism towards European/dual-use. A new European procurement regime would provide equipment for British forces at a reasonable cost and on time, but within a European industrial and technology policy framework that had successfully marginalized defence production.

- British foreign policy would also be better served by establishing more restrictive arms export controls. Britain is the world's second largest arms exporter, and the Government is therefore in an ideal position to take a lead on fostering wider international restraint. Furthermore, Britain's technology base can be strengthened by being shifted and targeted at 'national needs' like industrial renewal, envir-onmental restoration, renewable energies, and sustainable development.

- For this to happen, the pervasive power of the defence industrial lobby will have to be broken. As the Scott Report indicated, in ways that have hardly been met by the Freedom of Information Act as currently proposed, there is an unacceptable degree of secrecy over defence issues in Britain under the present system. Further improvements to the Freedom of Information are essential, as is a general acceptance of transparency in all matters of defence procurement and arms exports.

169

Should military intervention take place, it needs to be seen as a precondition for long-term measures for conflict prevention; but as we discuss below, agreement is extremely hard to reach on the criteria that should govern military interventions. However, there is scope for broad consensus on the important role of conflict prevention strategies. In this respect, there are other forms of action that can be taken to complement and render more effective the selective use of UN military intervention on humanitarian grounds. We should, as argued in Chapters 4 and 5, seek changes to the international system of trade and development in order to fight poverty and rising inequality between the poorest and richest within and between nations. This is justification enough for non-military interventions in areas at risk of conflict or experiencing it. These positive and preventive interventions are of various kinds:

- Generous aid programmes designed to foster good governance, better living standards for the poor, and better education, especially for women, as measures that will help prevent conflict and instability and create conditions for sustainable growth.

- Reform of the international trading system's rules to create more equitable conditions for developing countries, and to prevent over-exploitation of resources and environments.
- Programmes of debt relief, along with support for policies for better governance and diversion of spending from military budgets to social and educational investment.
- Fundamental reform of the crude structural adjustment programmes imposed on Southern governments, which have intensified inequalities and helped inflame existing social tensions (as in the case of, for example, Algeria and Rwanda).

- International support for collaborative resource management strategies linking countries in regions where vital resources such as access to fresh water could become a cause of instability and even war (for example, in the Middle East). Watersheds that straddle international boundaries need to be managed sustainably through cooperative strategies, such as the US-Canada agreement on management of the Great Lakes system. Support for joint management by neighbouring states of vulnerable and strategically vital resources is an essential part of a programme for conflict prevention and long-term sustainable development.
- Disaster anticipation and prevention strategies drawn up by UN agencies, disaster relief NGOs and governments and civil society organizations in areas at risk of major environmental disasters, in order to plan settlements and infrastructure to minimize disruption and loss of life from disasters such as floods and hurricanes, and to build up regional centres of emergency aid for rapid mobilization.
- Development of micro-credit and insurance schemes for people in areas vulnerable to natural disasters, so that local economies can become more resilient and less dependent on disaster relief monies, and so that economic disruption is reduced, which could otherwise lead to conflicts.
- Support for conflict prevention and reconciliation work, by NGOs in partnership with local agencies and communities.
- Sanctions regimes against pariah governments (such as Iraq) that target the financial and military resources and strategic interests of the ruling group, rather than impose blanket restrictions on the economy which hurt the poor most (as also in Iraq).
- Support of international agreements to prevent prolifera-

tion of nuclear, chemical and biological weapons, and to ban landmines.
- Above all, prevention of conflicts by curbing arms trading and production, measures to remove small arms from circulation, and strict controls to cut off the supply of arms to regimes engaged in conflict and repression (see below).

Improved policies for aid, trade, arms control and development are the best long-term hope for preventing conflicts, which are intimately connected with deep poverty, inequality and corruption. If we wish to avoid military and non-military interventions as far as possible in future, then the West needs to take more seriously investment in preventive strategies which will also increase the economic and environmental security and resilience of developing countries. And if we wish to have, as a last resort, effective military action for humanitarian reasons by the UN, then we must fund the UN and its peacekeeping resources adequately.

Curbing the Trade in Arms:
A Vital Part of Conflict Prevention

An essential element in preventive strategies is rapid reduction in arms exports to repressive regimes and war zones. If we are serious about preventing conflicts we should stop fuelling them through weapon sales. As noted earlier, military spending represents a staggering opportunity cost, reducing the sums that could be invested in sustainable development programmes that would reduce and prevent conflict and create the conditions for democracy, stability and a decent quality of life for all.

The trade in arms is not simply about sales of major military items such as missiles, aircraft and heavy weaponry. The spread of so-called small arms – which include assault rifles and machine guns – has been a major force behind the resort to violence by organized criminal organizations, private militias and insurgents around the world. Some 500 million military small arms are in circulation worldwide.[13] Numerous governmental and NGO initiatives have been set up to try to halt proliferation of small arms, as well as of weapons of mass destruction.

The arms trade is poorly regulated in the democratic world, with much weaponry reaching the hands of repressive regimes, private armies and criminals. While it is hard to control the export of weapons between repressive governments, it should be a priority among democracies to ensure that their part in the arms business does not contribute to aggression, murder and the use of torture, and to sparking and prolonging wars. This points to the need for tough regulation of the arms export and brokering business to prevent weaponry reaching repressive governments, war zones and regions where tensions are rising.

The UK is in a position to act as an exemplar and eliminate its arms trade with repressive regimes and war zones in the South with virtually no overall economic impact. But despite the Government's wish to operate a more ethical foreign policy, licensing of exports of arms and military spare parts to repressive governments has continued – for example, to Zimbabwe in 2000 for use in its intervention in the Congolese civil war, and to states with bad human rights records such as Saudi Arabia and Indonesia. The UK sells weapons to over 140 countries, many of them dictatorships. It is an immoral trade, and not even one that is economically important, despite the huge opportunity costs it represents to us and to the buyers of UK weaponry. The arms trade in 1998 accounted for less than 3 per cent of UK visible exports and around 0.5 per cent of jobs. A policy of rigorous reform of export licensing to eliminate sales to all regimes failing an 'ethical policy' test would be a powerful signal to the market and would shift the arms industry over time towards other business opportunities.

The Last Resort: Military Intervention in Conflicts

Curbing the arms trade and focusing investment and ideas on conflict prevention are the keys to a sustainable long-term policy on international security. But conflicts will not vanish, and each time a war breaks out in which civilians and regional stability are threatened, arguments follow about the extent and nature of intervention by the United Nations and/or the developed nations.

The argument for humanitarian intervention in conflict as a last resort is powerful. It draws on international law intended to protect civilians and prisoners in wars, and on international law on human rights. If we know of genocide; the deliberate slaughter of civilians; the torture and killing of prisoners of war; or the gross abuse of human rights (as in East Timor in 1999), then there is a moral duty for the 'international community', represented by the UN's forces, to intervene if we can. At this point realpolitik takes over. When military intervention is impossible, since it would provoke a greater conflict than the one it aims to suppress – as in the case of an intervention in a major power's territory – then we have to confine our actions to protest, diplomacy, trade sanctions, arms embargoes and humanitarian aid. True, this dilutes the moral universalism that inspires UN action; but because we cannot intervene everywhere, it does not follow that we should not intervene anywhere, regardless of the scale of suffering. Without an ethical dimension to security policy, however qualified by the limits to humanitarian intervention, countries and peoples are at risk of being condemned to indefinite suffering, with no prospect of recovery and the conditions for progress and sustainable development.

173

When it is possible, and is the subject of international consensus sanctioned via the UN, intervention should be undertaken provided that various other conditions are met. Among the most important are, that the situation is well understood; that clear goals are set for the operation; that the make-up and skills of the intervening forces are appropriate to the issues on the ground; and that a large and well-equipped force should be used, backed up by adequate funding for UN peacekeeping and conflict prevention and resolution work by NGOs and other agencies in partnership with civil society leaders on the ground.

These conditions have rarely been met in full in recent years. The failures in Somalia and Bosnia, and the disastrous delay in acting in time to intervene in Rwanda, were rooted in poor funding for the UN, inadequate planning and a lack of nerve on the part of Western governments in the face of the inevitable risk of casualties.[14] But if we wish UN agencies and forces to act on humanitarian grounds, as we should when genocide and suffering among civilians are at stake, and when there is little or no risk of precipitating a worse conflict by intervening, then the means must be willed as well as the ends. UN peacekeeping budgets, as shown in Panel 12 (page 158), have shrunk as member states (above all the US) have failed to make payments. And peacekeeping forces have been starved of the resources from the best trained and equipped national armies, as a result of Western governments' fear of casualties among their troops.

Failures of will of this kind undermine the humanitarian motive for action, which remains a powerful argument for military intervention. But when missions are better designed than

---

Witness Box 24: United Nations Association (UNA)

The United Nations Association (UNA) works very closely with the United Nations Environment and Development Committee (UNED-UK) on many sustainable development issues. We seek to cooperate whenever possible and often express our views within the UNED context rather than separately. For UNA, however, there are a number of key issues relating to sustainable development that do not appear as key issues for UNED:

1 *Deadly conflict avoidance:* For genuine sustainable development to become a truly global reality, the world of the 21st century must develop strategies for deadly conflict avoidance. The level and widespread areas of violent conflict in the world today are so appalling – with civilians the major victims – that sustainable development is simply not possible in them. Sub-Saharan Africa and various regions in Asia are the main areas of such conflict.

The United Nations Security Council (especially) and its regional bodies – such as the Organization of African Unity (OAU) and the OSCE – need to display much more political determination to devise and implement preventive strategies as a contribution, not least, to sustainable development.

The tenth anniversary (in 2002) of the publication of *An Agenda for Peace* and its supplement would be an ideal occasion on which to take stock of the (lack of) progress since it was published in 1992.

2 *Meeting financial targets:* Donor governments have, with very few exceptions, failed to meet the UN target of 0.7 per cent of GNP being allocated to official development assistance. The UNDP *Human Development Report* has recorded the considerable meanness of governments over many years. In the UK under the last Government, the figure reached its nadir of 0.26 per cent. Even the current Government has raised it to around only 0.3 per cent by the end of the present parliament. Given the broadly progressive policies now being pursued by the UK Treasury and DFID over debt relief, the UK is slowly becoming one of the leading donor countries of the industrialized world; but it needs to do more and to boldly encourage others to follow suit.

More generous and carefully targeted development assistance is urgently needed. It must tackle the root causes of poverty and injustice and not just play the Good Samaritan role in immediate humanitarian programmes.

3 *Disarmament:* The appalling level of global military expenditure needs to be tackled urgently and more comprehensively than ever before. Governments' rhetoric on the relationship between disarmament and development is considerable – remember the Peace Dividend of the early 1990s and the way in which military budgets were going to be trimmed and development finances enhanced? Small arms and light weapons, just as much as weapons of mass

> destruction, need to be more fully integrated into the process. The added complication of the grotesque misuse of agricultural tools – machetes, hoe handles and the like – as used in Rwanda in 1994, for example, must be addressed; but the context in which disarmament can really start to be realized must be developed, otherwise it will remain a mere pipe dream.
>
> Much rhetoric, little action is the order of the day, and this must be turned around urgently.

they were in the early and mid-1990s, and well-supported and equipped troops are deployed, positive results and local relief from suffering can be secured. It is always far more desirable to avoid interventions, and to rely on preventive strategies; but this can be a counsel of perfection in a world beset by emergencies. As Alex Ramsbotham of Real World member the United Nations Association (UNA) has said:

> 'the fact that conflict prevention is at present so inadequate suggests that there are situations where more emergency measures are required ... we can distinguish between the neo-imperial imposition of western ideals and the obligations of richer, more stable countries to uphold their responsibilities to poorer or less stable states, whose predicament we have often had a significant role in creating.'[15]

The debates will go on as new conflicts arise. But whatever stance we take on humanitarian military interventions, there is no doubt that prevention is better by far than cure. We need to take conflict prevention far more seriously as the key to long-term sustainable development in vulnerable societies and to collective security for the world.

Arguments for Preventive Security Policy: The Case for Self-Interested Action

The arguments above have been based to a large extent on an ethical stance. But as noted earlier, even if we reject arguments rooted in ethical principles, there is a powerful case for investment in preventive security measures and conflict resolution on grounds of Western self-interest. This is based on a number of factors.

First, as noted earlier, many conflicts are linked to criminal activity, as factions within states fight for control of resources for illegal trading and profiteering. This is the issue behind much conflict in Colombia (drugs trading); Congo (minerals); and Sierra Leone (diamond trading). The value chains of illegal trading stretch deep into the West, underpinning organized crime and creating a kind of shadow globalization process as national mafias and corrupt officials and businesses establish complex networks, using force to exert control over land and high-value resources. Organized crime is the fastest route for many from deep poverty to affluence: in the process whole countries are plundered; the poor exploited yet further; and good governance is subverted. Combating corruption is emerging as a vital issue for development aid programmes, and also for efforts by multinational enterprizes to pursue social and environmental responsibility initiatives and to trade ethically around the world.[16]

The rise of organized crime networks and the spread of drugs into the West is destabilizing, socially and economically. It breeds poverty and crime in the rich countries. Western demand for drugs fuels production in the South, which in turn benefits 'drug barons' in South and North and distorts agricultural economies in the developing countries. It puts Southern peasants at the mercy of drug cartels and militias and forces them away from growing other crops. Tackling the root causes of illegal trading, as in the case of drugs, is thus not simply a matter of helping Southern communities to develop more sustainably, but also an issue of self-interest and fundamental security for the West.

In addition, the costs of conflicts and corruption in the South and ex-Communist world spill over into the West. The rich world is inescapably the main paymaster for conflict interventions, many of which are made necessary by fighting using arms supplied by the West in the first place. Moreover, the costs of fighting organized crime and funding military interventions hugely outweigh those of conflict prevention. There is also the issue of the costs of refugee movements to consider (see Panel 13, page 179).

The aftermath of the Cold War has seen an upsurge in the number of refugees worldwide, as people flee from war zones, oppressive governments and environmental disaster areas; and the opening up of frontiers as globalization proceeds has also encouraged new migration as people in impoverished countries seek better conditions elsewhere.[17] The image of waves of feckless refugees and migrants attracted by the welfare systems of the rich world is unfounded. But there is indeed a risk of unsustainable development around the world leading to truly dangerous displacements of populations in the new century, especially as a result of environmental disasters (see Panel 14, page 180), which by the end of the 20th century were displacing more refugees than were wars.[18] The answer is for the rich world to recognize how it gains from its modest inflow of new people from the developing world, and also why it needs to take steps to raise the quality of life in poorer countries in order to prevent future crises over refugee movements.

This highlights the need for preventive action by governments, such as radical cuts in greenhouse gas emissions and policies to safeguard populations in vulnerable areas by improving resource efficiency (for example, improved water conservation measures); promoting joint resource management systems between governments in such regions; and developing disaster readiness initiatives as outlined earlier. This is a vital area for funding by the rich countries, but so far Western donor countries have failed to provide adequate resources to UN agencies concerned with refugee welfare, the Red Cross and other NGOs, and to build the idea of environmental security into strategies for sustainable development. As Sara Parkin has noted, the growing risk of environmental turbulence, and nations' shared state of dependence on nature's services, point to the possibility of the environment becoming a 'diplomat' for the 21st century, acting as a focus for cooperation instead of a catalyst for conflict.[19] But this will not happen automatically: development policy needs to focus more effectively on anticipating environmental change and shocks, and on preventive measures to limit the damage done to economies, social stability and relations between states.

Migration: Fears and Realities

In addition, there are fears in the West of being 'swamped' by 'bogus' refugees and economic migrants. These have been exploited by the hardline Right, and much has been made in Britain and the rest of the EU of the rise in applications for asylum following the Yugoslav wars and the persecution of Romanies and Gypsies in Eastern Europe. In reality the number of 'bogus' refugees is low, and many resort to appeals for asylum as the only way to gain legal status as an immigrant. Many refugees, moreover, return to their home countries after the end of a conflict or emergency, rather than seeking to make their futures in richer countries. Since the early 1990s the number of immigrants into the EU has fallen, and many migrant workers are in fact 'cross-border commuters', moving to and fro across EU frontiers, rather than settling within them.[20] But there is no doubt that on balance an increase in immigrants can benefit the developed world, and also their country of origin in some ways:

- Many migrants bring valuable new skills and resources, and transfer funds back to their home countries as well as contributing to the 'host' country.
- Many migrants are keen to take jobs shunned by the native population, and contribute to tackling labour shortages (such as Germany's shortfall in software specialists).
- The EU is facing a future of potential labour shortages in the light of declining birth rates. According to UN estimates, the EU could need as many as 13.5 million new workers each year over the next half century, just to maintain its dependency ratio between people of working age and the pensioner population. Much of the shortfall can be met through opening up more opportunities for paid work of decent quality to those now unemployed and inactive; through combating discrimination based on ethnic origin, sex, age and disability, all of which deprive the labour market of people with skills to offer; and through new uses of technology to substitute for labour. But there are gains – fresh ideas, skills, vitality, links to other cultures and markets, and life-enhancing diversity in Western cities and towns – to be had from the West's modest intake of refugees and economic migrants.

So there is a good case for a more generous and imaginative approach to immigration on the part of the developed world. This needs to go hand-in-hand with strategies to prevent conflicts and environmental crises in the developing world, and to stimulate more economic opportunities and greater quality of life in the poorer countries, in order to ensure that unsustainable development does not create crises that genuinely do lead to massive problems of migration.

Panel 13

Refugees and Migrants in a Connected World

The number of refugees receiving assistance from the UN rose sharply through the 1980s and reached a peak in 1995 at over 27 million. The total declined in 1996–99, but remained at over 21 million. Moreover, the UN total excludes 'internally displaced' people (estimated at 30 million) fleeing oppression, war or disaster, but unable to cross a frontier and receive official aid; and some 5 million people live in 'refugee-like' conditions but do not qualify for assistance from the United Nations High Commissioner for Refugees (UNHCR). So there may be some 57 million refugees and internally displaced people – nearly the population of the UK.

Warfare has usually been the key reason for displacement, along with oppression by governments; and the environmental disasters that often accompany conflicts (such as famines) exacerbate the problems. But at the end of the 1990s the Red Cross reported that for the first time the number of people displaced by environmental crises and extreme weather events (see Panel 14) outweighed the total forced from their homes by war.

Sources: L Brown et al, *Vital Signs 1999–2000* (London: Earthscan, 1999); UNHCR, *State of the World's Refugees 1997–1998* (Geneva: UN High Commission for Refugees, 1998); Red Cross, *World Disasters Report* (Geneva: International Red Cross, 1999)

Achievements and Failures in Sustainable Development Policy: Closing the Security Gap

Against this complex background, what progress can be identified over recent years, and what is needed in the run-up to Earth Summit 2002 on environment and development, at which the broad concept of security outlined earlier will be a key issue? There are many signs of progress, from action taken by the UK Government and others around the world in moving towards a more holistic and preventive approach to security and conflict. The advances include:

- some measures by the UK to tighten controls on arms exports to repressive regimes, and the EU's code of conduct on the arms trade;
- the announcement in September 2000 of plans to tighten licensing controls on UK arms dealers brokering sales between overseas countries;

180

Panel 14

Environmental Disasters

Natural disasters seem to be growing more frequent and more severe in their economic, social and ecological impacts. Global warming is forecast to increase the risks of climate disruption and extreme weather such as hurricanes, storm surges, cyclones, droughts and flooding. The poor in the tropical regions of the developing world remain most vulnerable, as a result of living in the most risky areas, in coastal and estuarine regions, and in badly designed urban dwellings and neighbourhoods. Moreover, the poor are the least likely to be insured against economic losses, which have increased dramatically in real terms over the last three decades. But if climate disruption from global warming is as severe as scientists warn, then the developed world will increasingly be at risk, both from extremes of weather and from the economic and political instability – and the risk of conflict over environmental resources –

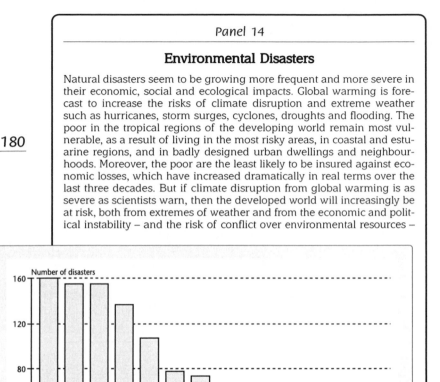

Natural Disasters, 1993–97

Source: UNEP, *Global Environment Outlook 2000* (London: Earthscan, 1999)

that disasters can bring to developed and developing countries alike. The 'El Niño' events of 1997–98 – stemming from a periodic rise in sea temperatures in the Pacific and possibly magnified by global warming – indicate how climate disruption can create problems whose effects ripple across many countries.

Sources: Red Cross, *World Disasters Report* (Geneva: International Red Cross, 1999); UNEP, *Global Environment Outlook 2000* (London: Earthscan, 1999)

- support by the UK for UN peacekeeping missions, notably in Bosnia, Kosovo and Sierra Leone;
- the UK Government's proposal to develop and host an international training institution specializing in peacekeeping;
- support for the International Court of Justice, and action to bring Bosnian war criminals to justice;
- support for the Landmines Convention;
- support by the UK for the nuclear-armed states' declaration in 2000 of a long-term aim to see all nuclear weaponry eliminated;
- the ambition to develop an ethical dimension in foreign policy;
- a strategy to design aid and debt relief programmes to support good governance, education and social policy.

These are substantial advances. But talk of the much-vaunted 'ethical foreign policy' of New Labour has faded away, and much more remains to be done to integrate preventive security thinking in UK policy, and even more, in the approaches of the USA and other members of the UN security council. Key security gaps remain:

- The need for more development of a more democratic and accountable global process and body within the UN framework for governing conflict prevention and peacekeeping initiatives, and for devising clearer criteria, better 'due diligence' preparation, and clearer objectives for military interventions. (In Chapter 6 we explored the contribution of democratic reform and innovations in democratic process and structure to sustainable development strategies globally and at the national and local levels.)
- The inadequate funding of the UN and its slowness in internal reform, both of which undermine its status and encourage unauthorized interventions.
- Inadequate funding for UN peacekeeping missions.
- The need for a standing UN army, which should include a strong UK contingent: this would help overcome the problems of assembling UN forces to react to outbreaks of war or instability, and of recourse to unilateral action;
- The development of a security dimension to international strategies for promoting sustainable development, recognizing the need for preventive investments in anti-poverty measures and governance in regions of tension, and in regions vulnerable to environmental disasters, especially

those likely to arise as a consequence of climate disruption.

- The need for a EU-wide debate on developing the preventive dimension of a pan-European security policy, and for the EU to act more strongly as a force for international action to reduce arms spending and prevent nuclear proliferation and the spread of other 'weapons of mass destruction' such as chemical weapons.

- The need for much faster progress in the UK towards ending arms exports to repressive governments and war zones; and tighter international controls on the arms trade, including small arms, and the illegal drugs trade.
- In the UK, development of the DDA as pledged by New Labour, and a higher policy priority for measures to help reorient the local and regional economy in the UK to reduce dependence on the arms industry.
- In the UK, strong implementation of Government's plans for tighter regulation of the arms export licensing process, including prior scrutiny of export licence applications; controls on licensed production and brokerage; a tough 'end-use' regime; and a commitment from Government to ending the system of Government-backed export credits for arms sales, and to abolishing the DESO, which offers assistance to arms exporters.

The challenges are great, but advances have been made, despite the disasters of recent years, towards the ideal of global peace-keeping. Closing the security gap is, however, fundamental to the prospects for global and national success in reversing unsustainable trends. Without stable and peaceful societies under good government, no progress can be made towards implementing sustainable development strategies for the good of all. And without a major reduction in the arms trade, resources will go on being wasted on a huge scale, which could be put to use for sustainable development worldwide, and above all in the poorest countries. Conflict, disorder and corruption are enemies of sustainable development because they erode economic stability, human rights, and justice and democracy, without which positive change cannot be made.

Making It Happen: Closing the Sustainability Gaps

'The beginning of a new millennium finds the planet Earth poised between two conflicting trends. A wasteful and invasive consumer society, coupled with continuing population growth, is threatening to destroy the resources on which human life is based. At the same time, society is locked in a struggle against time to reverse these trends and introduce sustainable practices that will ensure the welfare of future generations.'
United Nations Environment Programme[1]

'Lecturing poor countries about weak governance, while providing precious little money for technological advance, public health and other needs, is cheap all right. But it does not work... The prosperity of the richest countries is at an all-time high, and so is their capacity to look beyond their own immediate needs. At the same time, the crisis of the poorest countries is acute, and the shortcomings of the current strategy of globalization painfully evident... [The] world's leaders ... have a chance to will both the ends and the means for the kind of globalization that can serve all the world. They must seize that chance.'
Jeffrey Sachs[2]

Beyond 'Business as Usual': Towards a Richer Quality of Life

The paradox of the Millennium is that we have reasons simultaneously for unprecedented hopes and also for deep fears about the prospects for progress in the new century. The hopes stem from the analysis we can now make of the problems humanity faces, and the knowledge we have of the technologies, policies, values and market arrangements that can mitigate or eliminate them. The fears arise from the knowledge that we are making too slow progress in revitalizing institutions, adjusting market rules and fostering innovations in order to meet the environmental and social challenges, and seize the opportunities to make huge gains in quality of life and security for all.

The problems are rooted in the deeper paradox: that much of the 'business as usual' which has created better living standards for hundreds of millions of people and made possible rapid technological and commercial growth is itself a source of our greatest dangers. We are finding it – unsurprisingly – hard to reform the system of economic growth and market forces that have delivered the goods for so many for so long. Yet the longer we delay, the harder it will be to save the best of the Western model of progress from its own unintended and most destabilizing consequences.

The crises of global environmental degradation; deepening inequalities between and within many nations; the chronic poverty afflicting billions amid the immense wealth of the global economy; and the threats to peace and stability that arise from these problems, all threaten the many advances we have made, in the rich world and in many developing countries, in improving living standards and health, protecting the environment, and securing a democratic social order. The model of economic and social development that has swept all before it for 50 years is in danger of becoming once again, as in the 1930s, its own worst enemy, as it accentuates divisions between the richest and poorest and generates levels of resource depletion, waste and inequality that undermine the environmental services and social capital on which the system depends.

We must build the ideas of sustainable development into market mechanisms and the processes of democratic accountability and corporate governance. The aim is to govern and humanize the 'globalizing' economy, not reject its potential to bring gains in quality of life; to build into it correcting mechanisms that make it work within the limits of environmental services and key resources; to strengthen local and regional economies by promoting fair and sustainable trade rather than the current model of unfair and damaging 'free' trade that favours the rich; to convert governments and the business world to what we called earlier the 'lasting value' economy – a system in which markets work to deliver environmental sustainability, social equity and genuine economic progress and innovations that enhance our quality of life.[3] The aim is to make markets work for the benefit of communities, not the other way around.

We Know What to Do: We Simply Need to Start Doing It

There is no great mystery about the potential for change or the ways in which it can be directed. The evidence is mounting that promoting environmentally sustainable technologies, environmental tax reform, and sustainable harvesting of resources can all lead to gains in well-being, domestically and around the world. The West can reduce its over-consumption of 'environmental space' without reducing quality of life, in order to allow the developing world to grow – while adopting more sustainable development strategies – and raise living standards among the poor.[4]

We also know that it is not only a matter of justice and moral duty to be wise stewards of the environment, and to reduce inequalities in health, opportunity, power and income. Degraded environments and inequitable, unhealthy and conflict-torn societies are not only morally intolerable, but also bad for prosperity and enterprise: business self-interest, which can be opposed to environmental care and social justice, actually needs both.[5] More and more business leaders recognize this, and those who do not risk having to learn the lesson the hard way from their competitors, workers, customers, regulators – and families.

None of this means that we face a future filled only with 'win-win-win' options as we bring our economic, environmental and social strategies into alignments that can reverse unsustainable trends and promote changes that benefit the poor and the environment. There are short-term costs and losers, and real political obstacles. The transition to a much more resource-efficient economy, realizing the potential for a 'Factor 10' gain in efficiency of energy and material use, means that we will have to shift workers and resources out of fossil-energy-intensive sectors and into new services and sustainable technology enterprises. But in this respect the revolution in prospect is no different from all the other structural changes and upheavals of capitalism – such as the IT and e-commerce revolution, or the drastic 're-engineering' of manufacturing in the late 1970s and 1980s. We are urged by politicians and business leaders to accept these upheavals and their social costs as inevitable interim pains on the way to a better way of life and a better way of business.

So it is with the transition we need to make to sustainable, accountable and equitable forms of capitalism, and to a renewed culture of civic cooperation and democracy. But there are crucial differences. This revolution is one that cannot be imposed from above, by business leaders and politicians, in the same way as 'globalization' is currently experienced by so many workers and citizens. And it is not one that seems to generate great wealth and opportunity only for the few, as so many market booms and financial innovations have done. Finally, it is not an upheaval that seems to accelerate and overturn old assumptions in bewildering ways, like the 'dotcom' revolution of the turn of the Millennium.

The transition to sustainable development demands democratic revitalization. Because there are no top-down blueprints, and because it is about rethinking assumptions about what we value in the economy, environment and community, it calls for open and far-reaching debate at all levels of society, and between nations. It demands equity, because it rests on the idea that there are limits to our exploitation of nature and humanity in pursuit of growth, and because it recognizes the ethical imperative of reducing the grotesque inequalities of power, health, wealth and opportunity within and between countries. And it must, in some ways, be a gradual, patient process, because it challenges so many short-term interests and because it rests on the idea that we should take a precautionary approach to major innovations and technologies, concentrating on reversing damage and on careful planning for the use of land, scientific knowledge and technological fixes for environmental problems.[6]

But although the 'sustainability transition' is bound to be a long-term process of policy experimentation, market and technology innovation and changes in values, we cannot wait any longer to begin the serious work of change, acting on the strategies that have already been long debated and accepted in principle. The accumulation of ecological problems that will take decades to stabilize and overcome, is an example of issues that simply get worse, for us and above all for our children and grandchildren, the longer we simply discuss them or hope they will go away.

The Global Leadership Gap

In many areas – such as transport policy, renewable energy, eco-taxation – the principles behind the arguments for change have been accepted on most if not all sides. In policy on debt relief and aid for better education, health, development and governance in the South, the same is true. And in the idea of sustainable development we have the key principles, policy tools, criteria for funding and planning proposals, and targets for resource efficiency and poverty reduction that are needed to create a coherent, consistent and achievable action plan for the new century.

There is no shortage of money, ideas, well-meaning declarations and targets for action from the leaders of the developed world. They have the historic opportunity to make a difference to the human prospect, above all for the poor in the developing world, on a scale not seen since the Marshall Plan. The Western world, ever since the fall of Communism in 1989–91, has been in a position of immense economic, political and technological strength, with the capacity to pioneer a new economic order based on the vision of sustainable development, and to help the developing and ex-Communist countries gain in quality of life, income and stability.

But these leaders have a delivery problem. The gap between their analysis and plans, and the resources and changes they actually bring to bear, is huge. The end of the Cold War did not produce the hoped-for upsurge of statesmanship and global vision in the West, but fostered a complacent and short-sighted political culture apparently interested only in boosting its own unprecedented affluence. The grossly inflated budget, platitudinous statements, and air of detachment from global reality, of the 2000 Okinawa Summit of G8 leaders, summed up a decade of squandered opportunities and hopes after the end of the Cold War. The post-1989 political leadership of the West risks being remembered not for seizing an historic chance to build a sustainable and just economic and political order, but for wasting time and resources while the state of the global environment and the prospects of the poorest continue to worsen.

What is lacking is political willpower and courage to promote experiments in policy innovation from which we can learn and improve and stimulate yet wider public discussion and understanding about the challenges and opportunities ahead. NGOs and enlightened businesses have a major role to play in raising public awareness and demand for change, so that the failures of nerve and imagination on display in the governments of the rich world can be overcome. It is not too late for a change of heart and of direction by the leaders of the G8 nations, by the heads of the great corporations, and by the global economic agencies. Earth Summit 2002, the ten-year follow-up to the Rio summit on environment and development, offers a chance to make good the wasted opportunities of the past decade.

188

The Sustainability Gaps

This brings us back to our fundamental analysis of the state of the sustainable development transition. Huge advances in understanding have been made, not only in the science of environmental problems, but also in our approach to social problems. Since the Rio Earth Summit governments, international agencies, major businesses, NGOs and research communities have all made progress in embracing the idea of sustainable development and in beginning valuable reforms in policy, production and investment.

But the progress made has been patchy, halting and grudging. We are relying still on a handful of enlightened businesses, which are struggling to make the transition in the absence of powerful incentives from market regulation; on a handful of enlightened governments – including that of the UK – which have accepted the vision of sustainable development in many ways, but which are struggling to 'join up' their policies with their thinking; and on NGOs which have been a powerful force for change and for formal and informal regulation of the market, but which are struggling still to frame the messages of sustainable development in a way that connects them with the hopes of the mass of citizens, and which face challenges of accountability just as corporations do. We face, as a result, many 'sustainability gaps' between aims and achievement, between diagnosis of problems and action to tackle them.

Closing the Gaps: Programmes for the Transition to Democratic Sustainable Development

In the preceding chapters we have tried to assess these gaps, and to outline the broad programmes of innovation, learning and market reform that can help to reverse unsustainable trends, close the gaps and open up opportunities for progress towards greater well-being and security for all. The essential feature of these programmes for sustainability is that they recognize the linkages between environmental, social and economic progress; between peace and security and the health of the environment and community; and between sustainability and the renewal and extension of democracy.

These programmes are not about a rigid blueprint for change; still less do they amount to a new ideological world-view. They point to goals of democratic sustainable development that all democratic parties, businesses and civil society organizations, and citizens can recognize as desirable, for us now and for future generations. These are:

- a better quality of life for all, especially for the world's poor;
- a cleaner, healthier environment, rich in biodiversity;
- a fairer and more decent society;
- a more open and accountable business world;
- a fairer and more democratic approach to the management of globalization;
- protection and enhancement of the Earth's environmental systems and resources, in order to provide for future generations;
- careful and thorough debate on far-reaching innovations and proposals for change (including everything in this book!);
- a recovery of trust between citizens and Government; and
- a renewal of respect for what nature provides for us, and for the fundamental life support systems of the Earth.

The ideas discussed in previous chapters offer a programme which can define 21st century politics, but which does not force our choices into a rigid mould. We summarize the main features of a long-term strategy for the transition to sustainability below.

A Long-Term Programme for a Sustainable World

- *Making the lasting-value economy, based on a low carbon/low waste, high value/high innovation strategy:*
  - using ecological tax reform and recycled revenues to promote business innovation in technology in order to increase dramatically the productivity of our energy and

material use, and making deep cuts in waste, pollution and greenhouse gas emissions by 2050;

– using ecotax revenues to stimulate the 'green collar' economy and create jobs in energy conservation, waste minimization and recycling, clean production systems, renewable energy, sustainable forestry, organic and low-input farming, and low-emission transport services;

– adopting measures of growth and value that incorporate the social and environmental 'externality' costs of economic development;

– mandating new forms of environmental and social reporting and accounting by business, public and NGO bodies.

- **Ending exclusion at home: a sustainable new deal:**
  – recognizing the connections between poverty and unsustainable development, and using investments in environmental regeneration and revenues from eco-taxes to eliminate fuel, food and transport poverty and regenerate local economies;

  – benefits and welfare-to-work programmes for 'excluded' citizens should offer a richer range of opportunities to meet responsibilities by entering the social economy of mutual enterprise, volunteering, neighbourhood regeneration and local trading, as well as the 'mainstream' economy.

- **Promoting sustainable development in the international economic system: a global new deal:**
  – reforming global economic governance, above all the currently unfair, unsustainable and 'unfree' trade system, to ensure that developing countries can grow equitably and in an environmentally sound way;

  – providing leadership from the rich world in reducing resource consumption and arms production and trading, in debt cancellation, and in redesigning debt and aid strategies to promote sustainable growth and good government in the poor countries;

  – the principles of this 'new deal' idea should be applied globally, recognizing the responsibilities as well as the rights of rich and poor countries towards their environments and peoples, and the responsibilities of the rich world to reduce its share of global resource use;

– this 'new deal' would promote a transfer of funds and technologies from North to South to allow environmentally sustainable growth in the poor countries. It would establish principles for sustainable trade regulation by the WTO, and a clear duty on the World Bank and other global agencies to promote and uphold sustainable development accords. It would include rules for transnational corporations to establish accountability to their stakeholders, regulate competition and ensure that investment takes place in line with international standards on environmental and social protection.

- *Renewing democracy for richer choices:*
  – innovating in democratic processes at local, national and international/global levels, in order to improve public engagement in decision-making and to foster national and international debate on innovations, risks and long-term impacts of our choices as consumers and citizens;
  – enhancing the accountability to citizens of public and private bodies through reform of company law and the development of strong mechanisms for transparency and social and environmental accountability;
  – innovation in civic and moral education at all levels to promote better understanding of, and richer debate about, the choices and challenges ahead in moving towards sustainable development;
  – revitalizing the land use planning system to improve accountability and transparency, and to focus on alternative development plans that will maintain and enhance environmental, social and economic capital at all levels of activity.

- *Helping make a safer world through preventive action on security:*
  – reforming the UN and funding it so that the UN agencies can work better to achieve genuine international security, which must now be founded as much on tackling environmental and social risks as on military ones, given the potential for instability from environmental disasters and social tensions around the world;
  – recognizing that peace-keeping operations of the UN need to be well planned and well funded, and staffed by professional and well trained civilians and troops;
  – investing, as a priority over reactive measures to conflict,

in preventive strategies that focus on environmental improvements, better living standards for the poor, social policy reform, anti-corruption measures and conflict resolution in the most vulnerable areas; and pursuing determined policies to reduce and eliminate weapons of mass destruction, to curb the arms trade, and to drive down military budgets all over the world to release funds and human energies for sustainable development.

192

• ***Making truly 'connected' policy:*** all of the above need to be pursued together, as one coherent programme, following the analysis and principles of sustainable development. They must be designed, tested and phased in as a connected set of measures for a sustainable 'modernization' of society and economy. Only sustainable development gives a robust framework for radical and coherent 'joined up' policy-making that recognizes not only the connections between policy domains, but also those between economic development and quality of life; between the developed world and the poorer countries; between technological potential and environmental risk; between the interests of the present generation and those of our children and grandchildren.

We need to see bold use by policy-makers and their partners in business and civil society of a policy toolkit for 'future-proofing' of plans, strategies and products. At every turn we need to ask: 'What does this proposal imply for future resource use, equity and quality of life here and in the developing world?' Such a toolkit will include new indicators of genuine progress in the economy and society, targets for radical improvements in resource productivity and cuts in fossil fuel use, and elimination of perverse subsidies in economic policy and tax systems. In a profoundly interconnected world we need truly connected policy-making.

A Short-Term Programme: Action for Earth Summit 2002

Some sustainability gaps are narrower than they were just a decade ago. Perceptions have changed and new policies are being developed; but the gap between what is being said and what is being done remains huge. Earth Summit 2002 will be a challenge and an opportunity for Government, business and

NGOs to demonstrate their commitment and capacity to work together with citizens in the UK and globally to close the sustainability gaps and make a better world. It is essential that this summit does not become yet another platform for warm words and empty promises from world leaders.

We identify here principles and measures that Real World members see as priorities if we are to make significant progress at Earth Summit 2002, and to harness the UK's potential for leadership and partnership in democratic sustainable development:

- *Quality of life:* Government should build on the ideas in its Sustainable Development Strategy document and commit itself to establishing an annual quality of life statement from the Prime Minister on progress towards sustainable development targets, and to developing measures of sustainable economic welfare and sustainable consumption as 'headline' indicators alongside the GDP growth-rate. It should also develop, with business and NGOs, standards for business reporting, auditing and accountability on environmental and social responsibility that could be the basis for international measures.

- *Environmental sustainability at home:* Government should set the pace among OECD countries by introducing targets for reductions in the UK's use of 'environmental space'. It should include agreements with business sectors on specific targets and tax incentives for major gains in resource efficiency, aiming for 'Factor 10' goals and deep cuts in greenhouse gas emissions by 2050. It would also involve promotion of environmental technologies with the same commitment and prominence as is given to information technologies and e-commerce; commitment to an action plan on radical reduction in global warming emissions through energy saving and renewable energy investment, as recommended by the Royal Commission on Environmental Pollution;[9] and development of close links between NHS reform and environmental policy, focusing on preventive measures to improve environmental and public health.

- *Environmental sustainability worldwide:* Government should take a lead in promoting urgent action by the USA to ratify the 1997 Kyoto Summit accords as a first step, and in developing an effective and equitable CO_2 emissions reduction system worldwide, significantly improving on the targets and mechanisms proposed at Kyoto and investigating emissions trading systems which could transfer funds to developing countries; and strengthening accords on protection of biodiversity in North and South. Government should also promote take-up of targets by the OECD countries for reducing their share of 'environmental space', and development of funds to finance implementation of measures in developing countries to safeguard protected habitats and resources.

- *Poverty elimination worldwide:* Government should press for, and take the lead in adopting, a New Deal-type commitment to the poorest countries, wiping out debt in return for adoption of 'good government' strategies and spending on health, education and environmental priorities. This should be the centrepiece of a strong commitment by countries to pursuing the UN's targets for poverty elimination and advances in health and education worldwide by 2015.

- *Trade policy and globalization:* Government should lead urgent debate and seek consensus between governments, NGOs and business on radical reform of the WTO, IMF and World Bank, in order to devise fair trade rules for the poorer countries, and to ensure that global accords on social protection and environmental sustainability take precedence in disputes over trade rules. It should also press for new international rules on the accountability of multinational corporations. A further priority for Earth Summit 2002 is reform of international intellectual property rules, especially concerning genetic resources, to recognize forms of ownership other than patents, and to establish a just balance between public and private interests, and particularly the interests of people in the South.

- *Democratic renewal:* Government should be a leader in the renewal of democracy at home, and in promoting more democracy at the global level. It should move towards further devolution of powers and resources to reformed local authorities and new neighbourhood bodies in the UK; it should pursue a more radical programme to revitalize democratic institutions in the UK, and complement this with experiments in participatory democracy. At the global level it should lend its weight to proposals to reform the UN and the global economic agencies to improve democratic accountability and transparency of decision-making.

- **Peace and security:** The UK should take a lead in introducing new measures to control and reduce the international arms trade, and in implementing Government's plans for supporting and improving international peacekeeping resources.

Conclusion

The progress being made on all these fronts towards a more sustainable environment and richer, more democratic global community is real, despite the crises, failures and miseries that are all too evident across the world. It is not yet rapid enough, or imaginative and determined enough; nor is the sense of outrage at the damage being done, and the opportunities we are missing for sustainable development, potent enough. More must be done by Government and all parts of the sustainability movement, to promote rich and constructive debate and action across society. It is not only governments and business, but also NGOs such as the Real World members, that have to rise to the challenge of bridging the sustainability gaps. But we know that the potential of sustainable development to make a better world, with gains in quality of life for all, is immense.

The UK has become a world leader in acknowledging that potential and beginning the process of learning and innovation that will change policies, markets and values for the better. Government and its partners in business and the NGO community need to build on this, helping the UK to become a world leader in achievement, setting an example to the world and in the process shaping a richer future for its citizens, enterprises and future generations.

It can be done, and Earth Summit 2002 will be the right stage on which the UK and our partners in the democratic world can stake a claim to pioneering the sustainable development needed globally in the new century. Fulfilling the potential can bring a better quality of life for everyone. All we need to do is seize the challenge. At the Millennium, Britain, and much of the democratic world, was searching for a 'Big Idea' to inspire it with a new sense of purpose and direction. Creating the sustainable economy and making a better environment for all is as big an idea as we could find. It holds enough challenges and opportunities to inspire us for a century to come.

References

Foreword

1   J Porritt, 'Optimism of the will', in WWF, *A new century, a new resolution*, WWF/*The Guardian*, 1 January 2000
2   Kofi Annan, quoted in S Townsend, *Variety and Values: A sustainable response to globalization?*, British Telecom, London, 2000
3   M Jacobs/The Real World Coalition, *The Politics of the Real World: Meeting the new century*, Earthscan, London, 1996
4   K Worpole, 'The path not (yet) taken: The politics of sustainability', in K Worpole (ed), *Richer Futures: Fashioning a new politics*, Earthscan, London, 1999

Chapter 1

1   C Handy, *The Empty Raincoat*, Hutchinson, London, 1994, p15
2   E O Wilson, 'Vanishing before our eyes', *Time*, Special Earth Day Edition, April/May 2000
3   VSO, *Material World*, Voluntary Service Overseas, London, 2000
4   See for example G Mulgan and H Wilkinson (eds), *The Time Squeeze*, Demos, London, 1995; P Macnaghten et al, *Public Perceptions and Sustainability*, Lancashire County Council, Preston, 1995; B Burchell et al, *Job Insecurity and Work Intensification*, Joseph Rowntree Foundation, York, 1999
5   See for example J Murphy, *Peace and Plenty*, Model Reasoning Ltd, London, 1999
6   J K Galbraith, *The Affluent Society*, revised edition, Penguin, London, 1999
7   M Jacobs, 'Quality of life', in M Jacobs (ed), *Greening the Millennium?*, Blackwell, Oxford, 1997
8   See for example the 'Economic Optimism Index' produced by the opinion research organization MORI
9   M Jacobs/The Real World Coalition, *The Politics of the Real World*, op cit
10 See D McLaren et al/Friends of the Earth, *Tomorrow's World: Britain's share in a sustainable future*, Earthscan, London, 1998, Ch 3; T Jackson et al, *An Index of Sustainable Economic Welfare for the UK*, CES/New Economics Foundation, London, 1997

11 See UNEP, *Global Environment Outlook 2000*, Earthscan, London, 1999
12 A Adonis and S Pollard, *A Class Act*, Hamish Hamilton, London, 1997
13 See Robert Reich, 'Trouble we're in', *Prospect*, November 1998; J K Galbraith, *The Affluent Society*, op cit
14 See 'Is there a crisis?', *The Economist*, 17 July 1999
15 See UNDP, *Human Development Report 1999*, Oxford University Press, New York, 1999; World Bank, *World Development Report*, World Bank, Washington, DC, 1999
16 T O'Riordan and H Voisey (eds), *The Transition to Sustainability: The politics of Agenda 21 in Europe*, Earthscan, London, 1998
17 Sara Parkin, British–German Environmental Forum Conference, London School of Economics, 20–21 March 2000
18 DETR, *A Better Quality of Life: A strategy for sustainable development for the UK*, The Stationery Office, London, 1999
19 DETR, *Quality of Life Counts*, DETR, London, 1999
20 DETR, *A New Deal for Transport: Better for everyone. The Government's White Paper on the Future of Transport*, The Stationery Office, London, 1998
21 See Social Exclusion Unit, *Bringing Britain Together*, Cabinet Office, London, 1998
22 See the statement by the Chancellor, Gordon Brown, on debt relief, 'Smash the chains', *The Guardian*, 21 December 1999
23 Clare Short, 'The challenge of our age', *New Statesman*, 16 August 1999
24 See M Jacobs, *Environmental Modernization*, Fabian Society, London, 1999
25 UNEP, *Global Environment Outlook 2000*, op cit
26 Klaus Töpfer, quoted in *The Guardian*, 16 September 1999
27 M Engel, 'Hanging on the telephone', *The Guardian*, 8 February 2000
28 J Hills and O Lelkes, 'Social security, selective universalism and patchwork redistribution', in R Jowell et al (eds), *British Social Attitudes: The 16th report*, NCSR/Ashgate, Aldershot, 1999
29 See for example A Barmett and P Carty, *The Athenian Option*, Demos, London, 1998
30 A Park, 'Young people and political apathy', in R Jowell et al (eds), *British Social Attitudes*, op cit
31 See S Zadek, *Ethical Trade Futures*, New Economics Foundation, London, 2000, for scenarios on the development of ethical trade standards; on consumer power, fair trade and sustainability see N Robins and S Roberts, *Consumption in a*

197

Sustainable World, IIED, London, 1998; S Zadek et al,
Purchasing Power: Civil action for sustainable consumption, New
Economics Foundation, London, 1998

32 See J Vidal, 'Monsanto – we forgot to listen', *The Guardian*, 7
October 1999; J Borger, 'How the mighty fall', *The Guardian*,
22 November 1999

33 See R Grove-White et al, *Uncertain World*, op cit; J Elkington,
Cannibals with Forks, Capstone, Oxford, 1997; A Stirling and
S Meyer, *Rethinking Risk*, SPRU, University of Sussex,
Brighton, 1999

34 See R Willis and B Rose, *Steps into Uncertainty: Handling risk
and uncertainty in environmental policy making*, ESRC/Green
Alliance, London, 2000; ESRC, *The Politics of GM Food: Risk,
science and public trust*, University of Sussex, Brighton, 1999

35 R Scase, *Britain Towards 2010: The changing business environment*, ESRC/Office of Science and Technology, London, 1999

36 Quotation from Tom Burke in talk at the British-German
Environment Forum conference, London School of Economics,
20–21 March 2000

37 See R Murray, *Creating Wealth from Waste*, Demos, London, 1999

38 See K Worpole (ed), *Richer Futures*, op cit

Chapter 2

1 P Hawken, A B Lovins and L H Lovins, *Natural Capitalism: The
next industrial revolution*, Earthscan, London, 1999

2 A Marr, 'The ghost in the mirror', *Resurgence*, no 201,
July/August 2000

3 F Fukuyama, *The End of History and the Last Man*, Penguin,
London, 1992

4 See G Mulgan, *Connexity*, Chatto & Windus, London, 1997;
W Hutton and A Giddens (eds), *On the Edge: Living with global
capitalism*, Cape, London, 2000

5 M Jacobs/The Real World Coalition, *The Politics of the Real
World*, op cit, pp 8–9

6 See J Gray, *False Dawn: The delusions of global capitalism*,
Granta, London, 1998

7 On critiques of traditional measures of growth and progress
see T Jackson et al, *An Index of Sustainable Economic Welfare
for the UK 1950–96*, Centre for Environmental Strategy,
University of Surrey, Guildford, 1998; see also I Christie and
L Nash (eds), *The Good Life*, Demos, London, 1998; M Jacobs,
'Quality of life', op cit

8   UNDP, *Human Development Report 1999*, op cit
9   See World Bank, *Annual Report 1999*, World Bank,
    Washington, DC, 1999; World Bank, *Entering the 21st Century:
    World development report 1999/2000*, World Bank,
    Washington, DC, 1999; OECD, *Employment Outlook*, OECD,
    Paris, July 1996
10 M Jacobs/The Real World Coalition, *The Politics of the Real
    World*, op cit, p 11
11 See A Giddens, *The Third Way*, Polity Press, Cambridge, 1998;
    I Hargreaves and I Christie (eds), *Tomorrow's Politics: The Third
    Way and beyond*, Demos, London, 1998; Tony Blair, *The Third
    Way*, Fabian Society, London, 1998
12 See A Giddens, *The Third Way and its Critics*, Polity Press,
    Cambridge, 2000; *Marxism Today*, special edition on New
    Labour and its critics, November 1998
13 See the debate between Will Hutton and Anthony Giddens
    on the economic and social background to the Third Way
    perspective, Chapter 1 in W Hutton and A Giddens (eds), *On
    the Edge*, op cit
14 M Jacobs, *Environmental Modernization*, op cit
15 See Perri 6, *Holistic Government*, Demos, London, 1997;
    Perri 6 et al, *Governing in the Round*, Demos, London, 1999;
    D Wilkinson and E Appelbee, *Implementing Holistic
    Government*, Policy Press, Bristol, 1999
16 Tony Blair, in DETR, *A Better Quality of Life*, op cit
17 M Jacobs, *Environmental Modernization*, op cit
18 See for example the comprehensive analysis of sustainable
    development and its implications for the UK in D McLaren
    et al/Friends of the Earth, *Tomorrow's World*, op cit
19 See G Mulgan, 'Timeless Values', in I Christie and L Nash (eds),
    The Good Life, op cit; E Straw, *Relative Values*, Demos, London,
    1998
20 See *A New Vision for Business*, Committee of Inquiry Report,
    Forum for the Future, Cheltenham, 1999; Jonathon Porritt,
    'Vision on?', *Green Futures*, January/February 2000
21 C Leadbeater, *Living on Thin Air*, Viking, London, 1999
22 See recent work by The Henley Centre on consumers'
    responses to the multiplication of consumer choices:
    www.henleycentre.com; see also I Christie, 'In and out of
    control', *Planning for Social Change 98*, The Henley Centre,
    London, 1997
23 See R Murray, *Wealth from Waste*, op cit, Chapter 2
24 C Williams and J Windebank, *A Helping Hand: Harnessing self-
    help to combat social exclusion*, Joseph Rowntree Foundation,

199

York, 1999

25 NEF, *Brave New Economy*, New Economics Foundation, London, 2000

26 See D Warburton (ed), *Community and Sustainable Development: Participation in the future*, Earthscan, London, 1998; Ken Worpole (ed), *Richer Futures*, op cit; M Carley and I Christie, *Managing Sustainable Development*, 2nd edn, Earthscan, London, 2000; M Carley and K Kirk, *Sustainable by 2020? A strategic approach to urban regeneration for Britain's cities*, Policy Press, 1998; P Healey, *Collaborative Planning: Shaping places in fragmented societies*, Macmillan, London, 1997; S Teles, 'Think local, act local', *New Statesman*, 22 August 1997

27 I Christie and L Jarvis, 'Rural spaces and urban jams', in R Jowell et al (eds), *British Social Attitudes*, op cit

28 F Hirsch, *Social Limits to Growth*, Routledge, London, 1977

29 Urban Task Force, *Towards an Urban Renaissance*, DETR, Stationery Office, London, 1999

30 B Plowden, 'Walk on the wild side', *The Guardian*, 31 July 2000

31 M Jacobs/The Real World Coalition, *The Politics of the Real World*, op cit; M Jacobs, 'Quality of life', op cit

32 G Mulgan, *Connexity*, Chatto & Windus, London, 1997

33 See C Wolmar, 'Driving back to happiness', *New Statesman*, 5 June 2000

34 See S Chen, *Citizens and Taxes*, Fabian Society, London, 1999

35 For a powerful and imaginative meditation on the challenges of truly long-term thinking in public policy and business see S Brand, *The Clock of the Long Now: Time and responsibility*, Phoenix, London, 2000

36 See for example P Healey, *Collaborative Planning*, op cit; Julie Lewis et al, *Participation Works!*, New Economics Foundation, London, 1998; A MacGillivray et al, *Communities Count!*, New Economics Foundation, London, 1998; N Wates, *The Community Planning Handbook: How people can shape their cities, towns and villages in any part of the world*, Earthscan, London, 2000; D Warburton (ed), *Community and Sustainable Development*, op cit; TCPA, *Your Place and Mine: Reinventing planning*, Town and Country Planning Association, London, 1999; TCPA, *Town and Country Planning*, special issue on participatory approaches in planning, May 2000

Chapter 3

1   Royal Commission on Environmental Pollution, *Energy: The changing climate*, The Stationery Office, London, 2000
2   M Jacobs, *Environmental Modernization*, op cit
3   See UNEP, *Global Environment Outlook 2000*, op cit, for a comprehensive overview of trends and projections for the global environment and for regions of the world
4   R Murray, *Creating Wealth from Waste*, op cit
5   K Brown, 'Homeless', *New Scientist*, 13 May 2000; WWF, *Global Warming and Terrestrial Biodiversity Decline: A modelling approach*, WWF, Godalming, UK, 2000
6   A Platt McGinn, 'Phasing out persistent organic pollutants', in L Brown et al (ed), *State of the World 2000*, Earthscan, London, 2000; T Colborn et al, *Our Stolen Future*, Penguin, New York, 1996
7   World Humanity Action Trust, *Governance for a Sustainable Future*, WHAT, London, 2000
8   See the IUCN's 'red list' on endangered species, updated in 2000, at www.redlist.org
9   For details of the work of the Ape Alliance see www.4apes.com
10 T Burke, 'The buck stops everywhere', *New Statesman*, 20 June 1997
11 See M Bunting, 'Global warning', *The Guardian*, 6 March 2000
12 As in the developing world, the poor in the UK face the worst environments and most risk to health from pollution and other threats. See the Friends of the Earth analysis of the impact of pollution on poor households in Britain: *Pollution Injustice*, Friends of the Earth, London, 1999
13 D McLaren et al/Friends of the Earth, *Tomorrow's World*, op cit
14 M Jacobs/The Real World Coalition, *The Politics of the Real World*, 1996, op cit, p 35
15 See for example M Jacobs, *The Green Economy*, Pluto Press, London, 1991; T Jackson, *Material Concerns*, Routledge, London, 1996; T O'Riordan (ed), *Ecotaxation*, Earthscan, London, 1996; P Hawken et al, *Natural Capitalism*, op cit; R Murray, *Creating Wealth from Waste*, op cit; D Wallace, *Environmental Policy and Industrial Innovation*, RIIA/Earthscan, London, 1995
16 M Jacobs, *Environmental Modernization*, op cit; I Christie, 1998, op cit; C Secrett, *Making Work: The environment*, Employment Policy Institute, London, 1999
17 C Leadbeater, *Mind over Matter*, Green Alliance, London, 2000

18 UNEP, *Global Environment Outlook 2000*, op cit, Chapter 5
19 See European Environment Agency, *Environment in the European Union at the Turn of the Century*, EEA, Copenhagen, 1999
20 N Haigh, 'Introducing the concept of sustainable development into the treaties of the European Union', in T O'Riordan and H Voisey (eds), *The Transition to Sustainability*, op cit
21 UNEP, *Global Environment Outlook 2000*, op cit, pp 362–64
22 Royal Commission on Environmental Pollution, *Energy: The changing climate*, The Stationery Office, London, 2000
23 See TCPA, *Your Place and Mine*, op cit
24 Urban Task Force, *Towards an Urban Renaissance*, op cit; Countryside Agency, *Rural Sustainability*, Countryside Agency, Cheltenham, 2000
25 R Murray, *Creating Wealth from Waste*, op cit
26 See I Christie, *Sustaining Europe*, Green Alliance/Demos, London, 1999; N Haigh, D Baldock, and D Wilkinson, *Possibilities of the EU Adopting Sustainable Development as the Supreme Goal*, IEEP, London, February 1997

Chapter 4

1 UNDP, *Human Development Report 1996*, United Nations, New York, 1996
2 Michel Camdessus, speech at UNCTAD, 13 February 2000, in A Simms, *Paradigm Lost*, New Economics Foundation, London, 2000
3 DFID, *Economic Well-Being: International development target strategy paper. Consultation document*, Department for International Development, London, 1994
4 Joseph Rowntree Foundation, *Child Development and Family Income*, by P Gregg, S Harkness and S Machin, York Publishing Service, York, March 1999
5 World Commission on Environment and Development, *Our Common Future*, Oxford University Press, Oxford, 1987 (The Brundtland Report), pp 8, 69
6 R Frank and P Cook, *The Winner-Take-All Society*, Free Press, New York, 1995
7 Roger Levett, personal communication
8 A Corden, 'Writing about poverty: Ethical dilemmas', in H Dean (ed), *Ethics and Social Policy Research*, Social Policy Association, University of Luton Press, 1996
9 R McKibbin, 'Make enemies and influence people', *London*

Review of Books, 20 July 2000

10   R Wilkinson, *Unhealthy Societies: The afflictions of inequality*, Routledge, London, 1996

11   DFID, *Economic Well-Being*, op cit

12   Ibid

13   B Boardman with S Bullock and D McLaren, *Equity and the Environment: Guidelines for green and socially just government.* A Catalyst pamphlet in association with Friends of the Earth, London, September 1999

14   J Gates, *The Ownership Solution*, Penguin, London, 1999, p 8

15   UNDP, *Human Development Report 1999*, op cit, p 101

16   Joseph Rowntree Foundation, *Income and Wealth: The latest evidence*, by J Hills, Joseph Rowntree Foundation, York, March 1998

17   Joseph Rowntree Foundation, 'Income gap remains wide despite mid-1990s fall in inequality', Joseph Rowntree Foundation Press Release, 30 March 1998

18   Ibid

19   See J Millar, *Keeping Track of Welfare Reform: The New Deal programmes*, Joseph Rowntree Foundation, York, 2000

20   Social Exclusion Unit, *Bringing Britain Together: A national strategy for neighbourhood renewal*, The Stationery Office for the Cabinet Office, London, Cm 4045, September 1998

21   See note 17

22   See New Economics Foundation, *Brave New Economy*, op cit

23   WCED, *Our Common Future* (The Brundtland report), op cit, p 55

24   WWF-UK, *Poverty Elimination and the Environment*, by N Mabey, World Wide Fund for Nature, Godalming, UK, 1998

25   BBC Radio 4, *Changing Places*. Booklet to accompany Radio 4 series, BBC Natural History Unit, Bristol, February 1999

26   B Wade, 'Paying the Dues', *The Guardian*, 26 April 2000

27   H Hudson, L Newby and N Hutchinson with L Harding, *Making LETS Work in Low Income Areas*, Sustainable Economy Programme, Forum for the Future, London, 1999

28   See also D Boyle, 'Angela Eagle and the philosopher's stone', *Town & Country Planning*, September 2000

Chapter 5

1   UNCTAD, *Trade and Development Report*, UNCTAD, 1999

2   Nelson Mandela, speech to Labour Party Conference, 28 September 2000

3   D Held et al, *Globalization*, Foreign Policy Centre, London,

203

1999; D Held et al, *Global Transformations: Politics, economics and culture*, Polity Press, Cambridge, UK, 1999

4   L R Brown et al, *Vital Signs 1999–2000*, Earthscan, London, 1999

5   C Short, 'The challenge of our age', *New Statesman*, 16 August 1999

6   Oxfam, *Globalization. Submission to the Government's White Paper on Globalization*, Oxfam, Oxford, May 2000

7   C Leadbeater, *Living on Thin Air*, op cit

8   UNDP, *Human Development Report 1999*, op cit

9   C Leadbeater, *Living on Thin Air*, op cit

10   UNDP, *Human Development Report 1999*, op cit, p 31

11   C Leadbeater, *Living on Thin Air*, op cit

12   *The Multilateral Agreement on Investment (MAI)*, WWF, April 1998. See also the highly critical and outspoken report on the MAI process by the House of Commons Environmental Audit Committee, issued in January 1999

13   Vandana Shiva, 'This round to the citizens', *The Guardian*, 8 December 1999

14   Christian Aid and CAFOD, *A Human Development Approach to Globalization. A submission by Christian Aid and CAFOD on the Government's White Paper on Globalization*, Christian Aid/ CAFOD, London, 2000

15   World Development Movement, *Making Globalization Work for People*, World Development Movement, London, 2000

16   Friends of the Earth International, *The WTO and Finance: Possible investment negotiations in the WTO*, Friends of the Earth International, Amsterdam, November 1999

17   World Development Movement, *Making Globalization Work for People*, op cit

18   UNDP, *Human Development Report 1999*, op cit

19   See J Elkington, *Cannibals with Forks*, Capstone, Oxford, 1997; and S Zadek, *Ethical Trade Futures*, New Economics Foundation, London, 2000

20   Ethical Trading Initiative, *Purpose, Principles, Programme*. Ethical Trading Initiative, London, 1998

21   UNDP, *Human Development Report 1999*, op cit, p 101

22   C Stephens, S Bullock, R di Lullo and B Giobellina, 'Act Local, Think Global? Or Act Local, Act Global? How international environmental and social justice can be achieved if local governments reach out to each other', in *EG-Local Environment News*, University of Westminster, London, June 2000

23   UNDP, *Human Development Report 1999*, op cit, p 46

24   Christian Aid, *Curbing corruption: A people's approach to debt*

relief, Christian Aid, London, 1999
25 Oxfam, *Globalization*, op cit
26 Memorandum from Concerned Non-Governmental
    Organizations, UK Export Credits Guarantees Department
    (ECGD), 'Minimum Conditions for Reform', June 2000
27 World Development Movement, personal communication
28 Christian Aid, *Campaign News*, June 1999
29 J Stiglitz, 'The Insider: What I learned in the world economic
    crisis', *New Republic*, 4 April 2000
30 Christian Aid, *Who Owes Who? Climate change, debt, equity and
    survival*, Christian Aid, London, 1999; A Donoso, *No More
    Looting: Third World owed an ecological debt*,
    www.cosmovisiones.com/DeudaEcologica/a_looting.html,
    2000
31 See Christian Aid, *Who Owes Who?*, op cit, and also D McLaren
    et al/Friends of the Earth, *Tomorrow's World*, op cit, Earthscan,
    London, 1998, Chapter 2

Chapter 6

1   Kofi Annan, Secretary-General of the United Nations, on two
    occasions: in his address to the General Assembly of the UN
    on 21 September 1998; and in *Partnerships for Global
    Community: The annual report on the work of the UN*, 27
    August 1998
2   Amartya Sen, 'Freedom's market' in *The Observer*, 25 June 2000
3   G Mulgan, *Connexity*, op cit
4   M Jacobs/The Real World Coalition, *The Politics of the Real
    World*, op cit, pp 110–111
5   P Wintour, 'Labour plan for people power, *The Guardian*,
    27 May 2000
6   Convention on Access to Information, *Public Participation in
    Decision-making and Access to Justice in Environmental Matters*,
    United Nations ECE/CEP/43, agreed in Aarhus, Denmark,
    23–25 June 1998; UNEP Press Release 31, 'Thirty European
    Countries adopt plan to make environmental information more
    widely accessible', 2 July 1998; Environment for Europe
    Process (www.unece.org.env.pp); Public Participation cam-
    paign website (www.participate.org/aarhus)
7   DETR, *A Better Quality of Life*, op cit (para 5.18). A footnote
    explains that the Freedom of Information Act will implement
    provisions in the Aarhus Convention.
8   A Sachs, 'Upholding human rights and environmental justice',

in L R Brown et al (eds), *State of the World 1996*, Earthscan, London, 1996, Chapter 8; UNDP, *Human Development Report 2000*, op cit

9   J Huckle and S Sterling (eds), *Education for Sustainability*, Earthscan, London, 1996

10 P Healey, *Collaborative Planning*, op cit; *Town and Country Planning*, May 2000, special issue on Planning and Participation: Modernizing Planning. A policy statement by the Minister for the Regions, Regeneration and Planning, DETR, March 1998; Town & Country Planning Association, *Your Place and Mine*, op cit; *Education for citizenship and the teaching of democracy in schools. Final report of the Advisory Group on Citizenship*, 22 September 1998, p 11, chaired by Professor Bernard Crick, Qualifications & Curriculum Authority/DFEE, London, p 16; see also N Pearce and J Hallgarten (eds), *Tomorrow's Citizens: Critical debates in citizenship and education*, IPPR, London, 2000

11 UNDP, *Human Development Report 1999*, op cit, p 238

12 Ibid, p 12

13 Ibid, pp 101–11

14 A Simms, T Bigg and N Robins, *It's Democracy, Stupid*, New Economics Foundation/World Vision/Charter 99, London, 2000

Chapter 7

1   M Ignatieff, *The Warrior's Honour: Ethnic war and the modern conscience*, Vintage, London, 1999, p 160

2   S Parkin, 'Environmental security: Issues and agenda for an incoming government', *RUSI Journal*, June 1997

3   IISS, *The Military Balance 1999/2000*, International Institute for Strategic Studies, London, 1999

4   SIPRI, *SIPRI Yearbook 1997*, Swedish International Peace Research Institute, Stockholm, 1998

5   Cited in L Brown, 'Challenges of the new century', in L Brown et al (eds), *State of the World 2000*, Earthscan, London, 2000

6   M Jacobs/The Real World Coalition, *The Politics of the Real World*, op cit, p 64

7   M Ignatieff, *The Warrior's Honour*, op cit

8   Michael Renner, 'Ending violent conflict', in L Brown et al (eds), *State of the World 1999*, Earthscan, London, 1999

9   Ibid

10 M Ignatieff, op cit, Chapter 3; see also *The Economist*, op cit

11 Christopher Clapham in dialogue with Alex Ramsbotham

'Should the UN get out of Sierra Leone?', *The Guardian*,
19 May 2000

12 M Jacobs/The Real World Coalition, *The Politics of the Real
World*, op cit

13 Cited in L Brown et al, *Vital Signs 1999–2000*, Earthscan,
London, 1999, pp 154–55

14 William Shawcross, *Deliver Us from Evil*, Simon & Schuster,
Bloomsbury, London, 2000

15 A Ramsbotham, 'Should the UN get out of Sierra Leone?', op
cit

16 See World Bank, *The State in a changing world: World
Development Report*, World Bank, Washington DC, 1997; World
Bank, *Entering the 21st century: World Development Report
1999–2000*, World Bank, Washington DC, 1999

17 See B Hall, 'Immigration and asylum in the EU', *Prospect*, June
2000

18 Red Cross, *World Disasters Report*, International Red Cross,
Geneva, 1999

19 Sara Parkin, 'Environmental security', op cit

20 'Europe's Immigrants', *The Economist*, 6 May 2000

Chapter 8

1 UNEP, *Global Environment Outlook 2000*, op cit

2 J Sachs, 'A new map of the world', *The Economist*, 24 June
2000

3 Ibid

4 D McLaren et al/Friends of the Earth, *Tomorrow's World*, op
cit; M Carley and P Spapens, *Sharing the World: Sustainable living and global equity in the 21st century*, Earthscan, London,
1998; P Hawken et al, *Natural Capitalism*, op cit; C Secrett,
Making Work: The environment, Employment Policy Institute,
London, 1999; New Economics Foundation, *Brave New
Economy*, op cit

5 See J Elkington, *Cannibals with Forks*, op cit

6 T O'Riordan and H Voisey (eds), *The Transition to
Sustainability*, op cit; S Brand, *The Clock of the Long Now*,
op cit

7 See New Economics Foundation, *Brave New Economy*, op cit

8 See M Hertsgaard, *Earth Odyssey*, Abacus, London 1999

9 RCEP, *Energy: The changing climate*, The Stationery Office,
London, 2000

Real World Member Organizations

Real World can be contacted c/o
Forum for the Future
227a City Road
London EC1V 1JT
Tel: 020 7477 7740   Fax: 020 7251 6268
Email: realworld@forumforthefuture.org.uk

Real World does not have a staffed secretariat. Information is available on our website www.realworld.org.uk or, ideally, by contacting one of our member organizations.

bassac
1st Floor, Winchester House
11 Cranmer Road
London SW9 6EJ
Tel: 020 7735 1075   Fax: 020 7735 0840
Email: info@bassac.org.uk
Web: www.bassac.org.uk

bassac is a broad association of local multi-purpose community organizations. Emphasizing cultural diversity and local accountability, the network meets the needs of local neighbourhoods in a wide range of ways. Providing services to the area through one-stop facilities and outreach projects, members touch need at grass-roots. Nationally, bassac provides advice and information, grants and consultancy, publications and signposting to its members, and seeks to influence debates affecting community development and renewal from the experience of its members.

Black Environment Network
9 Llainwen Uchaf
Llanberis LL55 4LL
Tel: 01286 870715   Fax: 01286 870715
Email: ben@ben-network.demon.co.uk

Black Environment Network is established to promote equal opportunities with respect to ethnic environmental participation in sustainable development. It uses the word 'black' symbolically, recognizing that the black communities are the most visible of all ethnic communities. It works with black, white and other ethnic communities.

Campaign Against Arms Trade (CAAT)
11 Goodwin Street
Finsbury Park
London N4 3HQ
Tel: 020 7281 0297   Fax: 020 7281 4369
Web: www.caat.org.uk

CAAT was set up in 1974 to work for an end to the international arms trade and the UK's role in it as one of the world's leading arms exporters, and for a reorientation of the economy from military to civil production.

Charter88
18a Victoria Park Square
London E2 9PB
Tel: 020 8880 6088   Fax: 020 8880 6089
Email: info@charter88.org.uk
Web: www.charter88.org.uk

Charter88 is the independent campaign for a modern and fair democracy. Its goals are the reform of Britain's system of government; political institutions that are just, open and accountable; and a culture that protects individual rights, encourages responsibility and values the participation of every citizen. Charter88 calls for a democratic Parliament; a Freedom of Information Act; a Bill of Rights; decentralization of power; a proportional voting system; and a citizens' constitution – a new contract between the people and those who govern in their name. Charter88 has no affiliation to any political party. It has grown from the original Charter, published in 1988 with 348 signatures, to over 80,000 people today.

Christian Aid
PO Box 100
London SE1 7RT
Tel: 020 7620 4444   Fax: 020 7620 0719

Email: info@christian-aid.org.uk
Web: www.christian-aid.org.uk

Christian Aid links directly with people living in poverty through local organizations. It supports programmes with the aim of strengthening the poor towards self-sufficiency. Christian Aid also seeks to address the root causes of poverty by spending around 10 per cent of its income on development education and campaigning at home. Christian Aid is the official relief and development agency of 40 British and Irish churches. It works where the need is greatest in about 60 countries worldwide and helps communities of all religions and those with none.

Church Action on Poverty (CAP)
Central Buildings
Oldham Street
Manchester M1 1JT
Tel: 0161 236 9321   Fax: 0161 237 5359
Email: info-churchaction@cwcom.net
Web: www.church-poverty.org.uk

CAP was founded in 1982 as an ecumenical Christian response to increasing levels of poverty in Britain. It has around 1,500 individual and group members, drawn from all the major Christian churches and beyond. CAP works towards the elimination of poverty in the UK through raising awareness, campaigning and acting as a vehicle through which the voices of people experiencing poverty can be heard nationally.

Community Action Network (CAN)
The CAN Centre
Elizabeth House
39 York Road
London SE1 7NQ
Tel: 020 7401 5310   Fax: 020 7401 5311
Email: canhq@can-online.org.uk
Web: www.can-online.org.uk

CAN is a national learning and support network for social entrepreneurs and aims both to promote the social entrepreneurial approach and to support social entrepreneurs delivering specific projects. Its objectives are to identify high-potential social entrepreneurs across the UK; ensure that socially excluded social entrepreneurs are targeted and supported, and link them in a network, both electronically and face to face; disseminate best practice and share learning and experience; provide useful information (eg legal, training and funding); raise the profile of social entrepreneurs by coordinating them, promoting knowledge of their work and communicating their point of view.

The Electoral Reform Society (ERS)
6 Chancel Street
London SE1 0UU
Tel: 020 7928 1622   Fax: 020 7401 7789
Email: ers@reform.demon.co.uk
Web: www.electoral-reform.org.uk

ERS is a membership organization, established in 1884, and dedicated to democratic improvement. It campaigns for improvements to the voting system to ensure that all votes have equal value; give effective representation to all significant points of view within the electorate; allow the electors to vote for their preferred candidates without fear of wasting their votes; and ensure the accountability of individual representatives to their electorates. ERS believes these criteria are best met by the single transferable vote (STV) system.

    ERS also campaigns for other measures that will lead to higher turnouts in elections and a better informed electorate.

Forum for the Future
227A City Road
London EC1V 1JT
Tel: 020 7251 6070   Fax: 020 7251 6268
Email: info@forumforthefuture.org.uk
Web: www.forumforthefuture.org.uk

Forum for the Future's mission is to accelerate the building of a sustainable society by taking a positive, solutions-oriented approach. It believes that the solutions – whether technological, economic or social – already exist, and that the challenge is to find inspiring and innovative ways to make those solutions work for others. It works in partnership with decision-makers in business, government, higher education and professional bodies, and publishes the bi-monthly *Green Futures* magazine.

Friends of the Earth (FOE)
26-28 Underwood Street
London N1 7JQ
Tel: 020 7490 1555   Fax: 020 7490 0881
Email: info@foe.co.uk
Web: www.foe.co.uk

FOE inspires solutions to environmental problems which make life better for people. FOE campaigns on a wide range of issues including food and biotechnology, toxic pollution, climate change, trade, investment, transport, waste, habitats, corporate accountability and economic modernization. FOE is the UK's most influential national environmental pressure group; the most extensive environmental network in the world, with 68 national member groups and around one million supporters across five continents; and a unique network of over 200 campaigning local groups.

International Institute for Environment and Development (IIED)
3 Endsleigh Street
London WC1H 0DD
Tel: 020 7388 2117   Fax: 020 7388 2826
Email: info@iied.org.uk
Web: www.iied.org

IIED is an independent, non-profit organization that promotes sustainable development through research, policy studies, networking and knowledge dissemination. While working mainly in the poorer countries of the South, it also works on northern agendas that have an impact on global environment and development issues. IIED's mission is to understand sustainable development and the forces of change in order to promote policies that deliver progressive benefits to the poorest, and better and more equitable management of natural resources.

The Iona Community
Community House
Pearce Institute
840 Govan Road
Glasgow G51 3UU
Tel: 0141 445 4561   Fax: 0141 445 4295
Email: ionacomm@gla.iona.org.uk
Web: www.iona.org.uk

The Iona Community is an ecumenical Christian community seeking new ways of living out the gospel in today's world – through its dispersed membership throughout Britain and beyond; through its residential centres on Iona and Mull; through action for social and political change, the promotion of an integrated approach to spirituality, and the renewal of worship.

Medact
601 Holloway Road
London N19 4DJ
Tel: 020 7272 2020   Fax: 020 7281 5717
Email: info@medact.org
Web: www.medact.org

Medact is the independent and radical voice of health professionals with a global vision of social and environmental justice. Concerned about conflict, poverty, nuclear hazards and environmental degradation, it challenges these major threats to health by means of advocacy, education and research. It speaks to the million-strong health sector in the UK, to decision-makes in government and international bodies, and to the wider public.

National Peace Council

162 Holloway Road
London N7 8DD
Tel: 020 7697 0949   Fax: 020 7609 9777
Email: npc@gn.apc.org
Web: www.gn.apc.org/npc

The National Peace Council was founded in 1908 and consists of over 200 local, regional and national groups working for peace through campaigning, research, education, humanitarian and conflict resolution projects, and the production of peace resources. Under the umbrella of the National Peace Council these organizations are working together towards the abolition of war and the building of a culture of peace.

Oxfam
274 Banbury Road
Oxford OX2 7DZ
Tel: 01865 311311   Fax: 01865 313770
Email: oxfam@oxfam.org.uk
Web: www.oxfam.org.uk

Oxfam GB is a development, relief, and campaigning organization dedicated to finding lasting solutions to poverty and suffering around the world. It believes that every human being is entitled to a life of dignity and opportunity; and works with poor communities, local partners, volunteers and supporters to help this become a reality.

Pesticide Action Network UK (PAN)
Eurolink Centre
49 Effra Road
London SW2 1BZ
Tel: 020 7274 8895   Fax: 020 7274 9084
Email: admin@pan-uk.org
Web: www.pan-uk.org

PAN is an independent, non-profit organization working nationally and globally with individuals and organizations who share its concerns to: eliminate the hazards of pesticides; reduce dependence on pesticides; and promote alternatives to pesticides.

Population Concern
Studio 325
Highgate Studios
53-79 Highgate Road
London NW5 1TL
Tel: 020 7241 8500   Fax: 020 7267 6788
Email: info@populationconcern.org.uk
Web: www.populationconcern.org.uk

Population Concern works with local and national partners in the developing world to improve quality of life for women, men and young people. This work concentrates on provision of sexual and reproductive health services, and the promotion and defence of individual choices, including women's access to education.

In the UK and Europe, Population Concern's programmes aim to educate and inform the general public and policy-makers about the continuing needs of individuals whose lives, security and happiness are threatened by a lack of basic information and services concerning their sexual and reproductive health rights.

Quaker Peace and Social Witness (QPSW)
Friends House
173-177 Euston Road
London NW1 2BJ
Tel: 020 7663 1000   Fax: 020 7663 1001
Web: www.quaker.org.uk

QPSW is the department of Britain Yearly Meeting of the Religious Society of Friends in Britain which undertakes work within the UK and elsewhere in the world, in support of, and in response to, the Society's testimonies to peace and social justice. The Peace Section of QPSW concentrates on peacemaking and peace-building in areas affected by armed conflict, addressing the systemic causes of violence at a global level, and creating a culture of peace with justice based on nonviolent change. The Social Witness Section of QPSW concentrates on addressing the causes of economic and social injustice, in the UK and internationally, and working for change in structures which lead to social injustice.

Save the Children
17 Grove Lane
London SE5 8RD
Tel: 020 7703 5400   Fax: 020 7703 2278
Email: enquiries@savethechildrenuk.org.uk
Web: www.savethechildren.org.uk

Save the Children works in over 65 countries, including the UK.
Emergency relief runs alongside long-term development and prevention work to help children, their families and communities to
be self-sufficient.

Town and Country Planning Association (TCPA)
17 Carlton House Terrace
London SW1Y 5AS
Tel: 020 7930 8903   Fax: 020 7930 3280
Email: tcpa@tcpa.org.uk
Web: www.tcpa.org.uk

Since its foundation in 1899, the TCPA has been at the forefront
of the planning movement, locally and nationally. It has a major
and enduring influence on the worldwide development of planning policy, law and practice.

TCPA's main priority today is to promote its concept of
environmental planning, as a contribution towards achieving
sustainable development. It prides itself on creative thinking and
developing practical environmental solutions through its extensive
networks, and contacts with senior politicians and policy-makers,
and its monthly journal Town and Country Planning. Membership
is open to all.

Transport 2000
1st Floor, The Impact Centre
12-18 Hoxton Street
London N1 6NG
Tel: 020 7613 0743   Fax: 020 7613 5280
Email: info@transport2000.demon.co.uk

Transport 2000's mission statement is 'To find solutions to transport problems and reduce the environmental and social impact of
transport by encouraging less use of cars and more use of public
transport, walking and cycling.' Transport 2000 is the national
campaigning organization concerned with sustainable transport.
Its vision is of a country where traffic no longer dominates our
lives; where public transport provides for many of our journeys;

where every child can walk or cycle to school in safety, and where a car is not necessary to enjoy the countryside or city life.

UK Public Health Association (PHA)
75–77 Ardwick Green North
Manchester M12 6FX
Tel/Fax: 0870 010 1930
Email: info@ukpha.org.uk
Web: www.ukpha.org.uk

The UK PHA is a voluntary organization, made up of individual and organizational members across all nations and regions of the UK. It aims to be an advocate of healthy public policy, working with and for people throughout the country. The UK PHA is concerned about health beyond the NHS, including an environment that promotes good health; employment and education opportunities for all; social and emotional support for individuals and communities and tackling inequalities to create a fairer and therefore healthier society.

United Nations Association (UNA)
3 Whitehall Court
London SW1A 2EL
Tel: 020 7930 2931   Fax: 020 7930 5893
Email: info@una-uk.org
Web: www.una-uk.org

UNA is a membership organization that exists to support the work and the strengthening of the United Nations in global affairs. It runs campaigns and, through its charitable trust, educational programmes. Linked to 80 other national UNAs, it belongs to the World Federation of United Nations Associations and enjoys consultative status within the United Nations.

The Wildlife Trusts
The Kiln
Waterside
Mather Road
Newark NG24 1WT
Tel: 01636 677711   Fax: 01636 670001
Email: info@wildlifetrusts.cix.co.uk
Web: www.wildlifetrusts.org.uk

The Wildlife Trusts have been one of the major forces speaking out for nature in Britain since 1912. The Wildlife Trusts are a

national network of 46 Wildlife Trusts, 52 Urban Wildlife Groups
and Wildlife Watch, our junior environmental action club. Caring
for over 2,300 nature reserves across the UK and with over
325,000 members worldwide, The Wildlife Trusts' aim is to work
through education, conservation and campaigning to create a sustainable balance between town, country and wildlife.

World Development Movement (WDM)
25 Beehive Place
London SW9 7QR
Tel: 020 7737 6215   Fax: 020 7274 8232
Web: www.wdm.org.uk

WDM is a democratic network of local groups and individuals,
committed to changing the policies of governments, international
agencies and companies for the benefit of the world's poor.
WDM's campaigns aim to cancel international debt and the harsh
economic conditionality applied by the IMF and the World Bank;
to change socially and environmentally damaging policies of
multinational companies and build support for international regulation of global business; to make trade and investment rules fairer; and to work with an international movement to promote equitable and sustainable alternatives.

WWF-UK
Panda House
Weyside Park
Catteshall Lane
Godalming GU7 1XR
Tel: 01483 426444   Fax: 01483 426409
Web: www.wwf-uk.org

WWF-UK was founded in 1961 and now has a global network of
27 national organizations, of which WWF-UK is one. Among its
founders was Sir Peter Scott, the naturalist and painter, who
designed the Panda logo. WWF's mission is to stop the degradation of the planet's natural environment, and to build a future in
which humans live in harmony with nature. It strives to do this by:
conserving the world's biological diversity; ensuring that the use of
renewable natural resources is sustainable; and promoting the
reduction of pollution and wasteful consumption.

Index